KYOTO AREA STUDIES ON ASIA

CENTER FOR SOUTHEAST ASIAN STUDIES, KYOTO UNIVERSITY

VOLUME 28

I0083871

Bali and Hinduism in Indonesia

The Institutionalization of a Minority Religion

KYOTO AREA STUDIES ON ASIA

CENTER FOR SOUTHEAST ASIAN STUDIES, KYOTO UNIVERSITY

The Nation and Economic Growth:
Korea and Thailand
YOSHIHARA Kunio

One Malay Village:
A Thirty-Year Community Study
TSUBOUCHI Yoshihiro

Commodifying Marxism:
The Formation of Modern Thai Radical Culture, 1927–1958
Kasian TEJAPIRA

Gender and Modernity:
Perspectives from Asia and the Pacific
HAYAMI Yoko, TANABE Akio and TOKITA-TANABE Yumiko

Practical Buddhism among the Thai-Lao:
Religion in the Making of a Region
HAYASHI Yukio

The Political Ecology of Tropical Forests in Southeast Asia:
Historical Perspectives
LYE Tuck-Po, Wil DE JONG and ABE Ken-ichi

Between Hills and Plains:
Power and Practice in Socio-Religious Dynamics among Karen
HAYAMI Yoko

Ecological Destruction, Health and Development:
Advancing Asian Paradigms
FURUKAWA Hisao, NISHIBUCHI Mitsuaki, KONO Yasuyuki and KAIDA Yoshihiro

Searching for Vietnam:
Selected Writings on Vietnamese Culture and Society
A. Terry RAMBO

Laying the Tracks:
The Thai Economy and its Railways 1885–1935
KAKIZAKI Ichiro

After the Crisis:
Hegemony, Technocracy and Governance in Southeast Asia
SHIRAISHI Takashi and Patricio N. ABINALES

Dislocating Nation-States:
Globalization in Asia and Africa
Patricio N. ABINALES, ISHIKAWA Noboru and TANABE Akio

People on the Move:
Rural–Urban Interactions in Sarawak
SODA Ryoji

Living on the Periphery:
Development and Islamization among the Orang Asli
NOBUTA Toshihiro

KYOTO AREA STUDIES ON ASIA

Center for Southeast Asian Studies, Kyoto University

KYOTO AREA STUDIES ON ASIA

CENTER FOR SOUTHEAST ASIAN STUDIES, KYOTO UNIVERSITY

VOLUME 28

Bali and Hinduism in Indonesia

The Institutionalization of a Minority Religion

Yasuyuki Nagafuchi

Professor Emeritus,
Nagoya Institute of Technology

Kyoto University Press

TRANS
PACIFIC
PRESS

Published in 2022 jointly by:

Kyoto University Press
69 Yoshida Konoe-cho
Sakyo-ku, Kyoto 606-8315, Japan
Telephone: +81-75-761-6182
Fax: +81-75-761-6190
Email: sales@kyoto-up.or.jp
Web: http://www.kyoto-up.or.jp

Trans Pacific Press Co., Ltd.
2nd Floor, Hamamatsu-cho Daiya Building
2-2-15 Hamamatsu-cho, Minato-ku, Tokyo
105-0013, Japan
Telephone: +81-50-5371-9475
Email: info@transpacificpress.com
Web: http://www.transpacificpress.com

Distributors

USA and Canada
Independent Publishers Group (IPG)
814 N. Franklin Street
Chicago, IL 60610, USA
Telephone inquiries: +1-312-337-0747
Order placement: 800-888-4741 (domestic only)
Fax: +1-312-337-5985
Email: frontdesk@ipgbook.com
Web: http://www.ipgbook.com

Europe, Oceania, Middle East and Africa
EUROSPAN
Gray's Inn House,
127 Clerkenwell Road
London, EC1R 5DB
United Kingdom
Telephone: +44-(0)20-7240-0856
Email: info@eurospan.co.uk
Web: https://www.eurospangroup.com/

Japan
For purchase orders in Japan, please contact
any distributor in Japan.

China
China Publishers Services Ltd.
718, 7/F., Fortune Commercial Building,
362 Sha Tsui Road, Tsuen Wan, N.T.
Hong Kong
Telephone: +852-2491-1436
Email: edwin@cps-hk.com

Southeast Asia
Alkem Company Pte Ltd.
1, Sunview Road #01-27, Eco-Tech@Sunview
Singapore 627615
Telephone: +65 6265 6666
Email: enquiry@alkem.com.sg

The publication of this book was supported by a Grant-in-Aid for Publication of Scientific Research Results (Grant Number 21HP5100), provided by the Japan Society for the Promotion of Science, to which we express our sincere appreciation.

ISBN 978-1-925608-34-2 (hardback)
ISBN 978-1-925608-35-9 (paperback)
ISBN 978-1-925608-33-5 (ebook)

CONTENTS

INTRODUCTION

In the Republic of Indonesia, Islam is the religion of the majority and Hinduism is the religion of a minority. However, the central government of the republic has a Religion Ministry (Kementerian Agama), which recognizes not only Islam, but also minority religions, including Hinduism, and maintains a pluralistic system of religious administration.[1] The aim of this book is to describe how Hinduism in Indonesia has been perceived, how it has been institutionalized by the state administrative apparatus, and the issues that the system faces in the twenty-first century.

Hinduism in Indonesia, which began with the perception that Balinese culture was Hindu, has structurally internalized (under the same name 'Hindu') both the expansion of rituals in Bali on a local level and the expansion of Hinduism on a global level. This distinctive aspect arose because of the historical formation of discourses on religion and institutional frameworks legitimizing those discourses under Indonesian religious policy. Those frameworks, which at first glance appear unrelated to religion, have played a significant role in assigning meaning to the religious discourse. By tracing the historical development of this institutionalization process, I hope to identify the unique characteristics of Hinduism in Indonesia.

The perception of Balinese Hinduism as a religion first emerged in the region that today constitutes Indonesia during its colonial period under Dutch rule, as part of what was called the Dutch East Indies. Colonial administration, which began in the seventeenth century with Batavia, Java, as its seat, necessitated a knowledge of indigenous culture so that a system of indirect rule could be implemented. This need prompted the accumulation of scholarship about the culture of the region. One aspect that attracted particular interest was the area's culture predating the spread of Islam. Based on their knowledge of other Asian regions, including India, scholars saw this culture as Hindu-Buddhist in character, a perception that further fostered a positive assessment of the culture. A latent anti-Islamic bias by Dutch scholars led them to assign a 'high' cultural value to this Hindu-Buddhist culture that preceded the region's 'contamination' by Islam. This perception was applied not only to past

1

history, but also to the extant culture on the island of Bali, which had not been Islamized. Part I of this book examines this aspect of Balinese society during the colonial era.

Chapter 1 focuses on the relationship between this scholarship and the ruling order that constructed the actual system of governance put in place when the colonial government established its administrative apparatus in Bali in the early twentieth century. The cumulative scholarship on the subject defined Hinduism as the essence of Balinese society. Extrapolating from this assumption, scholars saw Bali's class hierarchy system as a native Balinese tradition, and recognized the existence of royal families as part of that tradition. Ultimately, indirect rule was implemented in the form of autonomous regions headed by those royal families. When a powerful earthquake struck Bali in 1917 during this period, the Balinese took it as a sign of the collapse of the cosmic order they had known until then. The colonial government, which felt compelled to actively involve itself in the island's recovery from the earthquake, restored Besakih, which it had determined was the central temple of Balinese society, and held an inauguration ceremony there for the heads of the autonomous regions. That the colonial government went so far as to restore this temple indicates how thoroughly its governance was grounded in scholarship that perceived Hinduism as the foundation of Balinese society.

Chapter 2 examines reactions in Balinese society to the ruling order thus established. Bali was subsumed into the capitalist order through the colonial government's establishment of a land management system for tax collection purposes. Consequently, Balinese society was not immune to the effects of the worldwide Great Depression that began in 1929. Amid poverty exacerbated by the combination of colonial exploitation and economic crisis, movements arose among the Balinese populace to actively revive religious ceremonies and cultural activities. Balinese who worked as lower-level civil servants of the colonial administration participated in these movements and published numerous magazines. This led to an effort to reinterpret social customs within the framework of Hinduism. Thus was born 'another space' in which Balinese people appropriated the colonial government's perception of Hinduism.

The colonial period came to an end after several years of wartime occupation by Japanese forces. In the process of decolonization, the perception of Hinduism formed during the colonial era was reconstituted and incorporated into the religious administration of an independent state, the Republic of Indonesia. Part II discusses this period.

Decolonization in Bali was a geopolitically complex process. On August 17, 1945, immediately after Japan's surrender, the Republic of Indonesia, which had been preparing for this occasion for a year, proclaimed its independence. At the time, however, the republic comprised only a portion of what is Indonesia today. With the conclusion of the Second World War, the Netherlands sought to reassert its hegemony over Indonesia, setting up a pro-Dutch state in territory outside the independent republic with the aim of creating a Federated States of Indonesia that would absorb the republic. Bali was incorporated into the Negara Indonesia Timur (State of East Indonesia), which was set up by the Dutch in the eastern part of the archipelago. But Bali's connection to this entity went beyond geography; the man inaugurated as president of the State of East Indonesia was a member of the Balinese nobility, Cokorda Gede Raka Sukawati. In short, Balinese society was intimately linked to the Dutch.

In 1949 the State of East Indonesia collapsed and was absorbed into the republic, with the birth of the unitary Republic of Indonesia as it exists today. Yet, on the regional administrative level, the laws of the State of East Indonesia remained in effect until the enactment of a Unitary Regional Administrative Law in 1957. Formerly adjacent to the republic, yet part of East Indonesia, Bali had in a sense experienced the reality of a border zone in which a pro-republic camp and a pro-Dutch, pro-colonial camp opposed one another. As this factionalism intensified during the 1950s, attempts at unity failed and fear of violence proliferated. During this period, intellectuals began advocating a morality based on Hindu teachings, and a movement calling for social reconstruction gained momentum. The efforts of these intellectuals also produced religious schools, universities, and other educational institutions.

Meanwhile, the promulgation of the Unitary Regional Administrative Law saw Bali enter a new era as an autonomous province of the republic. In effect, this established an order that merged religious identity, the

3

territory of the island of Bali, political representation in the form of the Bali Regional Assembly, and the Balinese as an ethnic group. Chapter 3 studies the relationship between Hinduism and Balinese society as it evolved in this manner in the 1950s.

The state's religious administrative apparatus also confronted a new reality. The Japanese occupation forces had set up a Religious Affairs Office (Shūmubu in Japanese, Kantor Urusan Agama in Indonesia; Benda 1983: 111) in Indonesia with the aim of pacifying the Islamic community. The newly independent republic replaced this with a Religion Ministry through which it exercised administrative jurisdiction over religious matters. When the republic incorporated the regional administrative laws of eastern Indonesia, the Religion Ministry faced a serious problem: in this region, Bali was predominantly Hindu, while further east, Christianity was the majority religion and Islam was in the minority. Christianity had had a presence in Java since colonial times and was officially recognized as a religion by the ministry, but Hinduism was not. It was at this point that a movement grew in Bali to persuade the Religion Ministry to recognize Hinduism.

The fear was that if Hinduism failed to gain formal recognition, it would be treated as a mere 'belief,' devalued, and even excluded by Islam; however, the most significant concern was education. The compulsory education system provided time for religious studies, but Hindu education would not be permitted at schools if the religion lacked government recognition.

As mentioned above, Balinese society now possessed an order that merged religion, territory, political representation, and ethnicity—yet it was still unable to resolve factional strife. During this period, the movement for religious recognition was a singular example of united action. With the Balinese regional government at the forefront, participants in the movement included the Autonomous Religion Bureau, religious leaders, university faculties, and other intellectuals. The final outcome was state recognition of 'Hindu-Bali' as a religion. This was followed by the establishment of Parisada Hindu Dharma as the organization officially representing Hindu-Bali. Parisada would also support the priesthood responsible for carrying out religious ceremonies, which had formerly been under the purview of the kingdoms.

Another significant effect of the Unitary Regional Administrative Law on Balinese society was a change in perceptions of the status of the royal families. Under the regional administrative framework, the domains of these families were reflected in the designation of regencies, an administrative level below the province. However, the special status the families had enjoyed as heads of autonomous regions since the colonial era was nullified. In considering the ramifications of this for Balinese society, a crucial development was that the loss of status by the royals was accompanied by Parisada's acquisition of authority over the priesthood. The result was that the provincial governor, who was now the highest administrative authority in the province of Bali, took on the role previously occupied by the kings, particularly in the conduct of religious ceremonies. Together with the advent of a priesthood represented by Parisada, this shift revived the concept of a monarchy with the province as kingdom. Under the banner of belief in the 'one and only God,' the Republic of Indonesia became a pluralistic state that recognized Hinduism alongside Islam. At the same time, the island of Bali became a secular regional administrative unit, yet also retained its monarchic framework with the provincial governor as a revived version of the king. Chapter 4 looks at the relationship between religion and the state that produced this result

In 1965 the September 30 Incident in Jakarta led to the replacement of the Sukarno regime with that of Suharto, and a massacre of suspected communists occurred in Bali. Mount Agung had erupted in 1963, causing damage particularly on the east side of the island, and many Balinese had migrated to places like Lampung in southern Sumatra and central Sulawesi. Amid this confluence of regime change, a great number of deaths, and a migration of Hindus throughout Indonesia, Bali (under its revived monarchic framework) underwent sophistication as a symbolic space through ceremonies conducted under the aegis of Parisada. Chapter 5 examines Balinese society under the Suharto regime.

As Hindu Balinese migrated throughout the republic, what had originally been regarded as a religion exclusive to Bali became pan-Indonesian in character. The name 'Bali' was formally excised from the term 'Hindu-Bali' as Hinduism became recognized as a religion of the entire Republic of Indonesia. In Bali, meanwhile, Parisada, which saw

Indonesian Hinduism as rooted in the customary practices of Balinese society, recognized Besakih Temple as the center of the religion, maintained the temple, and carried out several successive, large-scale ceremonies. Before these ceremonies could be held, however, there had to be island-wide purification rites for the dead. In addition to the dictates of the Balinese calendar, a pragmatic reason for holding ceremonies at Besakih was the vast number of dead needing purification.

The Suharto regime viewed religion as the spiritual foundation of its New Order, and Besakih represented its Hindu manifestation. The government built an international airport in Bali and, capitalizing on the island's appeal since prewar days, promoted the tourism industry. With this dovetailing of the interests of the government and Balinese society, and the supply of wealth obtained through tourism, the 1990s saw the repetition of one major ceremony after another, further refining and consolidating a cosmology in which Bali was a symbolic space with Besakih at its center. The primary purpose of the ceremonies in Bali was to give every citizen access to the holy water created in these ceremonies. The provincial government devised a system under which representatives of the communities at the bottom of the administrative hierarchy would come to Besakih to receive holy water, thereby symbolically uniting every individual with the cosmos. This constituted the completion of a process of bureaucratization of the symbolic space that had come into being in the colonial era after the 1917 earthquake.

The Asian financial crisis of 1997 had a traumatic effect on Indonesia, and the Suharto regime, so long in power, collapsed the following year. The same period saw the proliferation of the internet and access to information on Hindu activities around the globe. These conditions conspired to expose the internal contradictions of Hinduism in Indonesia, resulting in a schism in Parisada, the organization that had played such a key role in the institutionalization of Hinduism by the state. Part III discusses this period, with Chapter 6 describing the events leading up to the schism.

Two major contradictions arose in Indonesian Hinduism. One was the result of the deterritorialization of Hinduism. From the standpoint of Hindus outside Bali, Parisada devoted itself exclusively to the performance of ceremonies and utterly neglected the role properly played by a true religion. A religion, they felt, should address the problems of day-to-day life and try to offer solutions, but Parisada showed no such inclination. The nationwide organizing of Hindus also brought to the fore the discontinuity that led to the schism. Behind the expansion of networks connecting Hindus in different locales lay a growing interest in the religion's activities in the social sphere. The desire to learn about one another's efforts and thereby develop possibilities for new undertakings grew in parallel with the organizing process. The formation of new groups in the social sphere signified the growing desire for a network among Hindus in general. Meanwhile, Parisada had decided in 1991 to move its administrative headquarters from Bali to Jakarta. This development served to expose both the systemic shortcomings of Bali-based Hinduism, with its lack of an organizational structure in the social sphere, and the discontinuous nature of the relationship between Hinduism on a national scale and Hinduism in Bali.

The second contradiction occurred within Balinese society. Formerly an agrarian society, Bali had become dependent on tourism. Urbanization rapidly advanced as people flocked to Denpasar, the provincial capital. As time went on, more and more Balinese were Denpasar-born. People born in Denpasar were divided in their views of their relationship to the ancestral villages where their parents had grown up. Some felt they could not sever that relationship, for two reasons. The first concerned ceremonies for the dead. Custom stipulated that these ceremonies were to be held in one's home village. Rites for the dead were a form of mutual aid in the sense that one must contribute to all such ceremonies in the village if one wished to hold them for one's own family. Nearly all villages established a system by which people working in Denpasar who were unable to help directly with these rites could donate money instead. This allowed people in the city to maintain relations with their home villages. The second reason was ancestor worship. To the majority of Balinese, the soul and the body are inseparable. If they feel physically unwell, they may go to a doctor of Western medicine and take a prescribed drug, but they will also look for a spiritual cause. The most commonly cited cause of illness is neglect of one's *kawitan* (ancestral origins). During the colonial era, ordinary people could not determine what these origins were. After independence, they were free to do so, and the search for ancestral origins grew into what might be termed the largest grassroots social movement in Bali. Ancestral deities are worshiped at village temples, and it has been an essential part of daily life in Bali to offer prayers and receive holy water at ceremonies conducted at those temples.

However, more and more people born in Denpasar were losing their ties to village life, whether intentionally or inadvertently, as a result of changes in human relations from their parents' generation onwards. Yet, even without those ties, they remained Hindu unless they actively converted to another religion. One's religion is even inscribed on identity cards; in effect, there is no such thing as a person without a religion in the Republic of Indonesia. In these circumstances, people in Denpasar who had lost their links to their home villages yet still felt compelled to identify themselves as Hindu were drawn to global Hindu networks such as the Sai Baba and Hare Krishna organizations. These networks expanded rapidly throughout Indonesia in the twenty-first century as information became readily accessible via the internet. Places of worship set up by such organizations proliferated in Denpasar and are now part of the landscape of twenty-first-century Bali.

Inevitably, conflict arose between Parisada, which based its authority on Balinese community customs, and people who pursued their faith through global Hindu networks. Those in the latter group believed that Parisada was concerned only with conducting ceremonies and did nothing to address the daily struggles faced by urban Hindus. Moreover, Parisada, despite its position as the representative organization of Hindus in Indonesia, adopted an exclusionary stance toward the global Hindu networks, declaring them to be a false form of Hinduism, with Balinese practices embodying the only true form.

Toward the end of the Suharto regime, Hindus outside Bali and those who identified with Hinduism as practiced in Bali joined together in criticizing the ritual-centrists who dominated the top echelons of Parisada. Within the organization, too, some members were seriously contemplating the proper role of Hinduism as a religion and had come to feel that the emphasis on rituals was not enough to deal with new realities. Even among people seeking to establish their ancestral origins, voices were raised in complaint that the ceremonies at Besakih were monopolized by priests belonging to a certain social status who had been granted special privileges during the colonial era. These criticisms surged in tandem with rising calls for democratization at all levels of Indonesian society in the wake of the collapse of the ruling order. The ultimate outcome was a schism in Parisada between the ritual-centrists and those who opposed them.

This book is based on my previous book, which was published in Japanese in 2007 (Nagafuchi 2007). Chapters 1 through 5 of the present book are an English translation of Chapters 2 through 6 of that earlier book, which was based on my dissertation for a doctorate in human sciences in 2004 from the Osaka University Graduate School of Human Sciences. Chapter 6 of this book is an English translation of 'Religion and proliferating pluralism of values: Negotiating the boundaries on Hinduism in Indonesia,' an article of mine that was published in 2005 in the Bulletin of the National Museum of Ethnology (Nagafuchi 2005). With the addition of this article, the present book provides an overview of the entire history of Indonesia's most representative Hindu organization from its founding to its rupture.

I conducted my initial research in Bali from 1984 to 1986 while studying at Udayana University on a scholarship from the Ministry of Education, Science and Culture of Japan. From 1991 to 1992, on a fellowship from the International House of Japan, I studied documents from the colonial era and other literature while I was a visiting scholar at the University of California, Berkeley, in the United States, and Leiden University in the Netherlands. During this time, I was granted the privilege of reading the subsequently published doctoral dissertation of Geoffrey Robinson, then at Cornell University, as well as other research materials he had gathered. I also had a chance to read the draft of a yet-to-be-published book by Henk Schulte Nordholt in the Netherlands (Schulte Nordholt 1996). During the periodic research visits that I made to Bali until 2003, Widnyana Sudibya, archivist of the ceremonies at Besakih Temple, provided me with much valuable information and documentation. To all, I express my gratitude.

Part I

Hinduism and the Colonial State

CHAPTER 1

A Character Defined, a Cosmos Destroyed

Ethical imperialism

After the Dutch military intervention of 1846, the colonial government had forced the kingdoms of Buleleng and Jembrana, which extended across the north and west sides of Bali, to recognize its suzerainty. In 1882 this region, which had been under the jurisdiction of the regional administrative district of Banyuwangi on the neighboring eastern end of Java, began a new era as an autonomous administrative district. This represents the formal beginning of Bali and Lombok as a regional administrative unit of Dutch colonial rule, though the extent of colonial authority was still limited. Singaraja, at the center of the kingdom of Buleleng, was designated as the administrative seat (Figure 1.1). Meanwhile, the same period was marked by an intensifying power struggle among the kingdoms of Bali, as exemplified by the collapse of the kingdom of Mengwi. Already threatened by the Dutch forces, the island's kingdoms clashed repeatedly in a quest for expanded hegemony. In addition to the royal families, Cokorda Gede Sukawati, raja of Ubud in central Bali, was rapidly expanding his power.[1] The administrators assigned to Singaraja kept careful watch over the ever-changing map of these power struggles.

In 1894, with the Aceh War progressing toward an outcome favorable to the central government, the increasingly expansionist government launched a military operation in Lombok, and the island—until then ruled by the Balinese royal family of Karangasem—came under Dutch rule. The rationale given for this armed incursion was one of ethical concern. This moralistic stance was directed at the king, who was viewed as a despot who exploited the populace to an intolerable degree. As government policy, moralism provided a useful cover for imperialistic behavior. However,

12

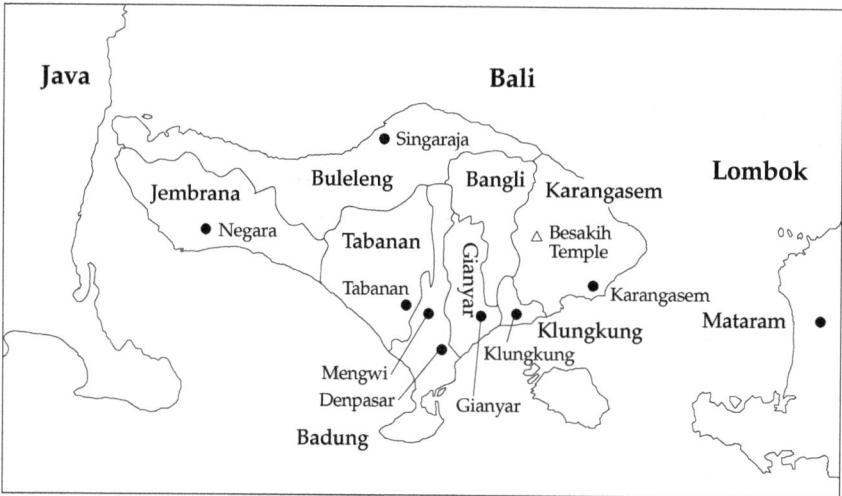

Figure 1.1 Bali and Lombok

F. A. Liefrinck, who served as Resident of Bali and Lombok from 1895 to 1901 (the period immediately following the offensive), sought to advance into southern Bali by developing peaceful diplomatic relations with the royal families. Karangasem became a Dutch protectorate in 1895, and the king, Gusti Gede Jelantik, was appointed regent; having witnessed the collapse of Lombok, he had quickly recognized the power of the Dutch and hoped, by accepting protectorate status, to preserve the status of the royal house. Gianyar followed suit, becoming a protectorate in 1900, as did Bangli in 1904.

When Liefrinck's term ended, so did the era of diplomatic negotiations. In 1903 the royal family of Tabanan authorized a cremation with human sacrifice, a practice that had been declared barbaric by the Dutch, and in 1904 the royals of Badung rejected Dutch demands for compensation for a ship that had been plundered off the coast of the kingdom. Viewing these acts as violations of the moralism espoused by the government, the Dutch treated both incidents as political issues and launched a blockade of the coast of Badung. In September 1906, Dutch troops landed at Sanur on the east coast. Their attacks on the royal houses of Badung and then Tabanan met with resistance from the royals, but ended with mass suicides in each case by the king and his court, in what was known as *puputan* (the finishing). In these incidents a throng of people, dressed in white, emerged from the palace and marched toward the Dutch troops. Then they stopped and, led by the king, began killing themselves. The Dutch opened fire and in the ensuing carnage corpses piled up around the palace. In 1908 a similar incident occurred when the government attacked Klungkung, the last remaining royal house in Bali, ostensibly to suppress opium smuggling. With the mass suicide of the Klungkung court, the colonial government completed its annexation of the entire island of Bali.

The process of occupation by colonial forces from the late nineteenth century into the first years of the twentieth century caused a clear split among the royal families of Bali into 'winners' and 'losers.' The winners were the king of Karangasem and Sukawati of Ubud, who had both sided with the Dutch when their own power was in ascendance and thus benefited from the advent of the Dutch era. The royal families of Gianyar and Bangli also managed to survive, albeit barely. However, the courts of Badung, Tabanan, and Klungkung were annihilated. Within the Dutch-established territory of Bali and Lombok, Bali was divided into northern and southern districts, with Buleleng and Jembrana (which had first come under Dutch rule) constituting the north. Denpasar was designated as the administrative seat of the southern district and an Assistant Resident took office there. A Dutch Controller was assigned to each of the administrative units based on the domains of the various kingdoms. Thus began the era of governance of Bali as a colonial territory.

Defining the Balinese

With the initiation of colonial rule in Bali, the first undertaking of the government was to identify the subjects of its rule. The objective was to define the people who would be under the purview of the legal system established to govern the indigenous population.[2] Since the nineteenth century, it had been the policy of the Dutch colonial government to implement a legal system that distinguished between Europeans and 'natives,' with a separate 'native court' for the latter. In the case of Bali, the population was classified as inheemsche bevolking (indigenous Balinese),[3] Balische Mohamedanen (Balinese Muslims), and vreemde oosterlingen (non-Balinese orientals). The latter two categories were combined into one, with a separate presiding head appointed by the government. On Lombok, a native court based on the same system as for the Balinese on Bali was established for Balinese Hindus, with a separate legal system for the Sasaks (Muslims who spoke a different language than the Balinese and made up most of the population of Lombok). Though distinctions were recognized among other ethnic groups besides the Balinese Hindus and the Sasaks (i.e. Balinese Muslims, Chinese, Bugis, etc.), the government did not set up special legal systems for these groups (Lekkerkerker 1920: 379–81).

The salient aspect of the legal system established for the indigenous populations of Bali and Lombok was its definition of indigenous Balinese as adherents of Hinduism. In other words, the law treated the indigenous people as a distinct entity whose defining characteristic was its religion, specifically Hinduism. Religion was a rigorously observed reference point for the legal system. First of all, the government defined the basic law as consisting of the 'traditional religious law'[4] of Bali, which will be described later. Moreover, it appointed Balinese priests to serve as judges in the native courts. The judges were selected by the Resident from candidates recommended by the Dutch Controllers of each district. Thus was born a legal system under which the Dutch government oversaw the enforcement by Balinese priests of what the government viewed as Hindu-based Balinese law.

The government had, in fact, recognized early on that the majority of people living on Bali were Hindu Balinese, as evidenced by statistical surveys conducted for the entire colonial territory. A 1920 survey did not classify Balinese living in Batavia or other districts outside Bali according to their religion, yet for Bali and Lombok it listed four nationaliteit or landaard (ethnic categories): Hindu Balinese, Muslim Balinese, Buddhist Balinese, and Bali Aga (old Balinese).[5] A 1930 survey divided the group 'Balinese' into Hindus and Muslims, with the other categories vanishing.[6] Of all the inhabitants of the Dutch East Indies counted and classified according to these surveys, the Balinese living on Bali were the only ones to be classified by religion as well as ethnicity. Considering that in the twentieth century, in the Netherlands as elsewhere, ethnicity rather than religion had become the predominant criterion for classifying populations, the case of Bali stands out as a unique exception to this practice.

In his analysis of the thinking of the colonial state as expressed through maps, museums, and population surveys, Benedict Anderson (1991: 184) describes this way of thinking in terms of classification and series as follows: 'The particular always stood as a provisional representative of a series and was to be handled in this light. This is why the colonial state imagined a Chinese series before any Chinese, and a nationalist series before the appearance of any nationalists.' Viewed in this way, one could say that the colonial government, in dealing with the territory of Bali and Lombok, imagined a 'Balinese classified as Hindu' series before any Balinese, and established a system of rule based on this classification and series. In other words, the colonial government defined the character of the people in its territory in advance of dealing with them as individuals, and accordingly treated the entire territory from a uniform perspective, as well as managing its society on the basis of that character. Thus the government identified 'natives' by grouping people according to a common character determined through classification, and governed these 'natives' through laws defined according to that character. In this case, the object of colonial rule—the distinguishing identity labeled 'Balinese'—was defined together with a character labeled 'Hindu.'

'Hindu' and the ruling system

After the establishment of Bali and Lombok, the government initiated a full-scale empirical study of Balinese society. Liefrinck, who (as mentioned earlier) kept a close eye on internal political developments in Bali, produced what could be practically termed 'ethnographic studies' based on surveys of Balinese society, primarily in the northern region. Together with reports submitted by his subordinate H. J. E. F. Schwartz based on first-hand observance of conditions in southern Bali, this empirical knowledge provided guidelines for the new era of Dutch rule in Bali.

Liefrinck's research also provided the impetus for research not only on the rule of Bali but on customary law in general.[7] However, the grouping of the Balinese under the religious category of 'Hindu' was set in place before this accumulation of empirical knowledge, and derived from scholarship that preceded the establishment of Dutch rule. Moreover, the stance of placing the villages at the lowest end of the governing system and basing governance on the rule of groups, not individuals, was an extension of the colonial experience in Java, and was only reinforced by the empirical research.

The legal system for 'natives' established in 1882 was without question a product of the Hindu-centric historical view of Bali. This viewpoint is prominently reflected not only in the religion-based identification of indigenous Balinese, but also in the source texts cited for the law. In 1910 the colonial administrator J. Fraser published an article titled 'De inheemsche rechtspraak op Bali' (The indigenous law in Bali) in the magazine *Indische Gids* (*Indies Guide*) (Fraser 1910). In this article the author summarized the legal system of 1882 on the occasion of the establishment of Dutch rule over the entire island and cited scholarly support for this legal system extending back into the nineteenth century. As legal precedents he cited three sources: the laws of villages and irrigation societies, legal codes written in Javanese or Balinese, and the laws of the royal courts. While recognizing a certain degree of autonomy for the laws of villages and irrigation societies, Fraser accorded legitimacy to the legal texts written in Javanese or Balinese as the authoritative sources to be followed in the native courts of the government. His reason for this was that the latter were Hindu; thus, the author saw the laws of the past as a more legitimate precedent than the laws actually in use at the time.

The government recognized a large number of legal texts as being Hindu in character; of these, in 1909 (the year after the establishment of Dutch rule over the entire island) it published the two texts accorded the highest legitimacy. Titled *Adi agama* and *Agama*, these documents were written in the English alphabet and in Balinese script, with the *Agama* treated as the more legitimate of the two (Lekkerkerker 1920: 10–13). The *Agama* had as its original source legal texts written in Javanese, but no text by this title existed. J. C. G. Jonker, a Dutch Orientalist who was the

17

fourth professor of Javanese at the University of Leiden at the time that Dutch rule was extended across Bali, had compiled the text in 1885—just after the establishment of Bali and Lombok—by revising a document (deemed incomplete and with a title open to varying interpretations) in the possession of the University of Leiden after comparing it with another document held by the British Museum. The latter text had been 'received' from the king of Buleleng in 1814 (Lekkerkerker 1920: 284–5; Hoadley and Hooker 1981: 51–86). Thus, a document based on texts removed from their place of origin to the colonizers' homeland was reintroduced to the colony as a 'classical' source text for the legal system installed there.

The work of restoring these source texts clearly reflects the relationship of scholarship to political hegemony. In this restoration process, which involved translation from Javanese to Balinese via Dutch, the matter of translation itself was of utmost significance to the Dutch government. V. E. Korn, a skilled colonial administrator who later produced a vast body of research on Balinese customary law, stated that even the Balinese priests found it difficult to comprehend Javanese in all its historical permutations, and that translation into Balinese with the assistance of Dutch scholars was essential if the texts were to serve any legal function (Korn 1932: 53–4). Geoffrey Robinson (1995: 33) asserts that 'There is perhaps no more striking example of the way in which Balinese "tradition" was manufactured by the Dutch colonial government' and that the translation of these texts also served as a justification of Dutch rule over Bali. In other words, the government could argue that the inability of the priests to read the texts was a clear sign of the decline of Balinese culture, and that it was the duty of the Dutch to restore the culture to its proper state.

This premise of a Hindu culture provided the foundation not only for the legal system but for the entire ruling structure. A caste-based view of the social hierarchy served as an ideology linking religion and politics. Under the British rule of India, caste was an indispensable tool for classifying colonial subjects, and the notion of caste as a system representing the indubitable essence of Indian or Hindu society had thoroughly permeated Western thinking (cf. Inden 1990: 49–84; Dirks 2001). It was the Dutch government that introduced the caste system as an ideology into Balinese society. Granted, the kingdoms had been supported by a robust class hierarchy, based on ranks of nobility, and the government treated this hierarchy as a ready template for the introduction of the caste ideology. With the government judging the status of these titles by the same standard of historical legitimacy that it had applied to the classification of legal texts, the existing hierarchy was absorbed into a rigid caste system (Boon 1977: 145–64; Korn 1932: 135–78; Schulte Nordholt 1986).

After the publication of Fraser's (1910) article 'The indigenous law in Bali,' the regional government held a three-day conference in Singaraja from September 15, 1910, to study administrative policy. Here the legal system of 1882 was validated on the basis of Fraser's article. Participating from the Dutch side were all the colonial administrators of Bali and Lombok, including the Resident, Assistant Resident, and Controllers; the seven participants from the Balinese side included native administrators and priests appointed to the native courts. Among the Balinese, the priests enjoyed the highest status, but the other participants were all of high social rank as well. The main focus of the conference was the establishment of the caste system. Heading a list of items for confirmation was a statement that the caste system was 'the principal foundation of Bali society.'[8]

When the colonial government introduced the ideology of caste to Bali, it perceived caste as follows. The Balinese population was divided into those accorded the title of *triwangsa* (three groups); everyone else was assigned the appellation *sudra* or the Old Javanese word *kula*. The ordinary meaning of *kula* was a group or family of the same origin, but this was expanded to refer to any person who was not of noble rank. The *triwangsa* were further divided into the *brahmana* (the priest class), the *satria*, and the *wesia*. The *sudra* were ranked below these three classes, and this ranking was treated by the government as a caste system.[9] The objective of the 1910 conference was to reify this conceptualized caste ranking as an actual social system.

The conference established a broad range of rules governing marriage, including penalties for adultery and elopement. Among its most significant decisions was the establishment of penalties for intermarriage between castes. These penalties targeted marriage between higher-caste women and lower-caste men. Intra-caste marriage was promoted to the priests as

19

a precondition for maintaining caste sanctity, although the Dutch declared that they would defer to the laws of Balinese society in the setting of punishments. Thus the caste hierarchy was made real through punishments meted out in the name of maintaining the order of bloodlines, based on local laws as interpreted by the government.[10]

The primary goal of implementing a caste system was to establish the authority of the Dutch government in the name of an inherently 'native' social system. In his article 'The indigenous law in Bali,' Fraser (1910) reconstructed the legal system as a product of the relationships among four distinct entities involved in implementing the law: village communities, district chiefs, kings, and priests. The village communities had their own laws and implemented their own legal systems. However, legal authority over disputes or crimes occurring between villages lay with the king. The king exercised his legal authority at the village level through the intermediation of district leaders. Meanwhile, custodianship of the laws that provided the basis for the king's authority was the responsibility of two or three priests, whose counsel was therefore indispensable to the king. In summary, the government placed the villages and the king at opposite poles, permitting a certain degree of autonomy on the part of the former but ultimately recognizing the latter as the highest political authority; at the same time the true 'owners' of the laws implemented by the king were the priests, who were thus positioned by the government at the pinnacle of the legal hierarchy of Bali (Fraser 1910: 867–9).

Having reconstructed the legal system of the period of kingships in this fashion, the government sought to shift sovereignty in this system to itself. On the one hand, it preserved the role of the priests as custodians of the law by establishing the native courts mentioned earlier. On the other hand, it placed itself, the government, in the position formerly occupied by the kings as executors of the law based on the counsel of the priests. The lineup of participants in the 1910 conference—Dutch administrators and Balinese priests—reflected the government's attempt to legitimize its rule by taking over the position of the executive authority within the indigenous legal system.

The process of setting up a colonial bureaucracy in Bali further reinforced the caste system. Specifically, there was an increase in the number of people of noble rank (i.e. members of the *triwangsa* class) among the Balinese appointed as indigenous administrators in each district. Korn (1932) points out that during the period of kingships, many district heads did not belong to the nobility, and acknowledges that it was the Dutch government that reinforced a caste-based hierarchy.[11] The government not only gave social rankings legal force, but also ensured that the bureaucracy that implemented its rule conformed to the Dutch perception of the caste hierarchy.

It was clearly a privilege to be appointed as an indigenous administrator. To be a government official not only guaranteed a salary from the government, but also legitimized one's own political authority, albeit under supervision. Indigenous officials were also exempt from forced labor. A 1922 law defining forced labor obligations specifically lists indigenous government officials, as well as priests, among the categories of those exempt from such duties.[12] With those recognized as *triwangsa* enjoying special access to such privileges, it is no wonder that the codification of social rankings sparked fierce disputes among the Balinese, as will be seen in Chapter 2.

The royal families were undisputed possessors of the highest rank in the social order. In this respect, the repudiation of the kings as executors of the law contradicted the newly implemented caste system. In districts where the royal families were disarmed and their members exiled from Bali, the government stepped into the position of authority vacated by the king and established a system of direct rule. However, in districts where the royals managed to avoid disarmament, notably Karangasem and Gianyar, they retained a strong voice in public affairs. There the government set up a system of indirect rule that incorporated the royal families into the administrative framework as district heads, and monitored the power of the lower-ranking indigenous administrators. In this manner the government deliberately created a caste-based hierarchy of political power (Robinson 1995: 29–30). At the same time, it abolished or restricted the traditional powers of the kings, which the government viewed as despotic. Under the traditional system, the royal families had the right to mobilize materials and labor for palace maintenance and ceremonies, as well as to demand labor in exchange for the right to use fields belonging to the royal families or the temples, a system known as *pecatu*. The regional government referred to these rights collectively in Balinese as *ayahan kadaleman* (palace service).[13] These privileges were abolished early on in territories annexed by force; for the royals on the winning side, an abolition order was promulgated for the first time in 1916.[14]

The colonial government established its combination of direct and indirect rule over Bali under the mantle of an ostensibly Hindu worldview, but mere months after its abolition of the *ayahan kadaleman* (a last vestige of the royal system), an event that shocked the government occurred. A Balinese kingdom was not merely a secular political entity, but a single cosmos that sustained the very order of the symbolic world. To abolish the privileges of the king was to abolish the rights that enabled him to maintain the cosmic order. Disruptions to this order could include epidemics, crop failures, and natural disasters such as earthquakes, and it was the duty of the king to restore order when such disturbances occurred. As far as the government was concerned, it had abolished the rights of the kings so as to solidify its rule. However, by stripping the kings of the right to muster materials and labor for ceremonies, the government had made it impossible for the kings to fulfill their role as restorers of the cosmic order. Shortly after the final gesture of the colonial government in replacing the royal system with the secular system of rule it envisioned, a natural calamity that struck Bali seemed intended to provoke the ultimate disturbance and test the government's resolve to change that system.

The earthquake of 1917

At 6:50 a.m. on January 21, 1917, a major earthquake shook southern Bali for some forty seconds. It struck at the time of morning baths, and people bathing in the rivers were swept into ravines, while (as was said to always happen during earthquakes) the sounds of gamelan instruments and bamboo pipes resonated in the air. Aftershocks continued into February and damage was extensive. According to official reports, northern Bali had only fourteen dead, eleven injured, and 1276 collapsed houses, but southern Bali suffered 1358 dead, 1060 injured, 64,488 collapsed houses, and 9927 destroyed rice storehouses. In Payangan, a village in the central southern district, 90 percent of houses were reported destroyed. The damage extended to the colonial government: Dutch homes in Denpasar collapsed, and numerous bridges and roads under construction suffered severe damage. The natural disasters plaguing Bali did not end with the earthquake—the following year a global influenza epidemic killed large numbers of Balinese, and the next year an infestation of rats spread through southern Bali, ruining the harvest. Thus Balinese society endured a succession of blows in the two years after the earthquake.[15]

The earthquake became a symbol of the collapse of the kingdoms' universe. After the quake, one priest wrote a document titled 'Destruction of the world,' in which he described the calamity as a decisive event in the downfall of the kingdoms, a process that had begun with their conflicts with one another in the late nineteenth century.[16] With the regent of Karangasem as their representative, the royal families presented a letter to the Resident of Bali appealing for recognition of the earthquake as divine punishment. As described in detail below, the letter asserted that the neglect of maintenance and failure to perform ceremonies at Besakih Temple had invited the wrath of the gods. In response, the colonial government set out to restore Balinese structures that had been damaged by the quake, but for purposes of cultural preservation rather than religion. The process leading to this decision involved a contentious debate within the government over the proper stance to adopt in relation to Balinese culture. Moreover, with the involvement of the government in the restoration process, Balinese culture became an object of conscious manipulation by the Dutch.

The actual course of developments that culminated in the government's involvement was an extremely convoluted one in which the central administration became embroiled. The colonial government was by no means monolithic, and each department expressed a different view on the issue. Soon after the earthquake, in early February, the architect P. A. J. Moojen sent a letter to the Governor-General. Moojen served as general representative of the culture circles founded in various colonial cities by Dutch enthusiasts of native culture. In his letter Moojen urged the Dutch government to take the lead in restoration work for the sake of cultural preservation.[17] Moojen was fascinated by Balinese architecture, and had spent time on his own in Bali before the earthquake to survey the architecture. After witnessing the collapse of the structures he loved, Moojen offered to take on the role of representative in charge of the restoration work on behalf of the government. His petition was also addressed to the Education and Religion Department, which left it to a subordinate agency, the Archaeological Service, to pass judgment. The head of the service took a negative view of Moojen's request as proposing an unwarranted intervention in native culture, and the Education and Religion Department adopted the same view.

After hearing the Education and Religion Department's opinion of Moojen's request, the central government asked the Resident of Bali and Lombok to render a judgment. The Resident reported on the current situation and asserted that circumstances demanded a reconstruction program led by the government in the interests of cultural preservation. The Resident stressed that the Balinese could not handle the reconstruction on their own and that, if anything, the Balinese themselves desired the government's assistance. He also responded favorably to the idea of hiring Moojen. In response the Archaeological Service reiterated its concerns about the risks of cultural intervention, adding that if, indeed, some minimal government guidance was required, it should be provided by an administrator of the Archaeological Service, not an architect and private citizen like Moojen. Moojen responded by writing directly to the Governor-General and attacking the anti-interventionist ideology of the Education and Religion Department. At the same time, the Resident sent a letter of recommendation to the Governor-General, reiterated the need for government aid toward reconstruction, and again urged the hiring of Moojen.

With opinions on the matter thus polarized, the Education and Religion Department asked the Royal Batavian Society of Arts and Sciences to conduct a survey on the appropriateness of government funding for reconstruction work and on the larger issue of preserving Balinese culture. The society dispatched a three-person investigative committee to Bali from August 20 to 29, 1917, and then prepared a report. The substance of the report consisted of specific instances supporting the views of the head of the Archaeological Service. The Education and Religion Department incorporated this report into a summation of its stance up to that point and presented it to the Governor-General.

The central government determined that its involvement was unavoidable in two areas: restoration of Besakih and other major temples, to which even the non-interventionist investigative committee had agreed, and funding toward reconstruction of the *puri*—the palaces of the royal families and other nobility. The government therefore asked the Archaeological Service to dispatch specialists to estimate the cost of temple restoration and to determine the funding required to rebuild the *puri*. The head of the Archaeological Service sent two specialists— an archaeologist and an architect—to Bali for an inspection tour from November 25 to December 14, 1917. However, the two specialists failed to engage in any serious investigations, either archaeological or architectural, and submitted only a brief report upon their return. While the inspection team was in Bali, the Resident conveyed his impressions in a letter to the Governor-General. He included a scathing attack on the earlier report of the investigative committee, stressed the significance of active involvement by the government in the reconstruction process, and again defended the position of Moojen.

With the specialists dispatched to Bali by the Archaeological Service failing to provide conclusive findings, the central government began to give more weight to the views of the Resident than those of the investigative committee, and to lean toward hiring Moojen. The Education and Religion Department responded to this shift by informing Moojen that work needed to begin immediately on the classification of buildings requiring reconstruction in order to calculate the amount of funding required, and asked Moojen to submit a plan to this effect. At the same time, the department began negotiating with Moojen over the specific conditions of a contract between Moojen and the government. In May 1918, Moojen entered into a formal contract with the government and began surveying the damage in Bali, classifying structures that required funding and calculating restoration costs. At the end of 1919 he submitted a report to the Governor-General, including in it his thoughts and suggestions on the preservation of Balinese culture (Moojen 1920). Reactions to this report from the Bali Resident, the Education and Religion Department, and the

Home Affairs Department were also submitted to the Governor-General, and the central government entered into the process of identifying objects of funding and calculating the amounts of government aid to be provided. The government also solicited advice from the Public Works Department and the Industry and Crafts Department, and, in this manner, finally began in earnest the work of restoring structures.

In short, the colonial government embarked on the restoration of structures at the urging of an architect and cultural enthusiast who presumably did not share the view of Balinese society that the destruction was a sign of the collapse of the kingdoms' universe. With Moojen and the various government departments holding mutually opposing views (the former, an ardent admirer of Balinese culture seen through the prism of architecture; the latter, holders of piecemeal cultural impressions acquired in the course of carrying out their administrative duties), debate continued to rage over a succession of issues: what should the government and the Balinese leaders do, and under what authority? Why must the Dutch government provide financial aid for the purpose of cultural preservation? Who or what should be the recipients of that aid? How should the actual work be carried out? Over the course of this debate, culture came into relief as an object to be defined and manipulated. In other words, by allowing for intervention in culture through the medium of discourse, the earthquake made culture more visible.

Meanwhile, however, throughout this debate, the discourse of the Dutch government regarding cultural preservation continued to be at odds with the Balinese perspective. On the one hand, the royal families accepted the Dutch viewpoint as part of their eager embrace of the modernity brought by the colonial era. On the other hand, they succeeded in securing power in what the government viewed as a traditional religious domain. The struggles among these actors would become more conspicuous in disputes concerning the *puri*, Besakih Temple, and the culture in general.

Issues with *puri* reconstruction

The contradiction inherent in the policies of the colonial government—
which, on the one hand, embraced the caste system as a guiding principle
of colonial rule and, on the other, stripped the royal families at the top
of that hierarchy of their privileges—was nowhere made more apparent
than in the issues surrounding reconstruction of the *puri*. Because the
royals now served as government officials, their residences served a
dual function as public buildings where government business was done.
Yet the process employed to repair any *puri* suffering physical damage
depended on royal privileges that had been established under the old
monarchic system. The government, which had been actively rescinding
these privileges right up until the earthquake, could not take a hands-
off approach to the damage to *puri* that now served as public buildings,
but neither could it leave reconstruction of the *puri* to the royal families
whose powers it had rescinded. Thus the government found that it had
no choice but to take an active part in the reconstruction process.[18] At
the same time, concerns from the standpoints of culture (that the *puri*
must be preserved as culturally significant structures) and economics
(that any government expenditures for this purpose should be kept to a
minimum) added further complexity to the situation. Within the Home
Affairs Department, the issue of rebuilding the *puri* became a subject of
intense debate.

The conflict over ownership of the *puri* and their use as public buildings had been dealt with earlier, in 1912, when the colonial government
provisionally decreed that the former royal residences were not private
property but public buildings for regional administrative purposes.
However, the government also instituted changes in the administrative
units themselves, and in some districts implementation of this decree
became problematic. Moreover, the government advised the districts
that officials' residences and the *puri* should be separated. In 1913 district
heads were living in the *puri* of Karangasem, Gianyar, and Bangli, but
their ownership was restored to private hands and a system adopted
whereby the government would rent them as places of government
business, paying a fixed amount of rent in addition to salaries.

Because maintenance of the *puri* had been part of the aforementioned *ayahan kadaleman* system, the abolition of that system led to the government agreeing to pay fixed monthly amounts to cover building maintenance and other essential expenses. However, when the earthquake struck mere months after the prohibition of the last vestiges of the old system, the *puri* suffered damage far too extensive to be covered by the monthly payments. The king of Gianyar, who now had to pay cash to purchase materials and hire labor, formally requested (in his position as district head) reconstruction funds for the *puri*. The Gianyar king was the only one to quote an actual figure in a request for assistance, and so the rebuilding of the *puri* in Gianyar became a political issue.

Upon receiving the request and recognizing that the measures taken to abolish the *ayahan kadaleman* system represented to the royals a drastic reduction of their past powers, the Resident made a substantive proposal. First, because he could not determine on his own whether the requested amount was appropriate, he asked the central government to send an architect to Bali to make an assessment. Second, he suggested that, while there was no choice but to provide funding in the wake of the old system, the government could still allow the royals to exercise their past privileges within limited time frames and conditions, thereby enabling the government to restrict its funding to just a part of each *puri*. The objective of this proposal was economic: to minimize expenditure on the part of the government.

The Home Affairs Department in Batavia cautiously rejected the Resident's proposal. Deciding that even under restricted conditions it could not reinstitute a system that had already been prohibited, it indicated its inclination to adopt a policy to dispense financial aid. It was the department's judgment that, insofar as everyone on Bali—not only local officials—had suffered losses from the earthquake, re-approval of the *ayahan kadaleman* system for economic reasons might well help the Balinese procure materials and labor for reconstruction of the *puri*, but would also force local people to supply those materials and labor under duress. As the Home Affairs Department grew firmer in its resolve to pursue a policy of monetary aid as a trade-off for the old system, its focus shifted to the practical question of how much money to allocate for which *puri*. To that end, the Home Affairs Department urged the Education and Religion Department to actively respond to the Resident's request that an architectural expert be dispatched to Bali. When Moojen was hired as just such an architectural expert to calculate reconstruction costs, he avoided direct involvement in the political issues surrounding the *puri*, limiting his assessments to the cultural value of the *puri* as architectural structures. Unlike the Home Affairs Department, Moojen viewed the reconstruction of the *puri* strictly as a matter of cultural preservation.

One direct reason for the Home Affairs Department's aversion to dependence on the old system concerned a disturbance involving inhabitants of the Sukawati district on May 17, 1917. The police responded with gunfire and several Balinese were killed or injured. The incident began when residents of four *banjar* (communities) in Sukawati, who had refused to perform uncompensated labor for the *puri* of Gianyar, marched on the Gianyar palace to protest punishments imposed on them for failure to fulfill labor duties. Upon receiving a report from the district head about this activity, the Controller of Gianyar and the Assistant Resident ordered the mobilization of the police to suppress the demonstration, which resulted in the use of firearms. The march by some 150 people, headed by leaders dressed in white, was the first protest action to take place after the earthquake. One of the leaders declared that the protest was directed not at the government but at the royal family, and the government viewed the protestors as motivated by resistance to labor services demanded for *puri* reconstruction, not to compulsory labor for the government. This incident reinforced government doubts that reconstruction work could proceed smoothly if conducted as an extension of the old monarchic system (Lekkerkerker 1920: 205).

In the course of these debates, the Home Affairs Department displayed a keen interest not only in government policy and expenses, but also in the symbolic significance of the *puri* as architectural structures. Whereas Moojen exclusively emphasized the cultural value of the structures, the department was far more sensitive to the symbolic authority evinced by the buildings themselves. Having intentionally avoided addressing the issue of cultural preservation, it now began expressing concern about the Balinese mode of construction of the rebuilt *puri*. The concern was that the indigenous official of Gianyar continued to be viewed by the Balinese as a king and that if a Balinese mode of structure was rebuilt on this occasion, it would only remind people of the kingly authority of the past. The Home Affairs Department intuited that the royal palace was a highly symbolic space that epitomized the power of the king. Meanwhile, however, the Resident proposed a specific means to utilize the old royal privileges. He suggested that the Dutch government take over usage rights to the rice fields that belonged to the king and use the harvest to hire groups of Balinese builders and sculptors to handle the sculpture work on the rebuilt *puri*. The goal was to shift the privileges of the king to groups of commoners in a way that would also enhance the cultural preservation process. It is unclear whether this proposal was actually adopted and carried out, but it shows that the Resident was searching for a way to use royal privileges to the benefit of the people, as he perceived it. The Resident also thought it important that what he considered the cultural activities of architecture and sculpture, heretofore the purview of the royals, be opened up to the public. In short, the Resident sought to address issues associated with the abolition of royal privileges in terms of effecting the transition to a more secular culture.

In the debate over reconstruction, the decision to rebuild the *puri* in a Balinese mode of architecture ultimately presented the government with a contradiction. Just when the government was attempting to carry out a thoroughgoing implementation of its policy to abolish royal privileges, events had occurred that highlighted more forcefully than ever the reasons why the old system of royal privileges existed in the first place. The result was that, even with the government paying the reconstruction costs, the rebuilt *puri* were more gloriously ornate than they had been before the earthquake, according to the testimony of a member of a royal family (Agung 1993: 63). Though the prestige of the royals had certainly been undermined, in the end the rebuilt *puri* became a means of showcasing their authority, just as the Home Affairs Department had feared.

The debate over the *ayahan kadaleman* system was strictly an internal one among government departments; to the general Balinese populace, it was not revealed that the source of reconstruction funding was the government. All that was apparent to the public was that the rebuilt *puri* were more dazzling than ever. Their reconstruction represented the final phase in the absorption of the old kingships into the colonial system of rule. However, the consequences of this process were not what the ruling government had in mind.

Restoring Besakih Temple

The 1917 earthquake was a major turning point in the history of Besakih Temple (Stuart-Fox 2002: 300). On March 6, just over a month after the quake, the regent of Karangasem, the district heads of Gianyar and Bangli, *punggawa* (subdistrict officials), and priests gathered along with several thousand Balinese at Besakih and performed a religious ceremony. Those assembled believed that the neglect of the temple for sixteen years since 1901 and the failure to perform ceremonies there had invited the wrath of the gods and caused the earthquake. The spontaneous belief that the earthquake was divine punishment originated with the Balinese royal families, and the March 6 ceremony was conducted to beg the gods' forgiveness (Kemmerling 1918: 23; Nieuwenkamp 1922: 205).[19]

Immediately after the ceremony, a meeting was held at which it was decided to rebuild Besakih Temple as quickly as possible. With the Karangasem regent acting as representative, a written resolution to this effect was submitted in the name of all the people of Bali to the Resident, seeking his approval.[20] Upon receiving the letter, the Resident gathered the Assistant Resident, Controllers, priests, and other Balinese representatives for deliberations. The result was an agreement by the government that, in general, matters concerning Balinese religion or faith were to be left to the Balinese people. The government granted permission to restore Besakih Temple and did not oppose the procurement of restoration funds by the Balinese, even agreeing to provide financial assistance in view of the cultural value of the temple. Thus, even before the central government had accepted Moojen's advice, the Resident had promised to provide funding for Besakih, and this was a major reason why the Resident so consistently supported Moojen.

The letter submitted by the Karangasem regent consisted of eleven points, the first being that the neglect of Besakih Temple, due to hostilities among the various powers on Bali, had caused the earthquake. The document went on to discuss who would be responsible for reconstruction and subsequent ceremonies, the relationship of the Dutch government to the reconstruction project, how funds would be procured, and how the reconstruction work would be implemented. Finally, it touched on the relationship of religious faith to political sovereignty and, in that context, the relationship between Bali and the Dutch. The key point of the document was its assertion that the restoration of Besakih and the renewal of ceremonies there must be pursued as a cooperative undertaking of the Dutch government and the Balinese.

At the time of the earthquake, Moojen and the colonial government were already persuaded of the historical value of Besakih Temple and maintained a scholarly interest in seeking more facts about it. According to Stuart-Fox (2002), four accounts could be ascertained that mentioned the origins or pre-twentieth-century circumstances of the temple. Two stories were already known in the nineteenth century, having appeared in the historical text *Usana Bali*, which was translated into Dutch by Friederich (1847). The other two accounts related important episodes, one concerning the relationship between Besakih Temple and Hinduism, the other the relationship between the temple and the Balinese kingdoms. These latter accounts first became public knowledge during the colonial era and were incorporated into scholarship on the subject (Stuart-Fox 2002: 262–3). No source text in Balinese could be confirmed for the episode about the relationship with Hinduism, and it was thought to be an oral transmission that first gained notice in the 1930s; the oldest verifiable mention was a reference in a publication by Korn (1932).[21] The episode touching on the relationship with the kingdoms was found in 1932 in an inscription, an archaeological study of which was published in 1934.[22] The existence of a primary temple, recognized for its cultural value by scholars and objectified as a symbol of Balinese culture, was politically convenient for the government. By agreeing to the restoration of the temple, the government could present itself, both inside and outside Bali, as a benevolent ruler that understood the indigenous culture in a manner befitting the era of ethical policy. This was also the reason that an inauguration ceremony for autonomous rulers was held at Besakih Temple, as described in the next chapter.

In the activity surrounding Besakih Temple in the immediate aftermath of the earthquake, the Resident and the rest of the colonial government apparatus took a passive role. The Resident, who ultimately accepted the petition from the Balinese, took a general stance, recognizing the cultural value of the temple and the rationale of cultural preservation inspired by Moojen's appeals. It is not known how the government reacted to the claim that divine punishment was the cause of the earthquake. No record has been found, for example, of any government analysis of the names of the deities mentioned in the letter, or of the reason for citing them. It seems likely that the government viewed the Balinese logic as none of its concern, or ignored it altogether. By contrast, within Balinese society, the government's approval of the petition submitted by the Karangasem regent took on a significance far beyond matters of culture. To the Balinese, it redefined the relationship between the temple and a political center that had shifted under colonial rule. Thus the restoration of Besakih produced the same paradoxical results as the reconstruction of the *puri*. The abolition of royal privileges notwithstanding, the colonial government's hands-off stance in relation to religious activities meant that the royal families could retain their mobilizing powers within the domain of religion, even if the funding itself came from the government.

Well into the nineteenth century there existed in Bali, at least on the ideological level, widespread recognition of Besakih as Bali's supreme temple—an institution that transcended the political boundaries among kingdoms—and a belief that it would be desirable for the kingdoms to jointly administer the temple (Stuart-Fox 2002: 291–6). In practice, however, at the end of the nineteenth century only Klungkung, Karangasem, and Bangli played a material role in the management of Besakih, and the temple was not a focus of concern during the power struggles among the kingdoms. Ideology notwithstanding, the temple was left to decay.

The petition submitted by the Karangasem regent reflected the new political map, as redrawn with the arrival of colonial rule. The royal families of Gianyar and Bangli, which added their names to the document, belonged to the winning side. Since the mid-eighteenth century, Besakih had been part of the territory ruled by Karangasem, and Gianyar had not been involved in the operation of the temple. That these particular kings added their signatures to the petition could only be explained by the political realignment that resulted from developments during the colonial era. Acquiring the right to oversee the reconstruction of Besakih afforded these three royal families a prime opportunity to demonstrate their status within Bali. The result was that they were able to mobilize workers and procure funds on their own initiative. Ultimately, they were blessed with a chance to display their newly gained political power through the traditional medium of religious ceremonies.

Apropos of the relationship between the temple and the political center, the petition was a novel, unprecedented proposal. Rather than claiming the right to administer the temple for a particular king or kings, the letter identified Besakih as the responsibility of the entire Balinese populace. Therefore, the letter suggested, the proper course of action was to carry out the reconstruction with the participation of all Balinese. Until the nineteenth century, maintenance of the temple buildings was at least partly the responsibility of the king, who mobilized the maintenance workforce from people tending the fields he owned. Villagers living in the vicinity of Besakih also played a role in its management (Stuart-Fox 2002: 289–91). The petition, by contrast, proposed requisitioning funds from all Balinese according to the extent of each person's land holdings. The notion of all Balinese participating in projects associated with Besakih appeared for the first time in this document prepared shortly after the 1917 earthquake. Never before had it been argued that Besakih Temple was the concern of the entire populace, or that workers should be recruited on this basis.

Within the framework of the new political reality, the royal 'winners' sought to consolidate their power in the religious sphere. To this end they employed the clever tactic of confronting the Dutch with a cosmological rationale. Their letter cited the Balinese gods and the Queen of the Netherlands in the same context, paying homage to both:

We worship the Supreme God (Sanghijang Akasa Pertiwi), but at the same time we revere Queen Wilhelmina as Mother and Father of the Dutch East Indies…The two of them are like two great, high mountains. If they do not believe in each other, discord is certain to occur…With the Monarch of the Netherlands standing alongside the Supreme Deity (Sanghijang Darma), all earthly fears will surely vanish. The Monarch of the Netherlands is like the Waringin tree, casting a shadow of blessings over all. We trust that she will continue to do everything in her power to protect us, the people of the Dutch East Indies, in perpetuity.[23]

Such statements would appear to suggest that the royal families had assumed an extremely subservient stance in their acceptance of Dutch authority. However, even as the letter accords the Queen of the Netherlands the same deified rank as the Balinese gods, the relationship between the temples and the royal families remained utterly unchanged. In other words, within the cosmological domain at least, the Balinese were still the rulers of Bali. By placing the Queen alongside the Balinese gods, the writers of the letter achieved the reverse effect of incorporating the political reality of colonial rule into Balinese cosmology.

Disputes over the definition of culture

The post-earthquake debate over the wisdom of restoring structures on Bali under the aegis of the government, with Moojen in a supervisory capacity, presented a variety of viewpoints that cannot be reduced to a simple ruler-versus-ruled confrontation. Actors in the debate included Moojen, the Home Affairs Department, the Resident of Bali, the Education and Religion Department, the Archaeological Service, and the investigative committee dispatched by the Royal Batavian Society of Arts and Sciences. Even as their arguments revealed disparities between perceptions of Balinese culture as interpreted from nineteenth-century and subsequent scholarship, and between their perceptions of the actual state of Balinese society under colonial rule, the debate clearly evolved in the direction of designating specific targets for financial aid based on a recognition of cultural value. The parties split into two factions, with Moojen and the Resident calling for government intervention for the sake of cultural preservation, and the non-interventionists (represented by the Education and Religion Department and the investigative committee) urging minimal government involvement. As described earlier, the Home Affairs Department ultimately sided with Moojen and the Resident.

Moojen had first posited the necessity of government intervention in order to preserve Balinese culture. What he feared most was the introduction of non-Balinese elements, such as the use of Western construction materials like cement and steel, in the rebuilding process. The policy he advocated was one of ensuring that the restored structures adhered to Balinese tradition by using construction materials made in Bali, following Balinese texts on architecture as a reference, and entrusting the ornamentation and sculpture work to native Balinese. The concept of cultural preservation advanced in the architect's proposal was predicated on the retention of a Balinese mode of structure.

As mentioned above, the Resident assigned considerable weight to the fact that the request for funding came from the Balinese, but thought it necessary to hire a Dutch architectural expert to calculate the amounts of funding required. Accepting Moojen's assertion that cultural preservation was a legitimate matter of concern, the Resident incorporated into his own arguments Moojen's recommendation to 'provide the necessary instruction and guidance for distinguishing between authentic Balinese culture and the inauthentic.'[24] Noting that elements of Chinese culture and a distorted version of European culture had already been introduced to the island, and so as to prevent the occurrence of 'errors' in the rebuilding process, the Resident deemed it crucial to distinguish between that which was legitimate Balinese culture and that which was not.

The Resident, however, expressed doubts about relying on Balinese texts to determine the proper use of native Balinese materials. While it was true that indigenous texts indicated which materials were to be used for which components, they did not stipulate that any particular materials were forbidden. The Resident questioned whether such texts, written in an era when non-native materials did not even exist on Bali, could be properly employed as criteria for determining the correct form of construction in the present day. That aside, on the question of Moojen's qualifications as an expert in these matters, the Resident believed that if the objective was to rebuild the structures as they were before the earthquake, then there was merit in implementing a plan devised by someone like Moojen, who was familiar with pre-earthquake conditions on Bali due to his previous visits, and who had a deep personal interest in Bali's Hindu architecture. However, the Resident also expressed concern that Moojen's plan smacked of top-down supervision which, if implemented as written, would appear to be forced upon the Balinese, who might well be displeased with this prospect. The Resident suggested that in the case of the *puri* at least, reconstruction should be left to the royal families, with Moojen's ideas offered only in response to any requests for advice.

Upon receiving Moojen's appeal, the Education and Religion Department sought the counsel of H. J. E. F. Schwartz, who had served as Assistant Resident under former Resident Liefrinck, and at the time of the earthquake worked part-time as curator of Balinese exhibits at the Royal Batavian Society of Arts and Sciences.[25] The head of the Archaeological Service studied Schwartz's comments and concluded that Moojen's plan was basically unwarranted. First, the head cited the conservative inclinations of the Balinese in matters of religion and culture, adding that this tendency was the reason why the Hindu culture that had once flourished on Java still survived on Bali. He argued that the attitude of the Balinese ensured that the damaged temples and *puri* would be restored to their previous state in accordance with traditional faith and custom; furthermore, the Balinese had the organizing capacity to make this happen, and previous instances supported this assumption.[26] In short, he concluded, there was no basis whatsoever for the fear that the Balinese would deviate from their own traditions in the aftermath of the recent earthquake. The head declared that the deeply religious Balinese would take Moojen's proposals as unwarranted interference and that they would 'surely reject such leadership or supervision by a foreigner.'

The head of the Archaeological Service went on to say that Moojen's proposal was not only unnecessary, but dangerous. In calling for the preservation of Balinese culture, Moojen was himself displaying mistrust in the attitude of the Balinese toward their own traditions. Moreover, he warned, Moojen might claim to be limiting the purview of his supervision to the materials used, but this purview could easily expand. If it did, it would lead to real interference in Balinese culture and risk spawning a 'monstrous' version of the culture, as imagined by the Dutch, that had never existed in Bali. Moojen might boast that he had spent time in Bali and studied the culture, but his perspective inevitably remained colored by European architecture. The head of the Archaeological Service concluded by warning that reconstruction assisted in the manner proposed by Moojen could ultimately foment Balinese distrust in their own faith. The Balinese believed natural disasters such as epidemics and earthquakes to be the wrath of the gods and hence a religious problem. If aid from outsiders was introduced as a solution, he argued, it could weaken the bond of the Balinese with their faith.

The report of the Royal Batavian Society of Arts and Sciences began with a specific proposal. Temples were the primary concern, as they were considered the cornerstone of Balinese architectural culture. Addressing the current situation in which irrigation systems and the *puri* enjoyed higher reconstruction priority than the temples, the report called attention to the diversity of temples in Bali, classifying them into four categories: (1) family temples, (2) local temples, (3) larger district temples, and (4) the supreme temple, Besakih. It went on to recommend that any aid should first go to temples that were the concern of all Balinese. Regarding Besakih, which the society saw as fitting this description, it supported the assistance previously promised by the Resident (on condition that the costs be properly calculated) and expressed hope that this would provide a stimulus for further temple reconstruction by the Balinese.

The investigative committee also touched on questions of cultural epistemology, specifically the issue of transformation as a type of misappropriation of cultural forms. The discussion focused on the question of how to evaluate and address the danger that Balinese culture might lose its unique essence through transformation and by ultimately misappropriating European or Chinese cultural elements. At the opposite pole from transformation/misappropriation was the concept of cultural purity. An examination of the problem showed that the distinction between purity and transformation/misappropriation could not be defined in terms of beauty versus ugliness, nor of indigenousness versus foreignness.[27] Hence, the committee warned, it was no simple thing to distinguish pure culture from transformed/misappropriated culture. Citing the example of Chinese-made dishes that had become part of Balinese culture through their use as ornamentation in Balinese temples, the committee recognized the absorption of foreign elements by Balinese culture and condemned stereotypical attitudes of cultural purism that rejected any foreign cultural elements outright. It also denounced the ideology of cultural value-loss that attributed purity and beauty exclusively to older culture and viewed more recent Balinese culture as contaminated. The report went on to cite the historical legacy of ancient Javanese Hindu cultural and regional differences in architectural styles within Bali as frames of reference that must be given due consideration in any discussion of transformation/misappropriation.

In bringing up fears of transformation/misappropriation in the reconstruction process, the committee specifically addressed the problem of European influence. First, it distinguished between the *puri* and the temples. As the residences of powerful figures who admired the 'advanced' culture of the West and wanted to enjoy its conveniences, the *puri* already exhibited strong signs of westernization, but this trend did not extend to the temples, the report claimed (i.e. Western influence was confined to the *puri*). Moreover, the predilections of the rulers aside, the use of materials like concrete and steel in construction was favored simply because they were more durable than native Balinese materials. In this light, the committee cited two reasons for the transformation/misappropriation of European elements—first, the appeal of a 'higher' culture caused by the perception imposed by a ruling culture on its subjects of their own culture as ugly and inferior, and, second, the economic reason of durability. The assumptions that aesthetic judgment was an indicator of cultural superiority, and that it was inevitable that the inferior Balinese would yearn for the more advanced Western culture, typified a notion of civilization that ran through the entire discourse.

The committee arrived at its judgment on the propriety of a Dutch-led reconstruction program under Moojen's supervision by asking whether it was desirable or even possible to implement a policy of protecting

Balinese culture from transformation/misappropriation by removing the two reason mentioned above. The committee's position was that a distinction must be made between the Balinese and European viewpoints and that, according to the former, outside intervention was meaningless and Balinese culture was something to be modified at will by the Balinese themselves. Even if such modification resulted in what Europeans saw as a betrayal of their image of a pure Balinese culture, that was still, indisputably, Balinese culture. The very concept of cultural preservation, declared the committee, was not part of Balinese thinking, custom, or religion, but a European construct. In other words, the committee viewed culture as a kind of hothouse flower that would grow on its own as long as one made sure it was not exposed to rain or strong sunlight. Excessive intervention would only invite more transformation/misappropriation. Mention was made of the cultural changes that occurred in Buleleng, and particularly its main city, Singaraja, which absorbed European cultural influences earlier than anywhere else on Bali. Here government offices and schools were built, but new performing arts and musical forms also developed. Thus the committee indicated that it accepted some minimum degree of government guidance, but its overall stance toward culture was non-interventionist.

Regarding a government-led reconstruction process, the committee did not challenge Moojen's credentials as an architect or his knowledge of Balinese culture, but viewed the means of carrying out the project that he so forcefully recommended (i.e. under government guidance and instruction) as an extreme form of intervention. Even if Moojen's judgments in these matters were sound, the committee harbored strong misgivings that the implementation process itself would threaten the autonomy of the culture. It also feared that if the Dutch arbitrarily imposed their will in this manner in the name of cultural preservation, it would end up compelling Balinese society to provide excessive amounts of labor and goods. The committee concluded that only the bare minimum of government involvement in the reconstruction process was justified. While generally acquiescing to the idea of providing financial aid and professional advice for the temples and *puri*, its only specific recommendation was that costs be determined for aid to Besakih and its associated temples. As for hiring Moojen, the committee continued to take a dim view of this as a step that would invite excessive intervention. Instead, it requested that the government dispatch an archaeologist to devise a limited program for Balinese cultural preservation.

The Resident responded to the committee's report with a rebuttal based on the results of his own inspection tour. He began by criticizing the committee for an obsolete point of view that cloistered itself behind academic arguments and, worst of all, ignored the realities of Balinese society. The committee's argument was predicated on a dualistic perspective that placed Balinese thinking on one side and European thinking on the other, but this view, he declared, had no bearing whatsoever on the reality of Balinese society under Dutch rule. The very posture espoused by the committee—of encouraging the free development of Balinese culture by keeping 'outside' European interference to a minimum—was itself an outgrowth of the stereotypical notion of 'Bali versus the West,' which the Resident lambasted as an anachronism. He argued that Dutch instruction and guidance were needed in the proper use of the Western materials that were already being imported into Bali, and recommended Moojen as more suited to this task than an archaeologist. Analyzing the examples cited in the report, the Resident declared that the committee had erroneously judged Moojen's proposals to be excessively interventionist based on a distorted interpretation of the facts described in the examples. Praising Moojen's diplomatic talents and his experience in Bali, the Resident concluded that, while he recognized the need for archaeological research, he considered Moojen more reliable than an archaeologist who had never before set foot in Bali.

In the end the Home Affairs Department adopted the viewpoint of the Resident and progressed to the phase of identifying the targets and scope of assistance. Rejecting the stance of the committee as overly optimistic, the department concluded that the government, in its capacity as ruler, had an obligation to protect the culture, that Balinese society required not only monetary funding but also aesthetic advice, and that appropriate guidance was needed to foster a hoped-for 'new creativity in Balinese architecture.' More specifically, it outlined the following course of action: first, guidelines should be established to determine which structures to rebuild; then, based on these guidelines, structures should be identified and earmarked for assistance with the agreement of the owners. Finally, the government hired Moojen to oversee the execution of this policy, rejecting the candidates recommended by the Archaeological Service.

Underlying this debate was the question of how to identify, and how to deal with, 'legitimate' culture. The first party to propose government intervention was not an administrator but Moojen, a serious devotee of Balinese culture whose proposal was based on the perception that legitimate culture was easy to identify. Moojen believed in the existence of a true Balinese culture, and asserted that the goal of his efforts was to restore structures to their original state, keeping Dutch inclinations out of the equation as much as possible. Moojen's critics, on the opposing side, recognized the inevitability of cultural change and evolution, denied that there was such a thing as legitimate culture, and called instead for the free development of culture. There was no concept in Balinese tradition of legitimate culture, they claimed, nor of cultural preservation based on such a notion: 'legitimate culture' was a monstrous distortion of Balinese culture invented by the Dutch—one which, Moojen's opponents predicted, might well destroy Balinese culture.

The gap between these two views of culture was clearly temporal in character. The legitimate culture advocates saw the past as the standard for defining legitimate culture, believing that a Balinese culture that reflected the old traditions was the authentic version. The fact that Moojen (1926: 1–2) prefaced one of his own works by passionately relating how he had seen old Javanese Hindu culture in Bali reflects the degree to which the historical perceptions established by nineteenth-century scholarship onward formed the foundation of the cultural views of such advocates. Conversely, the debunkers of legitimate culture, in espousing free cultural development, embraced a view of culture that was more oriented to the future, not the past.

The most noteworthy aspect of these opposing perspectives on legitimate culture is that while they appear to be mutually antagonistic, both fail to recognize the creativity of the Balinese. Both positions share the viewpoint of Hurgronje (1906), the most famous scholar in the central government, who acknowledged the possibility of innovation only in 'civilized' societies. The future-oriented debunkers of legitimate culture at first glance appear more progressive in their views on culture than the advocates. However, even the debunkers predicated their stance on a belief in the cultural conservatism of the Balinese, and opposed the use of Western materials in Bali. They championed the free development of culture precisely because they were certain of the conservative character of Balinese culture. The fact that the debate revolved around the issue of transformation/misappropriation and came to focus on the influence of modernization introduced by colonial conditions can be attributed to the shared refusal by both sides to recognize Balinese creativity.

In reality, both Moojen and the Resident had witnessed first-hand the intense curiosity of the Balinese about the West. The regent of Karangasem gave his newly built villas names like Paris and Amsterdam, and local officials at the center of the *puri* reconstruction controversy sought to consult Moojen about rebuilding their residences in a Western style. Besides their residences, the royals on the winning side vied with each other over another status symbol—automobiles, which they festooned with elaborate ornamentation. The first automobile to travel the roads of Bali was a Belgian Minerva purchased by the Karangasem royal family, which was particularly proud of the luster of the car body. Finished from front to back with elegant decorations that gradually grew more detailed, the car boasted shiny brass bumpers and a horn that extended all the way to the rear. Its brilliance was further set off by the black trim on the roof and trunk. Inside, the seats were covered with deep green velvet and the windows with satin curtains, while silk cloth stretched across the ceiling. A crystal bottle of eau de cologne stood next to a vase holding artificial flowers made of silk. The exterior, originally painted the same shade of green as the interior, was repainted yellow at the time of purchase because the Balinese word for yellow, kuning, sounded like the Dutch word, koningin, for queen. Meanwhile, the royals of Gianyar bought a limousine, mounted a gold statuette of Garuda on the hood, and attached a yellow flag to the body (Djelantik 1997: 25–6; Agung 1993: 64).

What both sides in the legitimate culture debate shared in common was an opposition to what they viewed as the excessive modernism of the Balinese—in other words, they shared an institutional aversion to 'colonial modern.' The legitimate culture advocates naturally viewed the Balinese absorption of Western culture negatively. However, even the debunkers exhibited scorn for the Balinese attraction to the West, betraying an attitude of superiority in their belief that the Balinese felt their own culture to be ugly and inferior in the face of this 'higher' culture. Essentially, both sides feared that the indigenous culture would be swept away by forces of modernity that they themselves had introduced. This collective denial of Balinese creativity brought paradoxical results. On the one hand, the anti-interventionists espoused a future-oriented view of culture but were unable to accept pro-modernization attitudes on the part of the Balinese. If anything, it was the interventionists who recognized that the current state of Balinese society was one in which the Dutch and the Balinese were jointly engaged in the creation of a new reality. Even as they called for cultural preservation based on the traditions of the past, the interventionists acknowledged the attraction of Western modernity to the Balinese. Indeed, that is precisely why they formed a consensus that guidance and instruction were necessary to prevent the cultural changes already occurring under the influence of the West from going too far. It was on this point that the interventionists viewed the stance of the investigative committee as unrealistic, attacking the committee for inventing a false notion of distance separating Bali from the West. Thus the interventionists rejected the modernizing impulses in the Balinese, but bore witness to these impulses in calling for the preservation of legitimate culture.

For all this, the Dutch government's funding of reconstruction on Bali came to an unceremonious end in the 1920s. The cessation of aid resulted not from a clear-cut decision by the central government, but because of a change in Residents. The new Resident, H. T. Damsté, who was known as a skilled colonial administrator with a keen understanding of cultural matters, took a dim view of the reconstruction program. With his arrival, the projects underway were deprived of economic support. Damsté's view was that Bali was relatively wealthy compared to other regions under Dutch rule and that the Balinese themselves were capable of rebuilding destroyed structures with their own funds; as for the restoration of Besakih Temple, the funds already raised were sufficient for the task, any government leadership beyond the minimum required would be a mistake, and the work should continue with the Balinese in charge.

The suspension of the reconstruction program aroused in Moojen implacable feelings of distrust and frustration toward the new Resident, to whom he replied that all the government aid had been used up and the Balinese had already contributed more than that amount themselves.[28] Moreover, he said, the Balinese regarded the government funding as a gift and did not mind if it was replaced by a government order requisitioning funds from the Balinese people; all they asked was that the restoration of Besakih somehow be completed under the government's guidance. From Moojen's statements it can be inferred that the Balinese royal families already depended on the authority of the colonial government in order to muster a workforce.[29]

Despite the fact that Damsté, who contemplated Balinese issues within the larger context of the entire colonial territory and assigned weight to their economic aspects, clashed head-on with Moojen and his narrow focus on cultural concerns, the two men saw eye to eye on the question of preserving Balinese culture. Both were in Bali when tourists began visiting the island after the First World War, and both became increasingly concerned about the effect of tourism on Balinese culture.[30] Damsté lamented that the unique attributes of the Balinese were vanishing even from their mode of dress, and that their religious sensibilities were being deformed by 'our' Western education. If culture was to be a consideration, then special measures must be taken with Bali, such as appointing administrators familiar with Balinese culture. Damsté asserted that the Balinese should be educated about their own music and their 'admirable' script, and they should not be taught in Malay. For his part, Moojen applauded these declarations. Their mutual concern that Balinese culture would disintegrate without special safeguards became even more pronounced in the late 1920s, with administrators of the period sharing the view that Balinese culture was unique and merited serious attention. At the same time, the tendency to place Balinese society in the stereotypical, and ontological, category of 'Hindu' was also reinforced.

In the 1930s, Damsté's recommendations on cultural education were implemented as part of a policy of 'Balinization,' which, as will be seen in Chapter 2, provoked heated disputes among the Balinese. Meanwhile, Moojen, who had returned to the Netherlands after the suspension of the restoration project, served on the executive committee of the Dutch Pavilion at the International Colonial Exposition in Paris in 1931. The success of the exposition further entrenched among Europeans the reputation of Balinese culture as a last vestige of the golden age of Hinduism (Nagafuchi 1998).

The beneficiaries of the cultural preservation policy were, in any event, the royal families. What the Dutch perceived as culture was to the Balinese the domain of religion and custom. While the government assisted in the reconstruction of Besakih Temple and the *puri* in the name of cultural preservation, it declared a non-interventionist stance toward religion. However, the rebuilding of the *puri* enabled the owners (the royal families) to assert their authority in the religious domain, with Besakih at its apex. As the government's emphasis on the importance of culture grew stronger, so too did the discretionary powers of the Balinese in the realm of religion, further enhancing the authority of the royals.

During the initial period of Dutch rule over Bali that extended into the 1920s, it could be said that the regional colonial government readily acquiesced to the conclusion advanced by nineteenth-century scholars that Bali was a Hindu island. The process by which scholarship was introduced in the service of colonial rule is obvious; colonial administrators all shared the nineteenth-century conviction that Hinduism was not merely the name of a religion or civilization, but a glorious culture that legitimized their own rule. The dispute that followed the earthquake cleared a space in which royal privilege could be exercised, but it was the preconception about Hinduism in Bali that made the creation of that space possible. Indeed, the royals would find it increasingly difficult to extricate themselves from the confines of this Hindu framework. During the 1930s, as Bali directly experienced the effects of the Great Depression, ordinary citizens began to turn to traditional religious rituals. Then, as the colonial system entered a period of maturation with the reinvention of the kingdoms as autonomous regions and the institution of indirect rule, yet another space was created within the system, one independent of the royal families whose allegiance was to the colonial government. Important changes began to occur in the religious sphere that would carry over into the post-independence era.

CHAPTER 2

Another Space

A return to religious ritual

H. Beeuwkes, who was appointed Resident of Bali and Lombok by the Dutch colonial government in 1929, just as the world was entering the Great Depression, wrote in his Successor's Report, 'Since the visitation of the economic crisis on all of Bali, one can observe a heightening of awareness of religion' (he underlined the word 'heightening'). The Resident wrote that, throughout the region, he witnessed the restoration of temples, the performance of religious ceremonies, and the formation of gamelan ensembles. Moreover, he made these statements under the heading, 'A new culture'—the economic crisis had sparked a new interest in the world of religious ritual across Balinese society.

The Resident also reported the initiation of new activities not limited to ceremonies: in Gianyar groups were formed to read classical texts, while in Tabanan priests opened schools to teach religion. What particularly surprised the Resident was that even members of the younger generation of educated Balinese who worked for the colonial government were taking part in religious ceremonies and activities. These same young people were also busy organizing discussion groups. Conscious of the upsurge in nationalism already seen in Java, the Resident claimed that these groups were not part of a Java-like independence movement, or Indonesia Merdeka. In fact, the Resident welcomed this 'new culture' as a kind of 'renaissance' (MvO Beeuwkes 1932: 148–52).

In his analysis of the reasons for this revival of the world of ritual, Beeuwkes attributed it directly to the economic depression. The burgeoning ranks of the unemployed in every profession could no longer afford city pleasures like movies or the stambul theater, and their mass return to their home villages, the Resident postulated, spurred a revival of the traditional customs of village society. Stambul was a genre of provocative comedy

47

theater that had exploded in popularity (on par with cinema) as a form of urban entertainment in Indonesia. It offered revues by musicians and dancers who shouted and engaged in vigorous mechanical movements, sometimes parodying school training to great laughter. The name, derived from the city of Istanbul, added the Middle Eastern flavor imported via films to the comic theater then popular in Java. Adrian Vickers (1996: 19), for example, cites stambul as 'the most blatantly modern' of the hybrid styles of entertainment that appeared in the 1920s.

Beeuwkes viewed the young people who were previously engaged in wage labor but now returned to the cultural milieu of the village as the reason for the renaissance to which he refers. A reaction arose against the excessive infatuation with all things Western—in education, health care, entertainment, and technology—and the Resident speculated that this might reflect a fear by people that their neglect of religious duties had incurred the wrath of the gods. Even in the 1930s, he surmised, there was a widespread belief that the divine retribution visited upon the Balinese in the form of the great earthquake of 1917 had not yet subsided.

Even before the onset of the Great Depression, a legal decision had facilitated the return to religious ceremonies in Bali. In 1928 the regional government revised the slaughter tax, redefining the types of animals that would not be subject to the tax. A new category of exceptions was added at the top of the list: 'animals, including cattle, calves, pigs, and piglets, used for purposes associated with custom or religion,' provided the meat was not used for food.[1] Once the Great Depression arrived, this revision of the law had an impact on the performance of religious rituals. When the economic crisis was making itself felt most severely in Tabanan, various *punggawa* (subdistrict officials) circulated a document about the revised tax written by Gede Anom Manuaba, a judge of the native court. The document provided a detailed description of which animals should be used as offerings in which ceremonies, and how to conduct the ceremonies. The circulation of the document attracted the attention of people outside Tabanan as an indication of the government's acceptance of local autonomy in matters pertaining to religious practice. Sentiment also grew that if exemptions to the slaughter tax were to be made in Tabanan,

Bali's richest district and one blessed with ample farmland, then similar measures should be applied elsewhere in Bali.[2]

The performance of ceremonies at Besakih Temple resumed during the same period as the revision of the slaughter tax. In Bali newly completed buildings require a melaspas (purification ceremony) before they can be used. The purification ceremony for Besakih Temple, which had been rebuilt under the leadership of Moojen after the earthquake of 1917, took place over two days, April 1 and 2, in 1928. On May 12 that year a grand cockfight tournament, in which all the royal families participated, was held to raise funds for the operation of the temple (Stuart-Fox 2002: 305). Then, on May 12, 1930, a conference was held under the auspices of the royal family of Klungkung to study ceremonies to be held at Besakih Temple following the purification. A report on the conference states that all the royal families of Bali had been engaged in 'very earnest discussions in recent years' about ceremonies at Besakih Temple.[3] The conference concluded with a decision to hold a large-scale sacrificial rite, known as Panca Walikrama,[4] on September 29, 1933. In fact, September 29 was the date when a procession began to make its way to Klotok Beach in Klungkung, and the actual ceremony welcoming the gods took place at Besakih Temple for eleven days starting October 4.

The long wait until 1933 before this large-scale ceremony could be held at Besakih was due to the fact that the procession from the temple to the beach had to cross a river, and a bridge for this purpose had yet to be completed. A purification ceremony for the bridge, built by the Public Works Department, was held on October 19, 1932, and this made it possible to perform the Panca Walikrama. Thus implementation of the ceremony was dependent on a public works project carried out by the colonial government. Resident Beeuwkes saw the series of ceremonies at Besakih Temple as prime examples of the emergence of the new culture. Furthermore, he viewed the temple as 'national heritage' and, indeed, the improvement of the transport infrastructure led to an increase in tourists visiting Besakih (MvO Beeuwkes 1932: 18).

Subsumption into capitalism

The relationship between Balinese society and a capitalist economy is often discussed in terms of an association with the tourist industry. However, tourism did not approach a peak in Bali until the 1930s and, even then, the percentage of Balinese involved in the industry remained extremely low.[5] If anything, it was the tax system of the colonial government that enmeshed every Balinese without exception and cemented the relationship between Balinese society and capitalism. Among the diverse taxes levied by the government, the land tax implemented in the 1920s prompted the spread of a cash economy. With the increasing subsumption of Balinese society into a capitalist economy, it was inevitable that it would directly suffer the impact of the worldwide depression.

The authority to build dams, once the exclusive purview of the kings, was handed over to the colonial government; along with its job of maintaining roads and bridges, the Public Works Department began constructing concrete dams in order to stabilize water resources and expand rice paddies. At the same time, with the objective of organizing and streamlining Bali's irrigation systems, the government took over the *subak* cooperatives that had traditionally managed the water supply and organized the irrigation systems. In the 1920s, it became feasible to carry out quantitative surveys of farmland throughout the island. Immediately after the First World War, moreover, the colonial government sought to increase tax revenue with an eye to restoring the coffers of the homeland. At this time, cultivated acreage was recalculated and crop yield per unit of farmland was reassessed, with land taxes revised accordingly.[6]

Even as previously overlooked land was now calculated as a target for taxation, the tax rate itself was higher in Bali than any other region, and the colonial government viewed the Balinese as 'good taxpayers.'[7] They were able to cope with the markedly heavier tax burden only because their income from exports was also growing. Planning for a new port at Benoa to the south of Denpasar began in 1911, formal authorization was granted in 1913, and in the 1920s fully fledged harbor facilities were in place.[8] Benoa replaced Singaraja, which was not equipped to handle large amounts of cargo, as Bali's main import–export conduit. Roads were also improved in and around Denpasar, and commerce in Bali grew rapidly. The system supporting commercial activities also underwent a fundamental change from the era of the kingdoms. The monopoly on trade that had been bestowed upon the Chinese population by the kings disappeared, and the activities of individual brokers burgeoned. Balinese women joined the Chinese, who retained their old trade networks, in expanding an export-oriented economy in Bali.[9] Meanwhile, the government's requirement that land taxes be paid in colonial currency, not rice, accelerated the dependence of farmers on the market.[10] The land tax made it imperative to acquire colonial currency, so farmers were compelled to sell their rice, not trade it. The price of rice rose in the 1920s, barely enabling farmers to keep up with the new taxation system as long as the market price of rice remained at a level commensurate with the taxes they were paying (Robinson 1995: 54–9; Schulte Nordholt 1996: 283–6).

In an era when the livelihoods of Balinese farmers could no longer remain independent of the international capitalist economy that controlled the price of traded goods, the drop in exports and prices that accompanied the shrinkage of international trade in the wake of the Great Depression had a severe impact on Balinese society. Viewing this situation with concern, the regional government convened a conference, which included the royal families, to discuss reduced tax rates and the feasibility of accepting tax payments in rice.[11] However, the government insisted that priority be given to securing tax revenue and made no attempt to devise policies that would address the plight of the taxpayers.

The societal changes wrought by the depression were, in fact, profound enough to endanger the regime itself. The land tax system gave birth to a new social domain, invisible to the government, in which transactions that threatened to rip Balinese society asunder took place. The targets of taxation were not individuals, but fixed units of land known as *pipil* that were administered according to written records. As long as the tax calculated for a given plot of land was successfully collected, the government did not care who paid the tax or in what manner. It did not concern itself with the social relations between landowners and laborers (i.e. who paid whom, under what terms, or whether the payment was made in labor, cash, or rice). In these matters the government relied on the Balinese tax collectors,

51

known as *sedahan*, who had done this work since the era of the kingdoms.[12] Thus, in possession of unregulated discretionary powers, the *sedahan* began to acquire, at low prices, land relinquished by farmers who could not afford to pay taxes.[13] The increase in landless farmers generated more poverty, creating social conditions that might well have led to an explosion of discontent against those who exercised their discretionary powers for personal gain. Meanwhile, the regional government, which viewed the poverty issue solely in economic terms, failed to see that the land tax system brought with it structural factors that could intensify antagonism toward the regime itself. A number of tax collectors, however, recognized this animosity and feared for their own safety. Ultimately, it was these tax collectors who decried the plight of the farmers in articles contributed to magazines, and who sought a more tolerant method of tax payment.[14]

The desperate circumstances of Balinese society in the 1930s, however, were not generally recognized. This is primarily because the perception of Bali as a land of idyllic village communities had predominated among Dutch administrators since they first took over the island. The administrators shared a preconceived notion of Bali as a society of equals, where nearly everyone owned land that could be expected to produce large yields of rice. Plantations and forced cultivation of cash crops for export had heavily impacted rural society in Java, and the fact that Bali had virtually neither of these made this perception all the more credible. Furthermore, the image of the 'beautiful savage' that spread on a global scale in the 1930s exacerbated the idealization of the village community. In reality, however, even as Balinese dancers were astonishing Europeans at the Dutch Pavilion of the International Colonial Exposition in Paris in 1931, the economic crisis was already sending tremors through Balinese society. But ethnographers in the 1930s were not interested in issues like poverty; the renowned anthropologists Margaret Mead and Gregory Bateson studied Balinese village life, and Miguel Covarrubias, Jane Belo, Colin McPhee, and Walter Spies wrote extensively about their experiences living with their 'Balinese friends.' But even these individuals—who were ostensibly observing Balinese society with a sharper eye and from a different, more intimate perspective than the colonial administrators—ultimately viewed rural life on the island as one blessed by abundance, just as the administrators did.

The establishment of autonomous regions

During the period Resident Beeuwkes described as a cultural renaissance, the colonial government was incrementally solidifying the caste-based order that placed the royal families at the top. This process, in turn, further cemented the direct relationship between the ruling order and religious practice. In 1929 the government recognized the old kingdoms as autonomous political units known as Negarabestuur (*negara* in Balinese means state, bestuur in Dutch means administration), permitting the royal families to use titles indicating their rank and to exercise political authority in certain areas.[15] In 1931 a Paruman Kerta Negara (State Council) made up of representatives of the royal families was formed for the purpose of addressing Bali-wide issues, although it was not recognized as having administrative functions. This council signified the birth of the first unified political order covering all of Bali, one in which equal status was afforded to all royal families, not only those on the 'winning side.' Then, in 1938, the government redefined the old kingdoms as autonomous regions and conferred upon the royal families the status of heads of these regions. That same year, a Paruman Agung (Council of Royal Families) was formed, and in 1940, due to the overlapping memberships of the two bodies, the State Council was absorbed into the Council of Royal Families. The royal families were each permitted to adopt the high-ranking title of Anak Agung. The autonomous regions had their own independent sources of revenue and carried out administrative functions entrusted to them by the colonial government. In this way, the government completed the establishment of a system of indirect rule over Bali.

A ceremony of recognition of the heads of the autonomous regions was held at Besakih Temple on June 29, 1938, the day of Galungan, the most important Balinese holiday, when the ancestral spirits return to their homes.[16] The performance of an administrative ceremony on a religious holiday at a temple (rather than at the seat of government in Singaraja) reflected the religious considerations that lay at the root of the political policy of establishing the autonomous regions. From the days of his tenure as Resident, when he oversaw an end to the restoration work following the earthquake of 1917, Damsté had called for a reappraisal of royal family authority as a form of natural authority capable of exercising 'magical powers' to rebuild the religiosity of Balinese society, which was already on the decline.[17] The royal families further consolidated their authority, as represented by their power to mobilize labor at Besakih Temple; only the rulers of Karangasem, Klungkung, Bangli, and Gianyar had participated as Controllers in the 1933 ceremony at Besakih,[18] but when the autonomous regions were established, temple operations were taken over by the Council of Royal Families.

According to the discourse of reconstruction, which employed the metaphor of Balinese society as a single building, the structure's foundation was not the royal families, but the villages. It was the view of the regional government that village society, centered as it was around religious ritual, was particularly threatened by the loss of religiosity, and that a system of 'native rule' with the royal families at the top was the equivalent of a 'roof' to protect these traditions. Karangasem, whose royal family had long enjoyed something close to indirect rule since becoming the first territory to have its king designated as regent, was seen as a test case for whether such a system could really work as desired, without backfiring on the government.

The biggest problem associated with establishing the autonomous regions was the gap in status among the royal families. The government, having decided to confer equal status as heads of autonomous regions upon all the royal families (including those of the 'losing side'), nonetheless used Karangasem (the representative of the 'winning side') as its model in designing the autonomous region system.[19]

The specific means employed by the government to restore to village society what it perceived as an endangered religiosity consisted of research on customary law and philological studies to decipher Balinese documents. Before the autonomous regions were established, the regional government submitted a report to the central government for the purpose of outlining the actual state of affairs in the old kingdoms that were to become autonomous regions.[20] Identical topics were listed in the table of contents for every territory, in the following order: ethnographic descriptions of geography, population and ethnic classification of inhabitants, livelihood, religion, and language, followed by descriptions of economic conditions and the ruling order. While it is true that the report duly assembled the facts that could be determined about conditions in each territory at the time, it was predicated on the immutable perception of the Balinese as heirs to the Majapahit kingdom, and its presentation of Balinese history and customs was not based on surveys, but consisted of quotations from the research of Korn and R. Goris, who were already regarded as authorities in these matters, as will be described later. This ethnographic research provided the blueprint for the 'new building' that the system of indirect rule was to be.

The establishment of the autonomous regions was linked to policies that involved the colony at large. In the 1920s, it was a general policy of the colonial government (which feared the rise of nationalism) to rely on 'natural' authority by reinforcing the political position of indigenous representatives who were recognized for their 'traditional' status (Schulte Nordholt 1996: 265; cf. Sutherland 1979). It was also part of the government's 'ethical policy' aimed at promoting conciliatory relations with the indigenous population to delegate some administrative responsibilities to indigenous representatives. In parallel with the ethical policy, the government also implemented regional administrative reforms with the objective of streamlining its rule over the burgeoning colonial territories by decentralizing regional governance. One product of this policy was the creation of a separate administrative unit known as De Groot Oost (The Great East), consisting of the Lesser Sunda Islands from Bali eastward and territory from Sulawesi eastward, with Makassar as its administrative seat. The autonomous regions of Bali were established as part of this administrative reform.

A fierce debate ensued over the proper jurisdiction for Bali, which sat on the boundary between Java and The Great East. Scholars had emphasized the deep historical relationship of Bali to Java as heir to the latter's ancient Hindu culture, yet Bali was designated as part of The Great East, not of Java. The government, which saw an Islamist undercurrent in the national independence movement, wanted Balinese Hinduism to serve as a countervailing force and therefore sought to isolate Bali from the 'contamination' that might occur if its people made 'pilgrimages' to Java, the center of the movement. Bali's inclusion in The Great East provoked controversy from a different angle, however. The eastern side of The Great

East territory had a large Christian population. When the government was studying the inclusion of Bali in The Great East, a discussion ensued regarding the possible conversion of the Balinese to Catholicism, with which they were seen to share a ritualistic bent. The government had prohibited Christian mission activities in Bali, but this discussion sparked a contentious debate over the pros and cons of that policy. In the end, the pro-mission side was overridden by arguments in favor of preserving Bali's cultural uniqueness (Robinson 1995: 36–45; Schulte Nordholt 1996: 277–93). Ultimately, Bali's isolation from Java had the effect of reinforcing the island's Hindu culture, as well as exercising a profound impact on Balinese society, which will be examined in the next chapter.

Making the royal families the heads of autonomous regions ironically ensured them even greater stability in their social status. Not only did the permission to use top-ranking titles enhance their position atop the caste hierarchy, but the possibility of other indigenous administrators in the colonial government turning against the royals disappeared. During the era of the kingdoms, the royal families had been constantly in conflict with one another or with their own satellites and sought to sustain their rule through displays of power in the form of religious ceremonies. Now the fluidity of these kingdoms was a thing of the past. Moreover, the royals' position as heads of autonomous regions enabled them to seize religious authority as well. The colonial government had actually hoped for a restoration of religiosity in the villages, not among the royals, and had restored Besakih Temple (which would become a symbol of political authority) not for religious reasons but in the interests of cultural preservation. The royal families themselves were enamored with the new modernity that the colonial era had brought with it—and yet it was the royals whose religious authority was enhanced (cf. Geertz 1980; Schulte Nordholt 1981).

Order and discord

Before the emergence of the new culture, organized efforts to spread religious knowledge had begun on a small scale in the late 1910s.[21] The process that culminated in the establishment of the autonomous regions had fomented intense discord in Balinese society, and the organizations that were formed articulated those frustrations. The nature of their activities can be ascertained today from magazines produced by two such groups, Shanti Adnyana and Surya Kanta. Shanti emerged in 1923 from Suita Gama Tirtha, which was founded in Singaraja in 1921; in 1924 the group began to call itself Shanti Adnyana (and later Bali Adnyana). It came to be dominated by holders of noble rank and, on October 1, 1925, members who were not of the nobility and were upset by this development split and formed a new group, Surya Kanta. The disputes that arose between the two groups reflected a conflict between castes.[22] The two associations published their own magazines, respectively titled *Bali Adnyana* and *Surya Kanta*. Both publications had as their primary objective the study and dissemination of religious knowledge, and their most critical point of contention concerned questions about the legitimacy of authority based on caste.

If we compare the two magazines, *Surya Kanta* is the more explicit in its arguments. In this publication one senses an idealism that seeks moderate, pragmatic social reform. *Surya Kanta* articulated four goals upon its founding: (1) honor the *budi*, (2) improve economic conditions, (3) improve the circumstances of the *jaba*, and (4) reform customs in a way appropriate to the progress of the times.[23] *Budi*, usually translated as reason or wisdom, refers to the proper means of exercising sacred power for the sake of the kingdom; as will be explained below, this concept was central to attempts at a reinterpretation of kingships and royal authority (Tsuchiya 1982: 33; cf. Nagazumi 1980: 116). *Surya Kanta* also provided commentary on documents containing religious teachings in Balinese and Javanese, disseminated these teachings, and called for a more rational approach to religious rites, including simplification of the extremely expensive cremation ceremonies. The group sought to increase solidarity among people without noble rank, and introduced Gandhian philosophy. It did not confine itself to caste-related issues, but extended its discussions to calls for greater ethnic self-awareness and debates over the form Balinese society should take amid the changes brought about by the colonial era.

Particularly noteworthy is the use by Surya Kanta members of the title *jaba* to identify themselves. The term is Balinese for 'outside,' in opposition to *jero*, or 'inside'; when used as an appellation for people, *jero* connotes a person of higher rank than oneself. To use *jaba* to refer to oneself is to dare to declare that one is in an inferior position (i.e. excluded from the 'inside'). The choice of *jaba* as a self-appellation was a political statement by the members of Surya Kanta that reflected their recognition of the political reality created by the colonial system. People of noble rank used their monopoly on mid-level official posts in the colonial government apparatus to accrue exclusive privileges, while the majority of the population without rank were increasingly marginalized from the political arena. In addition, those of noble rank used religion and culture to justify their privileges, affirming the caste system with claims that such Hindu-based practices were part of Balinese tradition. Surya Kanta viewed caste privileges as a construct of the colonial era, pointing out that people without rank had served as political officials under the kingdoms that preceded the colonial era, an observation that Korn (1932) also made, as mentioned in Chapter 1.[24]

The reality-inspired self-appellation of *jaba* represented the concrete description of people without noble rank as a single category, and the definition of the marginalized members of the population as a countervailing force. The choice of the Balinese word further implied a negation of the Hindu term *sudra* for this class. This signified a tacit rejection by Surya Kanta of the stance of the government, which cited Hindu tradition as a basis for placing people without noble rank at the bottom of a caste system, as well as a confrontational posture, symbolized by use of the Balinese term, toward members of the nobility who claimed Hindu custom as a justification for flaunting their power.[25]

The use of the term *jaba* also implied recognition of the existence of its opposite, *jero*, and here one can see evidence of the idealism in Surya Kanta's intentions in relation to reform. The group always welcomed police officers as government representatives to its meetings, and kept its doors open to people of noble rank. It repeatedly emphasized that it bore no animosity toward the government or the Bali Adnyana group, even decrying such adversarial thinking as a sign of narrow-mindedness. Furthermore, Surya Kanta declared that its appeal to the *jaba* was not limited to those without noble rank, but extended to all Balinese, including the *triwangsa*, whose ranking had enabled them to occupy the high castes.

The group's goal, Surya Kanta stated, was to raise awareness among the Balinese of their own society and to call for reforms in that society.[26] When talking about reform, Surya Kanta viewed religious knowledge passed on among the Balinese people as the necessary starting point for any such reform. As the core activity of the group, dissemination of religious knowledge represented a democratic liberation of knowledge that had previously been the exclusive province of the priests. The group also had another objective to codify Balinese religion, inspired in part by the formation of religious organizations among Muslims and Christians in Java.[27]

Surya Kanta also used religious knowledge as a starting point to question the meaning of authority. Although it recognized hierarchical social rankings as part of religious custom, the group asserted that people should be aware of the obligations that came with the social position assigned to them, and that status brought with it a responsibility to work toward the development of Balinese society. Surya Kanta's ultimate goal, it said, was to normalize relations between *jaba* and *jero* (whose fates were determined at birth by the vested rights associated with noble rank) by converting antagonism between the two classes into a relationship between those in a position to fulfill their social obligations and those who held them in esteem for that reason.[28] Surya Kanta did not look to the authority of text-based religious knowledge for signs of the past glory of Hindu culture, as Dutch scholars had, nor for justification of the caste hierarchical system, as Bali Adnyana did. Rather, in the religious knowledge described in the texts, the group sought a new image of society for the future, one that would allow them to redefine social class as something independent of caste.

By contrast, Bali Adnyana gave vent to the very attitudes of intolerance and hostility that Surya Kanta criticized. Using the same term, *sudra*, as the government, this group viewed Surya Kanta as a movement by the *sudra* against holders of noble rank. Noting that many participants in Surya Kanta were teachers, Bali Adnyana warned that some of the *sudra* tainted by modern education were impugning the authority of the *triwangsa*. Furthermore, it claimed, this attack on the *triwangsa* was a communist-inspired movement that sought to abolish the class system; labeling it the 'Red Menace,' Bali Adnyana fanned fears that the movement could grow into one of resistance against the government.[29] Communist uprisings had occurred in Java in 1926 and 1927, and Bali Adnyana sought to frame the challenge to its authority as a comparable challenge to the government. Bali Adnyana was thus clearly part of the ruling establishment, using the authority of the government to reinforce conservative reaction. Even as the colonial government reduced the penalties for inter-caste marriage in 1927,[30] it increased its crackdown on activities that opposed the ruling order, and publication of *Surya Kanta* ceased that same year.

Lower-level civil servants and organized groups

In the 1930s, more than two decades after the advent of Dutch rule, the colonial environment in Bali began to undergo a transformation. Overwhelmed by paperwork, the Dutch administrators ventured into the field less often, preferring to spend what spare time they could find relaxing on the tennis court or at clubs. Few Dutch officials were now spurred by the kind of insatiable curiosity once evinced by Schwartz or Moojen to travel around Bali. Increasingly they socialized with the royal families, whose status as bureaucrats had been enhanced, and their dependence on administrative agencies run by indigenous Balinese grew. Contact thus diminished between the Dutch administrators and Balinese society. The report mentioned earlier, prepared in anticipation of the establishment of the autonomous regions, betrays the perspective of officials with only tenuous connections to Balinese society, which they viewed as they would a distant, newly constructed building. Meanwhile, the number of Balinese working in the administrative apparatus as teachers, tax collectors, or other lower-level bureaucrats was growing, and the actual work of governance increasingly fell to them. These civil servants, who had formed ties with one another during their school days, maintained contact even when assigned to outlying districts. As the ruling order approached a state of maturity, the gap between the Dutch administrators and Balinese society broadened, as did the scope of activities undertaken by indigenous lower-level government workers (cf. Schulte Nordholt 1996: 283–4).

Activities by various groups continued to proliferate in the aftermath of the Singaraja-based dispute between Surya Kanta and Bali Adnyana.[31] In the 1930s, organized groups that shared in common the support of lower-level civil servants expanded their activities throughout Bali and into other regions as well; they also began to form networks and to cooperate with one another. The greatest number of groups appeared in Denpasar, among them the Housewives' Mutual Aid Society, the Women Aware Society, the Workers' Association, the Literacy Education Alliance, and the Association for an Indonesian Society. Singaraja saw the birth of the Bali-Lombok Indigenous Teachers' Association, the Bali-Lombok Youth Unity Association, and Bali Dharma Laksana (the Association of Balinese for Orderly Action, hereafter referred to as BDL), which will be discussed in detail below. The Society for Women's Progress was formed in Klungkung, and the Education Society in Bangli. Organizations that were spreading throughout Indonesia, like the political party Parindra and the educational movement Taman Siswa, also established branches in Bali and began to engage in activities on the island.

With the single exception of Parindra, these groups were apolitical organizations that limited their activities to education and welfare; conspicuous among them were groups whose work centered on women. Noteworthy for its clearly stated objectives was the Women Aware Society,[32] which was founded by a group of teachers, including Gusti Ayu Rapeg, who had studied at a middle school for girls in Blitar, East Java, returned to Denpasar in 1935, and opened a school for girls the following year.[33] Gusti Ayu Rapeg rode her bicycle from village to village, preaching the necessity of education for women; she collected funds with which to send the best students to study in Java, campaigned for literacy education, and decried the injustice of polygyny and marriage by abduction. She is credited with designing and popularizing, out of a concern for etiquette, the *kebaya* blouse now considered part of Indonesian traditional dress (Parker 2000: 54–5; Wijaya 2000: 117–18).

Fearing the spread of the national independence movement, the colonial government kept constant watch over such group activities; adopting an apolitical stance was a conscious choice by these organizations. They functioned according to basic organizational principles, with members voluntarily assembling in the name of specific objectives and drafting bylaws under which the group operated. In this respect these organizations could be said to have developed out of a distinctively Balinese type of groupism. However, as BDL founding chairman I. G. G. Raka pointed out,[34] the organizations of the 1930s possessed characteristics not found in earlier Balinese groups: each one espoused an exalted social mission, extended its activities over a comparatively wide area, demanded professional work from its members, and required the payment of high membership fees. A condition that gave rise to these characteristics was the fact that all these groups were run by lower-level civil servants with guaranteed salaries. Thus it was the evolved ruling order that paved the way for group undertakings that created a unique new public space.

Of the many groups that arose during this period, the one that formed the largest organizational network was the aforementioned BDL. Its name was the same as that of a group formed for purposes of socializing and performing religious rites by Balinese students at middle schools in Malang and Surabaya.[35] These Balinese who had studied in Java formed the core of a group that set up the organization called BDL in Bali in 1936, just before the inauguration of the autonomous regions. Created by the merger of two existing organizations—Eka Laksana, which was formed in 1935 in Denpasar, and the Singaraja-based Bali Educational Fund—BDL situated its headquarters in Singaraja.[36] The group, which lasted until the start of the Japanese occupation in 1942, published its own magazine, *Djatajoe*. The core activity of BDL was the management of an educational fund, as indicated by the name of the Singaraja group that preceded it. BDL provided educational funding to the best student applicants out of funds acquired through membership fees (Pendit 1979a: 7–15; Putra 1989).

BDL made a conspicuous effort to reconcile an ethnic consciousness as Balinese with an identity as indigenous inhabitants of a colonial territory that would be sublimated into a national-unification consciousness under the name Indonesia. Its membership was classified into four categories: (1) regular members, (2) non-regular members, (3) honorary members, and (4) contributors. Non-Balinese were categorized as non-regular members. This arrangement was not meant to exclude non-Balinese, but to enable them to participate in an independent framework. Statements made in the pages of *Djatajoe* make it clear that BDL, in fact, had a very pronounced sense of itself as a Balinese movement. There were frequent declarations that the group aspired to 'contribute to the greater development of Balinese culture' and 'the unification of the Balinese people,' as well as such exhortations as, 'People of Bali! Let us become one under the leadership of BDL!'[37]

Contributors paid a high membership fee, about twenty-five times that of regular members,[38] and were accorded the status of honorary members, for whom regular duties were waived. Topping the list of contributors were rulers, along with a very few foreigners and some priests. From its inception, BDL welcomed any and all royals into its membership with the rationale that they were indispensable to the smooth running of the organization. However, with the expansion of BDL's operations concurrent with the establishment of the autonomous regions, two years after the group's founding, relations between it and the royal families deteriorated as the latter acquired new powers in their position as heads of the autonomous regions. BDL decided to send a representative to the newly formed Council of Royal Families to present it with a list of demands. With the group's demands growing more explicit as the authority of the royal families became more clearly defined, BDL adopted an increasingly confrontational stance toward the royals. It even looked into securing the right to choose a representative to the Volksraad (People's Council) in Batavia. Thus, while BDL was unquestionably an extremely moderate organization that looked to the royal families as its patrons, that very stance allowed BDL to give lower-level bureaucrats a voice in relation to the rulers at the top of the governing hierarchy.[39]

From the outset, BDL worked to expand its organizational network. Starting with branches in Denpasar and Karangasem in 1936, it went on to open branches where the royal courts were located, as well as in other locales such as Kubutambahan, Bubunan, and Sukawati. By 1937 BDL also had branches outside Bali, in Surabaya, Yogyakarta, Makassar, and, belatedly, Lombok. As of 1938, it had fifteen branches and 562 members, which rose to 591 in 1940. Of these, only eighteen were non-regular members, testifying to the essentially Balinese character of the organization.

In charge of the group's operations was a seven-person representative committee based in Singaraja. Individual branches were permitted to engage in their own activities independent of the committee, and reports on meetings at the branch level appeared in the pages of *Djatajoe*. Decisions on overall group policy were made at a general meeting convened once a year. A total of four general meetings were held, starting with an inaugural meeting in Singaraja from July 24 to 26, 1937. The purpose of these meetings was to discuss and vote on a list of proposals put forward by representatives from each branch, but at the same time they had the flavor of friendship festivals, with participants engaging in tennis, soccer, or badminton tournaments in the daytime, and holding music or dance recitals at night. Arts and crafts exhibitions were also held for the duration of the conferences.

Controllers, the officials on the lowest rung of the colonial government hierarchy, were always in attendance at BDL meetings—not only the general meetings, but those of the branches as well. Monitored and restricted in its freedom of discussion, BDL was inevitably forced into a subordinate position in relation to the government. Even so, the group is noteworthy for its modus operandi: individual branches would initiate proposals that were ultimately taken up and voted upon at the general meeting, with minutes of the deliberations published in a magazine. This process, democratic in the sense that demands from below were duly taken into consideration, demonstrates that BDL had the potential to create an arena for discourse at a remove from the government and its colonial system of orders unilaterally dispensed from above.

The general meeting took place every July, with the second meeting held in Denpasar, the third in Klungkung, and the fourth in Tabanan. The decision to hold the meetings in different locales outside Singaraja reflected not only an effort to strengthen BDL's expanding network, but also a consciousness of the political reality of the autonomous regions, as BDL feared that the autonomous region policy was a strategy to split up Balinese society.[40] Still, it was not easy for BDL to expand its territory and operations. As G. P. Merta, a key member, remarked shortly before the second general meeting, it was extremely challenging to coordinate and unify the organization. A major obstacle to achieving consensus was the diversity of the members' backgrounds, and Merta cited differences in education and birth-based social rank as especially problematic and lamented the difficulty of getting members to accept one another as part of the same group.[41]

The reasons for choosing the venues for the second and third general meetings were obvious. Denpasar was the economic hub of Bali, while Klungkung symbolized the unity of the Balinese people, being the domain of the royal family that was heir to the lineage under which Bali had once been unified as one kingdom. But the fourth choice, Tabanan, was not based on any clear consensus; if anything, it reflected the realities facing BDL. Tabanan was a region with a particularly high appreciation of education. According to documents from 1929 and 1932, Tabanan boasted the second largest number of students at a level equivalent to primary school after the administrative center of the island, Buleleng, despite having no Dutch language schools (MvO Beeuwkes 1932: 144). Tabanan had the largest BDL membership of any region, and the group's activities extended into the hinterlands beyond the locale of the royal court. Meanwhile, the region with the least BDL activity was Gianyar. The ruler of Gianyar attended the second general meeting, which was the first time he had attended such a meeting. The Gianyar branch of BDL had the fewest members and correspondence between it and the representative committee in Singaraja was neglected. BDL activities tended to grow in the territories of royal families who maintained some distance from the colonial government.

BDL did not just operate on its own, but also cooperated with other organizations. Several groups would typically set up a committee together to work toward a specific goal. The Literacy Education Alliance mentioned earlier was formed jointly by BDL, the Women Aware Society, and the Workers' Association. Another example was the Women's Aid Society, which was formed in Klungkung in 1940 for the purpose of assisting orphans and pregnant women; this was a joint undertaking by BDL, the Society for Women's Progress, Parindra, Taman Siswa, and Trimurti (a religious organization formed in Klungkung).[42] BDL focused its energies on familiar issues close to home in order to make the group more visible to ordinary people and enable it to extend its reach. The representative committee had, in fact, been criticized for never once holding a meeting open to the public, and the lower-level civil servants active in BDL made a conscious effort to extend the group's operations to the populace at large (cf. Putra 1989: 91–2).

Organization of knowledge, circulation of discourse

The flourishing group activities and magazine publication in the 1930s was linked to colonial regional government policies that supported the organization of knowledge about Bali, the establishment of a postal service that made magazine subscriptions feasible, and an improvement in educational levels. These policies were closely aligned with the political process of setting up a system of indirect rule. Spurred by the government's need for research on customary law and philology to aid in setting up the autonomous regions, and by the attention focused on the unique aspects of Balinese culture during the process leading to the decision to assign Bali to The Great East, the organization of knowledge about Bali advanced from the late 1920s onward. Archaeological surveys also increased in frequency, with the proliferation of public works projects as part of the post-earthquake recovery (Kempers 1991: 85–7). With the inauguration of the Archaeological Service in 1913, surveys that had been limited to Java and Madura extended throughout colonial territory, and the Archaeological Service declared that a survey of Bali was needed. The Resident and other administrators assigned to Bali were also ardent supporters of archaeological research (Anonymous 1916).

L. J. J. Caron, who was Resident in the late 1920s, made the decision to establish a library that would be the ultimate symbol of the effort to organize knowledge about Bali. Caron wrote that the indigenous Balinese 'pay no heed whatsoever to their own ancient culture,' and argued the need for a historical study of that culture (MvO Caron 1929: 100). With so many 'discoveries' already accumulating in the fields of archaeology and philology, he called for the creation of a 'center for the study of the great Balinese culture,' specifically proposing that a facility be built to preserve the indigenous-language texts that were recognized as the core of the culture. At a conference held in Kintamani in June 1928, it was decided to establish a library in Singaraja with funding provided by the government. Named the Kirtya Liefrinck-van der Tuuk, the library was set up as a foundation that would hold more than 6000 titles. The name combined those of F. A. Liefrinck, the former Resident who had been the architect of colonial rule over Bali, and H. N. van der Tuuk, a pioneering linguist. Kirtya was a Balinese term for 'foundation' suggested by the ruler of Buleleng.[43] A magazine, *Mededeelingen* (Communications) *van de Kirtya Liefrinck-van der Tuuk*, was published for the purpose of listing documents held in the library, alphabetizing Balinese-language texts, and presenting research on Balinese society. The first issue of the magazine appeared on October 1, 1929, and publication continued through issue number 15 in 1941.

The performance of ceremonies at Besakih Temple in 1928 sparked a sudden interest in documents about religious rituals, and this was a direct impetus for the establishment of the Kirtya library with the support of the royal families. From the outset, there was a strong link between the collecting of texts and the ceremonies at Besakih. Then, in 1929, C. C. Berg, an authority on the Javanese language at the University of Leiden, visited Singaraja for a month and reaffirmed the scholarly value of the documents archived in Bali; around the same time, R. Goris, who had studied Sanskrit under Berg, was assigned to Bali, setting the stage for an organized effort to decipher the collected materials.

Importance was also placed on the exchange of knowledge between the colony and the Netherlands. In November 1915, the Bali Institute had been established in the ethnology department of the Colonial Institute in Amsterdam; the stated objective was to collect materials germane to the development of Balinese society and to 'smooth' relations between it and the Netherlands. C. Lekkerkerker, the archivist of the Bali Institute, had compiled a vast body of documentation on Bali up to 1919 and published it through the institute in 1920 with his own bibliographic annotations (Lekkerkerker 1920), and Goris and others of his generation were already putting this voluminous work to use. The Kirtya Liefrinck-van der Tuuk library formed ties with the University of Leiden, as well as the Bali Institute.

The organization of knowledge about Bali advanced further still in the 1930s. Definitive works in fields other than philology were published, the

prime example being a study of customary law by V. E. Korn (1932), who had
served as an administrator in Bali. Published in 1932, Korn's monumental
tome was a revised version of the doctoral thesis he had submitted to the
University of Leiden. Praised as the ultimate study of Balinese customary
law, the work became the 'bible' for colonial administrators assigned to
Bali. Then, in the late 1930s, a delegation from the Java Institute visited
Bali and held a conference on Balinese studies, an event that prominently
bestowed authority upon the knowledge that had been compiled. The
Java Institute was the most authoritative research institution in Java and
had served as the model for the Kirtya library. The delegation was in Bali
from October 18 to 23, 1937. Arriving from Surabaya on a luxury cruise
ship, the group held a reception on October 19 at the Bali Hotel. Members
of Bali's royal families and a representative of the rulers of Surakarta
delivered greetings, followed by speeches by such noted scholars as Goris
and the archaeologist W. F. Stutterheim. The next day the group embarked
on an inspection tour, visiting major temples and other structures dating
back to the days of the Klungkung, Karangasem, Kintamani, and Bangli
kingdoms. Wherever they went, they were treated to music and dance
performances, as well as exhibitions of craftwork. The delegation spent
its nights on board the ship, where Walter Spies and Colin McPhee played
the piano for them. They and other Westerners residing in Bali assisted the
delegation in its work and even presented reports on their own research.[44]

In parallel with the government's efforts to organize knowledge about
Bali, the 1930s also saw the vigorous growth of publication activities by
lower-level civil servants. Ironically, the impetus for this was provided by
Resident Caron, the initiator of the Kirtya library. As he prepared to depart
for his next post in Celebes, Caron made an impassioned plea for the
continued development of the library he had founded. Gathering library
staff, administrators, and indigenous representatives in Denpasar, he made
a speech about the significance and ongoing necessity of the library and
concluded by proposing the publication of a new periodical, separate from
Mededeelingen, to foster the indigenous culture of the Bali and Lombok
administrative district. A year later, under the new Resident, Beeuwkes,
the magazine *Bhawanagara* was launched in accordance with the previous
Resident's wishes. The preparation committee for the inaugural issue met

on April 22, 1930, and decided that library funds would be used only for the first issue; subsequent issues would be paid for with subscriptions. This condition was established less from economic considerations than from the fact that the preparation committee believed that operation of the magazine by the people of Bali and Lombok would help nurture the 'popular will.'[45] It was during the tenure of Resident Beeuwkes that magazine subscriptions became feasible with the full-scale operation of a postal service on the island. An expanded road network allowed mail buses to run smoothly, and the inauguration of a regular shipping service between Singaraja and Java made it easier to get mail from Europe. Resident Beeuwkes reported that the postal service dramatically improved in the three years from 1927 to 1929 (cf. Putra 1989: 65).

After a pre-inaugural issue, *Bhawanagara* published issue number 1 on June 1, 1931, and continued through issue number 12 of its fourth year in May 1935. Whereas periodicals of the 1920s, such as *Bali Adnyana* and *Surya Kanta*, were poorly printed and bound, resembled pamphlets more than magazines, and were published irregularly, *Mededeelingen* and *Bhawanagara* represented the advent in Bali of magazines of respectable appearance and heft. From its inception, *Bhawanagara* adopted an open stance that welcomed anyone's participation. The magazine depended on contributing writers, and any article written in good faith was accepted without concern over the qualifications of the contributor, and without restrictions on topics covered. In the pre-inaugural issue, Resident Beeuwkes acknowledged that *Mededeelingen*, which was written in Dutch, was a magazine for Europeans, declaring that *Bhawanagara*, on the other hand, would be a magazine written both by and for indigenous Balinese (primarily in the Balinese language but also in Indonesian as needed) and that he hoped it would become a 'forum for discussion' in which anyone could speak out.[46] The title *Bhawanagara* embodied the Resident's aspirations: it combined the word *bhawa*, meaning a state of perfection, with *nagara*, meaning country or land. The latter word connoted a sentiment of Bali and Lombok as 'our land.'

If we take the Resident's vision for *Bhawanagara* at face value, one would have to say that it was more fully realized by *Djatajoe*. The latter magazine did not begin publication until after the demise of *Bhawanagara*, so the two periodicals were never in competition with one another. Readers expressed dissatisfaction to the editors of *Bhawanagara* that, notwithstanding the vision espoused, it did not contain articles about 'more modern things.' The stance of the editors was that, while they had no reason to reject such articles if any were submitted, their primary mission was to focus on the 'need for society and culture in Bali and Lombok.' *Djatajoe*, however, did in fact address 'more modern things,' with the majority of its articles, written by various authors in Indonesian or Balinese, offering studies or commentary on the current state of Balinese society.[47]

The first issue of *Djatajoe* appeared in August 1936, the year after *Bhawanagara* ceased publication. The title is the Balinese for Jatayu, the valiant bird who appears in the Sanskrit epic *Ramayana* as an ally of Prince Rama. Jatayu does battle with the demon king Ravana, abductor of Rama's wife Sita, but is mortally wounded. When Rama finds Jatayu, the bird manages with his dying breath to apprise Rama of the whereabouts of Sita. The story of Jatayu is a famous one and is the subject of many theatrical performances; the name of the bird who gave his life for Rama is synonymous with struggle, death, and sacrifice.[48]

Every member of BDL was obliged to subscribe to *Djatajoe*, with sales of the magazine helping to cover the group's operating costs. When it first began publication, the editor-in-chief was I. G. N. P. Tisna, the son of the ruler of Buleleng, which would become one of Bali's autonomous regions. On the occasion of BDL's second general meeting, the editorship passed to Gde Paneca and I Wayan Bhadra. One of Bali's most prominent intellectuals, Bhadra remained active into the 1950s. After entering medical school at Surabaya, he had switched to the faculty of literature, then returned to his hometown of Singaraja (where he became the first Balinese employed at the Kirtya library) and wrote essays in Dutch for *Mededeelingen* (Diantari 1990: 97). Gde Srawana, known as the first author of a novel in Balinese, is actually a pen name of Bhadra's. He came from the same district as Nyoman Kajeng, editor-in-chief of *Surya Kanta*.[49]

The fact that its first editor was the scion of a royal family and his successor an employee of the Kirtya library would seem to suggest that *Djatajoe* was a conservative publication. Furthermore, Tisna's father had played a central role in the founding of the library and served as editor-in-chief of *Bhawanagara*, thus the social status of these editors would appear to be conclusive evidence of a hereditarily conservative leaning. But Tisna's personal history belies this assumption; if anything, his relationship with his royal father exemplifies the dualistic dilemma of being part of the ruling order and yet a critic of it.

Born in 1908 as the eldest son of the ruler of Buleleng, Tisna (who had two younger sisters and two younger brothers) was from birth the designated heir to the throne. Dropping out of the Dutch school in Batavia, to which he had received preferential admission as a royal prince, he continued studying Dutch on his own in Surabaya, but by straying from the path of a formal education he was at odds with his father, who had hoped to groom him as a government official. In 1929, after a period helping to run a farm, he headed for Lombok and worked for his father's shipping business. Tisna writes in his autobiography that he never received a salary from the colonial government, but as his father's assistant he was part of the colonial apparatus. In 1934 he returned to Bali and told his father that he wanted to start his own business as an exporter of copra and livestock, but his father rejected this idea.

Soon after this, Tisna began writing his first novel. According to scholars of Tisna, this work is clearly a declaration of independence from his father, as well as a critique of the ruling order with the royal families at its apex, and it is true that, in its pages, the kings of the nineteenth century (a period portrayed as one of endless conflict) receive critical treatment (Caldwell 1985). Tisna began studying Sanskrit with Goris, who had recently arrived in Bali, and developed a personal interest in the history of Balinese society. However, his greatest interest was not in the culture of the classics, but in new cultural genres emblematic of the modern colonial era, of which the novel was one. His tastes ran to the new form of gamelan known as kebyar, the janger dance with its comical movements, and the aforementioned stambul, and he formed his own performance group and played the violin.

In 1935 Tisna released his second novel, *Sukreni gadis Bali* (A Woman in Bali), which came to be viewed as his greatest work. Subsequently, he embarked for Vienna to further his study of Sanskrit, but fell ill on the way, lost his sight in one eye, and returned to Singaraja in a despondent state. Immediately upon his return he lost two of his children to smallpox.

After this string of misfortunes, he moved to Kintamani to convalesce, and began writing his third novel while observing the lives of the local people. He became the editor of *Djatajoe* after returning to Singaraja. Soon after his father became head of the autonomous region, Tisna rejected his own position as royal heir and the promise of royal income, and left the palace and moved to the district known as Lovina to the west of Singaraja. There he chose to spend his days writing novels, cultivating citrus fruits, playing the violin, and composing songs for the stambul theater.

A re-endorsement of religious authority

The inaugural issue of *Djatajoe* reveals a lack of editorial care: there is no unifying flow to the magazine, no thought given to the organization of the articles, no compilation of special features. The articles and essays seem to follow one after the other in no particular order, and the subject matter ranges from how to define modernity and how Balinese might best live in the modern era, to raising the consciousness and social status of women, and critiques of the impoverished state of society and the vicissitudes of the judicial system under the colonial government. As if in response to exhortations about a new culture by Resident Beeuwkes, the focus of debate throughout the issue is religion and culture.

If *Djatajoe* and *Bhawanagara* shared a common interest in religion and culture, as well as some overlap in contributors,[50] their respective stances on these subjects were antithetical. The very terms they used to express the concept of culture exemplify this gap. In the subtitle of *Bhawanagara*, 'a monthly dedicated to the improvement of Balinese culture,' the term used for 'culture' was peradaban. *Djatajoe*, on the other hand, most frequently used the term cultuur. Also making occasional appearances were the Dutch kunst, as well as kebudayaan, which became the standard term for culture in post-independence Indonesia, but neither of these found common use in either publication. The difference in terminology reflects a marked disparity. The stem of peradaban is adab, which usually refers to refined rules of etiquette or, in a larger sense, to a high level of cultural sophistication. By contrast, cultuur is not only an abstract term, but can be used to highlight awareness of one's own domain relative to others. In other words, peradaban is a general term indicating a level of culture (it can also be translated literally as 'level of civilization') that can be applied to objective descriptions, whereas the obviously European word cultuur is a term that, in combination with kita (our), can represent an articulation of one's own position.[51]

Both publications used the term *agama* for 'religion,' but where *Bhawanagara* consistently defined religion in this context as Hinduism, *Djatajoe* did not subscribe to a general understanding of Balinese religion as Hinduism per se. Granted, many *Djatajoe* writers used the term 'Hindu,' but one can also read arguments that the word is a geographical term and not appropriate as a name for a religion; that even if Hindu is the name of a religion, there are various forms of Hinduism around the world; and that the term is in fact meaningless. Other names in use, besides Hindu, included Siwa or Siwa-Buddha, based on sects to which priests belonged; *Trimurti*, based on the doctrine by that name; and *Agama Tirtha*, meaning 'Religion of Holy Water.' This last term was the name given to their religion by Balinese who used holy water in their religious ceremonies.

The debate on religion encompassed the entire spectrum of Balinese customs and lifestyles, expanding into a comprehensive study of all aspects of society. Hardly any of the discourse was limited to the essential nature or tenets of religion. At the heart of the discourse was an awareness that Balinese society was undergoing fundamental changes, and bewilderment over how Balinese customs should respond to such changes. An article that addressed this dilemma head-on had this to say: the use of multiple names for religion was itself a source of confusion, as well as proof that Balinese religion was not a pure entity but had a mix of influences, and that what was required was an inquiry into the names used for religion in the texts owned by the priests; it was nothing less than gross ignorance to know the popular names of various gods without knowing anything about the gods themselves; and one could not compel educated people to participate in religious ceremonies whose meaning they did not understand, and even if compulsion was attempted, they would probably not participate. Inevitably, such contributors found they could no longer blindly follow customary practices and wanted to ascertain their meaning. Writers who ventured a step beyond critiques of the current state of affairs declared that, at the very least, it was imperative to determine which practices should be continued and which should be discarded. This, they suggested, required the compiling and comparing of knowledge about religion and the publication and dissemination of the results of these studies in books and magazines.[52]

Although the phenomenon of educated people becoming more conscious of the practices of the society to which they belonged was certainly not unique to Balinese society, one noteworthy aspect of this emerging consciousness in Bali in the 1930s was the peculiar process by which it brought about a concentration of religious authority. In examining this process, one must first address a point of view that might be described as a form of textualism: the unswerving faith in the texts and a belief that one must look to them for the solutions to all manner of problems. This textualism reaffirmed the authority of the priests based on their position as both holders and interpreters of the texts, and legitimized the view of the priests as religious teachers whom the people, as their disciples, should obey and rely on for guidance. Granted, some writers did assert that the texts should be for the benefit of everyone, not just a privileged few.[53] But there were no indications in the pages of *Djatajoe* of any misgivings about the authority of the priests per se.

Balinese textualism did not treat one particular volume of text as the holy one, as in the case of Islam or Christianity. Indeed, a broad range of materials came to be embraced as text, for which reason it is essential to analyze how these texts acquired legitimacy and became codified as holy writ. In that regard, it is significant that the Kirtya library was established as a direct consequence of the performance of religious ceremonies at Besakih Temple. This textualism is, moreover, a reflection of the status of knowledge during the 1930s. In addition to the Balinese word *weda*, the Indonesian kitab suci was also in use as a term for 'text,' and this latter appellation extended to Dutch studies of Bali as well. In other words, research documents on Bali, most of them written in Dutch, were accepted by the Balinese as a kind of holy text. Those who could read Dutch enjoyed a status on par with the priesthood; thus Balinese texts and Western research both fell under the definition of text.

Textualism was linked to demands for the establishment of a clearly defined system of religious practices. In 1939, the year after the inauguration of the autonomous regions, BDL resolved at its third general meeting to present to the heads of the regions a list of specific demands regarding religion and customs. The regional heads were called upon to use the discretionary budgets at their disposal to publicize the views of the priests on religion and customs, and particularly to have them standardize Nyepi and abolish the rules of banishment for *manak salah* (wrongful birth). Nyepi, which serves as the starting point of the Balinese calendar, is a day on which one is to avoid using fire and to engage in as few activities as possible. Nyepi was taken up as an issue because the day so designated varied from region to region. The day, which also determines when major purification ceremonies are conducted, was finally standardized in the 1950s.

One rule of banishment for wrongful birth stipulated that if the birth of a child was judged to be in violation of custom, parents and child were to be banished from the village. Educated young people viewed this rule as a classic example of a 'backward' custom and had been pressing for its abolition. But efforts at reform had not led to a change in the custom. According to an article about a deity-invoking religious ceremony conducted in a Singaraja village on October 27, 1933, the ceremony was intended to render a final judgment on how to handle the birth of twins of different sexes, the most common type of wrongful birth. The voice of the invoked deity declared that the incident would not create defilement. This did not mean that defilement had not occurred, but that its effect extended only to the temple of the ancestral deity of the family to whom the birth had occurred, not to the entire village. Employees of the colonial government had been urging the abolition of the rules of banishment in the village for ten years at that point, but had evidently failed to persuade the villagers to alter their custom.[54]

From its second general meeting onward, BDL made plans to publish a number of texts. In 1937 the association also began publishing a calendar. The print run rose year by year—from 500 copies in 1937, to 1500 in 1938, and 1800 in 1939—and the calendars sold out as soon as they went on sale. A calendar that determined the dates of religious ceremonies was intimately linked to the customs of the Balinese; although not a form of text, such a publication represented BDL's intention to assume a leading role in guiding Balinese customs.

Around the same time, the colonial government of the region was also exhibiting a strong interest in calendars. In his Successor's Report of 1937, Resident G. A. W. Ch. de Haze Winkelman added a ten-page postscript describing timekeeping methods and calendars used for religious ceremonies.[55] Observing that several methods of reckoning time coexisted in Bali, the Resident classified them from oldest to newest in historical terms as 'Old Indonesia,' 'Hindu-Bali,' and 'Java-Bali.' He defined the twelve-month solar *saka* calendar as Hindu-Bali. The most commonly used *wuku* calendar (with a cycle consisting of thirty units of seven days) and the calendar used to determine market days (which employed three-day units) were allegedly based on Majapahit time-reckoning systems and were therefore assigned to the Java-Bali category. The Resident went on to analyze how days were determined for the religious ceremonies frequently held by temples and irrigation groups. The concern with calendars was an important starting point for efforts to unify Balinese customs, and in this regard BDL and the regent shared a common interest.

The pertinent aspect of these efforts is that, even as BDL expanded its activities in the realm of religion and customs, ultimately it was calling for leadership from the royal families who were the heads of the autonomous regions. These same royals, who flaunted their prestige by driving around in luxury automobiles, were utterly dependent on the colonial government, even when it came to rebuilding the palaces that had been damaged in the great earthquake. Despite the fact that records of the royal lineages were no longer kept after the earthquake, the royal families enjoyed renewed legitimacy from the new titles bestowed upon them as heads of autonomous regions, a state of affairs that was criticized not only by groups like Surya Kanta, but also from within the families, as evidenced by the example of Tisna. Meanwhile, through their supervisory role in religious ceremonies at Besakih Temple, which had been restored out of cultural considerations, the royals publicly flaunted their position as leaders in the religious realm as well. This met with the tacit approval of the government, which sought the aid of the 'magical powers' of the royal families in achieving their objective to rebuild the governing structure of Balinese society, which had fallen into such a sorry state. The members of BDL, however, definitely did not share the government's expectations for the royal families, neither in terms of reclaiming their old status nor in exercising 'magical powers.' Although, as lower-level civil servants, they could not make their criticisms too explicit, BDL members consistently maintained a confrontational stance in relation to the royals. Eventually, however, even BDL, with its ranks of young people who had benefited from a modern education, did not reject the authority of the royals in the spheres of religion and custom, but effectively re-endorsed it.

By affirming the unity of political and religious authority, this endorsement helped cement the system of religious practice in Bali from that time on. The specific motives or internal logic behind this endorsement are not revealed in the pages of *Djatajoe*. The direct cause was the situation created under colonial rule whereby a religious sphere was established, and the royal families were granted power over that sphere. If one is to seek further reasons, a useful reference point is the analysis by Kenji Tsuchiya (1982) in his research on the Taman Siswa movement, in which he cites a reinterpretation of the concept of royal authority as part of the quest for a sociopolitical order different from that of the West. Apart from the fluidity of the kingdoms formed by the royal families and their satellites, which is described by Schulte Nordholt, Tsuchiya follows Benedict Anderson's elucidation of the characteristics of royal authority in Java in emphasizing the context in which the power of the royals was exercised. The unity of sovereign and subject relationship, according to which subjects directly experience the sacred power embodied in the sovereign, extended from the king down to the lowest ranks of society; thus the kingdom was by definition a space permeated by the power of the king. With the West in apparent decline in the wake of the First World War, the Orient, with such figures as Mahatma Gandhi and the poet Rabindranath Tagore, emerged as a new alternative. Tsuchiya argues that in the 'space' of the schools, the Orient was presented as offering a different kind of modernity; however, even while incorporating modern concepts such as state, nation, and territory, it did not reject the concept of royal authority, and indeed reaffirmed it. The unity of sovereign and subject relationship was reinterpreted as a teacher–pupil relationship; thus the schools formed a competing system in relation to the royal families, who were now reduced to bureaucratic functionaries of the colonial government. The vision in which schools were expected to help secularize colonial society was betrayed by those very schools that were built under the 'ethical policy' the government promoted. Instead, the schools gave birth to an alternative choice (Tsuchiya 1982: 23–87).

The *budi* espoused by Surya Kanta as its first objective was, according to Tsuchiya, a unique concept spawned by the competing system of the schools as spaces appropriated by Balinese society under the colonial order. Surya Kanta's redefinition of *jero* and *jaba*, which was based on the notion of *budi* as the proper exercise of sacred power for the sake of the kingdom, can be viewed in the same light as the redefinition of the sovereign–subject relationship represented by the schools. When, in the 1930s, Taman Siswa established a branch in Bali and *Djatajoe* began mentioning Tagore and Gandhi frequently in its pages, the religious leaders championed by *Djatajoe* were none other than teachers creating the new order (as described by Tsuchiya 1982), and participants in BDL could be said to possess the same vision apparent in the redefinition of the concept of royal authority. In that sense they were by no means secularized modernists. To express surprise that educated young people should re-embrace religious ritual and royal authority was merely to reiterate the same colonialist perspective as that of the Residents who viewed education as a prerequisite for secularization. The discussions appearing in *Djatajoe* were in fact realistic. Writers seeking a new mode for Balinese society addressed the issues of democratization of religious knowledge and reform of the religious realm based on the political reality in which the royal families had become heads of the autonomous regions. They accepted the existence of the royals as holders of knowledge and the priests as its interpreters even as they posed new questions about the meaning of those roles.

The dilemma of 'Balinization'

Even as BDL declared that it would not involve itself in politics, the association's core activities in the area of education generated political tension with the colonial government. This was due to the competing reality, albeit in distinctly Balinese form, that the educational sphere came to represent. In 1925 the colonial government, which had sought to isolate Bali from Java by incorporating it into the territory of The Great East, issued an ordinance compelling Balinese to attend middle school in Makassar.[56] Like Surya Kanta, which protested the ordinance, BDL, which had been founded primarily by Balinese students in Java, was engaged in activities at fundamental odds with the political agenda reflected by this policy. For BDL's members, who had been exposed to the modern era through their education in Java and feared, above all, that Bali would remain a backwater region left behind by progress, the establishment of technical schools where students could learn the practical skills needed to make concrete contributions to the development of Balinese society was a far more critical priority than higher education per se. BDL appealed to the colonial government not to content itself with providing scholarships so that young Balinese could study in Java, but to build more schools in Bali. Meanwhile, BDL itself initiated a program of purchasing rice fields and converting the harvests to cash with which to build schools. It further declared that it was not enough to timidly make do with these efforts alone, and demanded that the heads of the autonomous regions sign on to a policy of earmarking part of their regional budgets for education, and for building schools and allowing BDL to run them.

There was also disparity between the educational philosophies of the government and BDL. In appealing for improvements in education, BDL evinced a strong faith in progress—even as it struggled with the question of how to bring Balinese society into accord with the modern era, the association did not question the virtue of progress itself. Conversely, the colonial government, which saw a negative side to progress in the rise of the nationalist movement led by educated young people, adopted Damsté's views on cultural preservation as a substantive part of its educational policy. Known as 'Balinization,' this policy of traditional education involved converting school buildings to Balinese architectural designs; teaching Balinese literature, woodworking, painting, and music; and introducing dance as part of the physical education curriculum.[57] As part of this policy, teachers traveled through their regions surveying local music and dance in what could be described as a form of ethnological research, then taught their students what they had gleaned.

The educational policy caused a profound dilemma among the Balinese, as described in an article that appeared in two installments in *Djatajoe* under the title 'Baliseering' (Balinization).[58] According to the author of the article, the widespread use of the term Balinization was particularly prominent in the field of arts education, which was marked by the emergence of teachers who actively put the concept into practice. In taking note of this phenomenon, the author does not fundamentally oppose Balinization; he fully supports the notion of cultural development, asserting that culture reflects the level of spiritual advancement of a people and that its development is crucial for the Balinese. By 'culture' he means literature and the arts, and education in these areas is something to be unequivocally commended. According to the author's analysis, the problem lay in the fact that educated Balinese had become an elite group alienated from the rest of society, forming their own independent clique, and the educational policy of Balinization emerged as a reaction to this situation. The author's aim is to re-examine, through his inquiry into Balinization, the form that education should properly take. This is the context in which he speaks of a 'profound dilemma.'

In the view of the author, the cause of the dilemma was an extremely narrow interpretation of Balinization; what, then, he asks, should the practice of Balinization be in the broader sense? Policies promoting respect for culture were permeated by a glorification of the past, and even some Balinese teachers extolled the virtues of returning to a 'golden age'—this, the author asserts, was the biggest problem with the narrow interpretation of Balinization. Perhaps Bali did, indeed, enjoy a golden age when life was blessed and complete. But, he argues, in the present-day Bali, when society was undergoing numerous upheavals, what was important was recognition that the Balinese were living in a period of transition. The new age had not yet arrived. Nonetheless, he said, Balinese must not return to the past, but advance into the as yet invisible future. The role of teachers was to contemplate what was needed to greet the new age and teach that to their students; the narrow interpretation of Balinization, the author claims, severely impeded the work of the teachers. A second problem engendered by the narrow interpretation was a decline of interest in other cultures due to the emphasis on Balinese culture. Just because Balinese in the past did not wear Western garments or shoes, this did not mean that those living in the present should go about their lives wearing only sarongs, the author avers. Nor could one get by in the present age speaking only Balinese, not Indonesian. If Balinization meant learning only about Balinese culture, then the Balinese would be nothing more than the proverbial 'frog in the well.' Students had to be taught about both their own culture and other cultures. In promoting the former, he said, Balinization was not meant to preclude the latter.

The author also directs criticism at the stance of the teachers who put Balinization into practice, declaring that these teachers did not hold any actual convictions about the goals of Balinization or the reasons for applying it in education, but simply felt compelled to follow the policy dictates of the government. Children accepted these teachings because they trusted their teachers; if those teachers functioned as nothing more than 'soulless machines,' they would severely hinder the spiritual growth of their young pupils. The author highlights the coercive aspect of Balinization through his interpretation of the term itself. In his article, written in Indonesian, he translates 'Balinization' as diper Bali, a reflexive passive construction that literally means 'to be made into Bali again.' Thus, the author perceives Balinization as a coercive, passively accepted phenomenon, not as an active choice. In point of fact, the government did install supervisors in charge of Balinization (Leider Demonstraties Baliseering), under whose guidance the Balinese teachers carried out the educational practices of Balinization.[59]

In drawing attention to this dilemma, the author calls for cultural education that both addresses the needs of society and is based on general educational theory. The appropriate form of education must be sought from a broad perspective that faced the changes of the times head-on. Touching on the state of the world and the rise of fascism in particular, the author declares that education by the same methods employed in the past would be of no use in helping Bali deal with trends in the world at large. What was needed more than anything else was a spirit capable of coping with epochal changes, which was precisely what parents expected education to instill in their children, and it was the duty of teachers to respond to that expectation. Education had to be rooted in the needs people shared as members of society and, in that sense, education was inextricably linked to human improvement. The author concludes by stating that if the Balinese were to free themselves from an educational system that had lapsed into narrow-minded regionalism and taught only about the past, then they must study general educational theory. This finely drawn critique perceives, in a policy that cloaked in good intentions its attempt through education to fence in culture, a violent effort to force that culture into a passive, closed state. In his critique, the author redefines culture as a requirement for a future-oriented society. This is an image of culture as a work in progress, a notion that neither the advocates nor the debunkers of legitimate culture in the debate that followed the great earthquake could have accepted.

Though they were far from constituting an outright oppositional movement, the words and actions that linked *Surya Kanta* and *Djatajoe* sustained a political tension with the colonial government and the royal families; they also revealed the ambiguous nature of colonial rule. The Hindu culture extolled through the scholarship of the nineteenth century was, in fact, adapted to the governance of Balinese society. Laws, castes, and statistical data were employed to turn Bali into a fully fledged Hindu society, and this Hindu character was further emphasized in the name of cultural preservation after the earthquake. Then, when the Great Depression struck and drove Bali into poverty, the government sought to rebuild Balinese society. Establishing the autonomous regions in an effort to streamline its administrative apparatus, it relied once again on the power of the royal families, which it had earlier rejected for their autocratic rule. However, the ruling order thus established gave birth to a space in which group activities and language-related movements could flourish, and with them an incipient critique of the ruling order. The leaders of these activities were lower-level civil servants working for the colonial government, and their activities were sustained by the transportation, postal, and educational infrastructure developed by the government. As colonial rule attained full fruition, it inadvertently created a new sociopolitical space, and it was in this space that the system of religious practice was redefined.

The group activities of the 1930s are extremely significant. Unfortunately, previous research has assigned only a limited meaning to them. Even when *Djatajoe* has been cited, it has only been as an example of the first signs of an emerging cultural identity; the actual content therein has not been accepted at face value, nor has an attempt been made to analyze the position of the contributors in the political sphere. Instead, emphasis has been placed only on the limitations imposed on these activities by the watchful eye of the government, suggesting that such groups merely accommodated the status quo. To date, the highest evaluation of these groups has been provided by Robinson (1995: 45–51), who treats their activities as a sign in itself that the policies of the colonial government had come to an impasse. He posits that even as the government revived the kingdoms in the form of the autonomous regions, Balinese society was already undergoing irreversible changes that precluded this revival, and group activities were themselves proof of these changes. But an analysis of those group activities makes clear that they did not simply signify an impasse in the status quo. Rather, they set the stage for critical reforms in the religious realm that extended into the 1950s. With the end of colonial rule and the establishment of an independent Republic of Indonesia, it was the young writers who had participated in the activities of BDL and contributed to *Djatajoe* who formed the core of political and religious leadership in Bali in the 1950s.

Part II

Hinduism and the Nation State

CHAPTER 3
Social Reconstruction and Morality

In 1945, with the collapse of the Japanese military occupation that had ruled Indonesia since 1942, a process of decolonization began. But even as the scenario of liberation began to unfold with calls for independence, Balinese society faced a dark and difficult reality. For one thing, the island was fundamentally impoverished. Not until the 1970s, when the tourism industry got into full swing, did Bali truly begin to recover from the economic hardships that had persisted since the Great Depression. It was also in a politically challenging position. The Proclamation of Indonesian Independence made by Sukarno, Indonesia's first president, on August 17, 1945, claimed independence only for the Republic of Indonesia; Bali did not become part of the republic until after the establishment of a unitary Republic of Indonesia in 1950. During those five years, which have been erased from contemporary histories of the Indonesian nation, the Netherlands, in an effort to retain political influence in its former colony, set up the Federated States of Indonesia, of which the republic would be no more than one state. In this way, the Dutch hoped to marginalize the power of the republic. The most directly Dutch-dominated state was the newly formed Negara Indonesia Timur (State of East Indonesia), of which Bali was the westernmost region. Thus Bali was cut off from the republic, whose territorial center was Java, and was treated as a border zone. The appointed president of the State of East Indonesia was a prominent Balinese. Under his rule, royal families close to him grew more powerful even as people who supported the republic and dreamed of total independence were drawn into a violent and prolonged struggle.

Actual independence arrived in 1950, but with the expanding influence of party politics, the political problems that afflicted Bali continued unabated. With the first post-independence election scheduled for 1955 and the rise of the Islamic parties that had been organized during the Japanese military occupation, the Balinese had no political conduit to Jakarta, the political center of the new republic. The sole exception was in the person of Sukarno, whose mother was Balinese and who had built a palace in Bali at Tampaksiring. Thus the Balinese divided their allegiances among Sukarno's Nationalist Party, the Socialist Party, and the Communist Party, which were relatively non-Islamic in orientation. Some royal families retained their authority during this period. Former members of the republican camp were angered at the incomplete state of independence under which the pro-Dutch camp had not been liquidated and even retained the right to participate in the political process. They were also frustrated that they had received inadequate acknowledgment of their voluntary participation in the struggle for independence, and no economic guarantees. Some members of this group hid in the mountains and mounted a guerrilla resistance movement. Interparty strife and violence continued unmitigated, with Bali remaining unstable and only precariously unified, even after joining the republic.

The situation did not begin to improve until around 1958, after the election and the promulgation of the long-pending Unitary Regional Administrative Law. Under this law, Bali became a single autonomous province, the royals lost their legal authority, regional assemblies at the provincial and district level were granted authority, and the law's ultimate purpose—to dismantle the colonial system of rule—was achieved, albeit in a less than complete fashion.

The decolonization process of the 1950s was closely linked to the institutionalization of religion. The establishment of Bali as an autonomous province meant that even though they were a religious minority within the greater Indonesian state, the Hindu adherents who made up the bulk of the Balinese population were now assured of a regional administration in which they could exercise hegemony. This convergence of Bali's religiosity, territory, ethnicity, and political structure came to decisively define Balinese society's position within the Republic of Indonesia. Meanwhile, however, the royal families, who had retained their religious authority in such matters as management of the Besakih Temple, were finally stripped of their legal status, spurring calls for a new religious order to replace the royals.

At the same time, the Bali Regional Assembly was pressing the government of the republic to grant official recognition of the Hindu religion and establish a Hindu department in the Religion Ministry, which the government had set up at its inception. The loss of the royal families' legal status and the rise of the movement for recognition coincided with the promulgation of the Regional Administrative Law, a situation that led to the formation of Parisada, which would acquire the religious authority once held by the royals and serve as the representative Hindu organization. In this way, a conduit was established for Hindus in relation to the state, while within Bali a quest was underway to establish a religious order that would address the realities of Balinese society in the 1950s. This quest took the form of efforts to eliminate violence by cultivating religious morality, as well as the establishment of a religion-based educational system. One pressing issue was the re-entry into society of participants in the independence struggle; groups were formed to promote this process, and their members called for a religion-based morality to serve as a new foundation for Balinese society. Meanwhile, with the republican government making religious education mandatory, the expansion of a Hindu-based educational system also became an urgent priority, and schools were built with the primary objective of providing a Hindu education.

Chapters 3 and 4 examine the institutionalization of Hinduism that occurred as part of the decolonization process and culminated in 1958 with the formation of Parisada. Chapter 4 takes a separate look at the movement targeting the Religion Ministry to secure official recognition of Hinduism—a process that directly exposed the relationship between religion and the state—including declarations made by the Balinese in this effort, as well as the reaction in Gianyar, where the royal family had been particularly powerful. The present chapter focuses on the process of building a broad-based religious order—one that extended to government administration and education—in an effort to resolve the dire problems faced by the Balinese and to rebuild Balinese society on a foundation of religious morality.

A border zone

The administrative reform of 1938 that established the autonomous regions turned Bali into a border zone on the boundary between The Great East and Java. During the Japanese military occupation, local chiefs were appointed as heads of the autonomous regions, and there was no fundamental shift in the ruling order on Bali. A boundary was maintained between The Great East, which was under the jurisdiction of the Japanese navy, and Java (and points westward of Java), which were under the jurisdiction of the army. After 1945, when the Japanese military occupation collapsed, the borderland that was Bali became the site of increasingly fierce armed conflict between republican and pro-Dutch forces in the course of the convoluted political process of decolonization.[1]

Hubertus Johannes van Mook, Lieutenant Governor-General of the Dutch colonial government, hoped for the re-establishment of Dutch rule in postwar Indonesia, but was compelled to abandon outright rejection of the republic under its new president, Sukarno. The Java-based republic had already begun to assert its authority under the Japanese occupation. Moreover, a cabinet had been formed under Prime Minister Sutan Sjahrir, who managed to suppress the forces calling for immediate, full independence and instead advocated for 'realistic dialogue.' Thus the republic embarked on a path of diplomatic negotiation with the Netherlands. It was in these circumstances that the government of the Netherlands floated the scheme of establishing the Federated States of Indonesia. The scheme became a reality with an agreement reached in Linggajati, near Cirebon in central Java, in November 1946. The Dutch government would recognize the already extant sovereignty of the republic in Java, Sumatra, and Madura, and both governments would cooperate in the formation of the Federated States of Indonesia, which comprised the republic, Borneo, East Indonesia, and other states.[2] The State of East Indonesia was heir to the territory known as The Great East; thus the agreement cemented Bali's identity as a region on the border between East Indonesia and the republic.

This boundary created a fundamental disparity in administrative structure. In the Republic of Indonesia on Java, British forces had intervened but did not install a civil administrator. In East Indonesia, by contrast, the Australian forces charged with governing the state turned to the Dutch forces for assistance, and a Dutchman who had been part of the colonial administration was installed as civil administrator. By permitting bureaucrats of the Netherlands Indies Civil Administration to handle administrative tasks, the Dutch quickly re-established their rule over the territory. Bali, for its part, was under the military jurisdiction of the British forces stationed at Surabaya, but under the civil jurisdiction of the Dutch (Agung 1985: 39–40). This represented a continuation of the colonial order, from which the voice of the republic had been effectively shut out. The republic viewed this as a serious violation of the Linggajati Agreement by the Dutch. As a result, the perception spread that East Indonesia was a Dutch puppet state, and that supporters of the federation were collaborators in the re-establishment of colonial rule and enemies of the republic. During the process of formation of the federation, hostility between the pro-federation side and pro-republic sides worsened, and Bali, as part of East Indonesia, became an adversary of the republic.

Though its capital was Makassar, the State of East Indonesia was actually founded in Denpasar, Bali. Concrete preparations for the creation of the state began with a conference held in Malino, a town south of Makassar, in July 1946. The committee set up at this time elected regional representatives who then met and declared the formation of the State of East Indonesia at the Denpasar Conference held from December 7 to 24 that same year (van Goudoever 1947). The conference concluded with the approval of the Regulations for the Formation of the State of East Indonesia (which defined the basics of the state's governing structure) and the election of a president and parliamentary chair. The president was Cokorda Gede Raka Sukawati, a Balinese who had served as both chair of the committee and of the conference. A native of Ubud, Sukawati had been the head of the Balinese dance troupe that was invited by Moojen to perform at the Dutch Pavilion of the International Colonial Exposition in Paris in 1931 and had represented Bali in the colonial parliament. A fervent supporter of the Dutch, Sukawati promptly appointed a prime minister, and the government of East Indonesia was established on January 13, 1947, with the formation of its first cabinet.

With pro-republic legislators participating in the East Indonesia parliament, the reality was more complicated than a simple scenario of a pro-federation East Indonesia standing in opposition to the republic. Though Sukawati had been elected president, he barely attracted more votes than his opponent, a republican, who was then elected the chair of the East Indonesia parliament. From a purely military standpoint, the republicans could not realistically expect to prevail in an all-out armed conflict across East Indonesia. In that light, they viewed the establishment of a state that guaranteed the right to parliamentary representation of its citizens as a relative improvement over complete acquiescence to rule under Dutch administrators. At the same time, it was a strategy of pro-republic East Indonesian legislators to amplify the image of East Indonesia as a puppet state of the Netherlands (Harvey 1985: 220).

With full independence for all the former colonial territories as their goal, the republicans continued to wage struggles in various regions. The Dutch, too, maintained a hardline stance and launched military offensives in Java on two occasions. Under international pressure, the first attack was followed by a ceasefire agreement (the Renville Agreement), but this was subsequently violated by the second offensive, sparking further criticism of the Dutch government. In 1949 the Dutch ceded sovereignty entirely to the Republic of Indonesia, spelling the end of the Federated States of Indonesia. As Dutch troops withdrew and republicans were released from incarceration, the balance of military power conclusively shifted, and member states of the federation began to join the republic. At the end of April 1950, after federation troops who had recognized the vulnerability of their situation attempted an abortive coup, Sukawati announced that East Indonesia would join the republic rather than secede from the federation to form an independent nation. In May a conference of representatives of the Federated States resolved that the states would merge with the republic, and the State of East Indonesia ceased to exist. The unitary Republic of Indonesia was born that August (Kahin 1952: 460–1).

Even after its ostensible dissolution, the administrative structure of the State of East Indonesia exerted a significant impact on the relationship between Balinese society and religion from 1950 onward. In the course of formulating this structure, the top priority of the new state had been to define the districts that were to serve as administrative units at the regional level under the central government in Makassar. Representatives from these districts would comprise the members of the central parliament. In point of fact, working with Dutch specialists in administrative law, the districts were determined through negotiations between each region and the aforementioned committee chaired by Sukawati. Resulting as they did from negotiations between committee members and regional political leaders, the districts were based not on such rational administrative concerns as area, population, or economy, but on commonly shared traditions of culture, religion, customary law, political alliances, and spheres of economic activity. These districts can justifiably be viewed, then, as the hastily negotiated products of political machinations that did not reflect practical necessities (Legge 1961: 41). What matters for the present discussion, however, is that they maintained the legacy of a colonial administrative framework based on the studies of customary law that began with Hurgronje, a legacy that was reflected in the ongoing repetition of political rhetoric by the Dutch government about the preservation of local cultural autonomy. Article 5, Item 1 of the Regulations for the Formation of the State of East Indonesia specifically mentioned 'the freedom to live in accordance with the characteristics of each district' in stipulating that cultural autonomy would be preserved (Agung 1985: 764).

In a speech at the Malino Conference, van Mook had compared the attributes of a unitary state with those of the federation, saying that while the former might be advantageous from the standpoint of economic efficiency, he favored the latter because it would maintain the distinctive traits of the former Dutch territories that derived from regional and ethnic differences. As Anderson (1991: 132) has pointed out, we cannot overlook the degree to which this stance amounted to a divide-and-conquer policy exploiting the enmities among ethnic groups that had accumulated during the colonial period. In any event, preservation of local characteristics based on customary law became a motivation for federation, and the Bali Regional Assembly would later exploit this same argument, as will be discussed later.

Even though substantially an extension of the colonial ruling structure, the definition of the districts proved to be a problematic task, and nowhere more conspicuously than in Bali and Lombok. Although autonomous regions had already been established in Bali, Lombok had no such political framework. In Bali a representative body for the district could be set up by assembling representatives of the heads of the autonomous regions, but Lombok lacked a system of this sort.[3] The political system that would function as an administrative apparatus varied with each territory, and every district posed different challenges that demanded solutions. The regulations defining the powers of the federation, the state, and the district in each area of administration were a complex jumble, and there was no clear vision of the overall organization of the federation of which the State of East Indonesia was a part. As Schiller (1955: 199) notes in his description of administrative systems in the federation era, from a legal standpoint it is unclear if the distribution of authority really functioned in practice for the duration of the federation. In other words, the federation and the state exercised political power that was fragile at best; the administrative system was never fully unified; and the political world evolved according to the dynamics peculiar to each district. In the case of Bali, the royal families made full use of the reinforced authority they had been granted.

A convergence of issues

The unitary Republic of Indonesia founded in 1950 did not achieve unification of the regional administrative system until 1957. In June 1950, when the merger of East Indonesia with the republic had already been decided, a regional administrative law[4] was promulgated to ensure the unity of regional administration within the State of East Indonesia and facilitate its merger with the republic. The Yogyakarta-based government of the republic, meanwhile, had already enacted its own regional administrative law in 1948.[5] After unification, the Ministry of Home Affairs of the republic inherited from the East Indonesian government the task of implementing its law, with the result that the two laws continued to coexist in the same nation, each applied in its original area of jurisdiction. This situation was not resolved until the 1957 enactment of the Unitary Regional Administrative Law[6] (Agung 1985: 764–5; Legge 1961: 22, 41).

Today Bali is accorded the status of an autonomous province. Under 1958 Law No. 64, passed by the Indonesian parliament in accordance with the 1957 law, the Lesser Sunda Islands were divided into three provinces: Bali, West Nusa Tenggara (consisting of Lombok and Sumbawa), and East Nusa Tenggara (consisting of islands further to the east). After the formation of the unitary republic, these islands had been combined into one administrative unit whose name was changed in 1954 from Lesser Sunda to Nusa Tenggara.[7] Singaraja on Bali was the administrative seat of the province of Nusa Tenggara, and remained the capital of Bali when the island became its own province (until the capital moved to Denpasar in 1960). Provinces were first-level administrative units, with districts established as second-level units by 1958 Law No. 69. On Bali the eight districts designated as second-level administrative units consisted of the former territories of the kingdoms previously designated as autonomous regions: Jembrana, Buleleng, Tabanan, Badung, Gianyar, Klungkung, Bangli, and Karangasem. Thus the regional administrative system of the province of Bali was reinforced within the Indonesian state. Today Bali celebrates August 14, the day that Law No. 64 took effect, as Province Formation Day.

The establishment of Bali province had, in fact, been settled in July 1958, when the central government accepted the proposal approved by parliament to divide Nusa Tenggara province into three provinces. On September 22 the Minister of Home Affairs visited Bali and, at the Bali Hotel, made an announcement about the new autonomous province of Bali. In November representatives of the three new provinces were appointed. I Gusti Bagus Oka, who had been governor of Nusa Tenggara province, was appointed governor of Bali. On December 1, at the Bali Hotel, a ceremony took place to formally abolish the administrative units of East Indonesia, and the new province of Bali was born.[8]

The demarcation of the new regional administrative districts represented a reform of the secular state apparatus. However, the determination of regional administrative units at the two levels mentioned previously was intimately linked to religious issues. At the first level, the territoriality of the administrative units of Bali, West Nusa Tenggara, and East Nusa Tenggara came to be associated with a religion-based division among

Hinduism, Islam, and Christianity respectively. Thus the distribution of religions brought about by the sixteenth-century 'religious revolution' was loosely reflected in the secular administrative units of the twentieth-century national state. At the second level, the legal status of the royal families that had retained their position as representatives was finally abolished, depriving them of legitimacy as the symbolic center of Bali's religious order. After the advent of the State of East Indonesia, the administrative units that imparted legal status to the royals' authority were the swapraja, which in Bali were successors to the autonomous regions established during the colonial era. Under the new regional administrative reform, however, the districts of Bali province were no longer treated as 'special districts' under royal authority. Instead, the swapraja were abolished and replaced by swatantra, administrative units represented by legislative assemblies, and the royal families lost their legal status. However, the new districts retained intact the territories of the old kingdoms, with the result that the district heads continued to be viewed as representatives of the old kingdoms.

The correspondence of the new administrative units with the distribution of religions was not planned, but was the product of a political settlement. When regional administrative reform was first considered, the central government of Indonesia did not consider making Bali an autonomous province; indeed, the probability of this happening remained very low until just before the plan was finalized. At a conference on the administration of Nusa Tenggara province held in February 1955, the Minister of Home Affairs suggested that the options ranged from keeping the province in one piece to dividing it into three, but made clear that it would be divided into two. The government proposal announced on October 20, 1957, by the Minister of Home Affairs to administrators and party representatives from Nusa Tenggara and submitted to parliament called for a division into two provinces: one consisting of Bali, Lombok, and Sumbawa, and the other of the islands to the east. Heeding the government's decision, the strategic commander of the armed forces announced in February 1958 that the two-province division should be expedited as quickly as possible.[9]

There were compelling reasons to divide Nusa Tenggara into two provinces. In terms of population, Bali was close to that of Lombok and Sumbawa combined, but in geographic area it was too small to be considered a first-level province. The province of Bali that ultimately achieved autonomy was, in fact, the smallest of Indonesia's provinces, excluding special districts. Economically, Bali in the 1950s was a very poor place that depended on rice rations from the government for its survival. Thus it would clearly be a challenge for Bali to bear the financial burden of maintaining and operating a first-level regional administrative unit; moreover, it was feared that the burden would fall squarely on the shoulders of its most impoverished residents (Legge 1961: 81–2). Historically, too, there was a strong link between Bali and Lombok, where a Balinese royal palace had once been built. There was little historical precedent for separating Bali and joining only Lombok and Sumbawa together. Finally, and most importantly, making a single province of Bali carried the risk of perpetuating the colonial order. Given concern that the political units that had solidified over the long period of colonization were ill suited to the administrative structure of the new nation, dismantling the colonial order was a crucial element of regional administrative reform. Resolving this issue in Nusa Tenggara required a rethinking of districts held over from the State of East Indonesia at the first level, and of the autonomous regions of Bali at the second level.[10] The Ministry of Home Affairs proposed a two-way split as the most practical plan for these various reasons, and the central government viewed it as the most prudent option from a national standpoint, one that had been prepared for over an adequate period of time.[11]

The province of Bali, which did not appear in the government's proposal, came about as part of a political decision made in parliament. According to Magenda (1989), who analyzes the three-way division from the standpoint of Lombok and Sumbawa, the option was agreed upon at the adamant insistence of the Islamic Masyumi Party. The 1955 election made Masyumi the largest party in West Java and all Islamic districts outside Java and Sumatra. The representatives of Lombok and Sumbawa both belonged to Masyumi, the most influential group representing regional interests in Jakarta. These circumstances gave birth to the proposal for a three-way split of Nusa Tenggara that would join Lombok and Sumbawa together. By rejecting unification with Bali, Masyumi rejected submission to the discretionary powers—notably budgetary—of an administration controlled by the Balinese in Singaraja, and created a province from the Islamic parts of Nusa Tenggara, which would have its own assembly. For Masyumi, this was a way to secure for itself a voice to stand up to the military, the real power behind the new ruling order (Magenda 1989: 387, 393, 855).[12]

The Bali side, too, wanted autonomy as a province so as to retain its own capital and a political system that would help sustain its cultural identity. From the outset of the regional administrative reform process, I Gusti Bagus Oka acknowledged that Bali would shoulder a heavy burden as Indonesia's smallest province, but declared that this would 'enable us to fulfill the obligation we have inherited at the behest of our ancestors to preserve the unity of Balinese culture.' A prevalent view among the Balinese was that if the island was not recognized as a first-level province, it would be proof of the central government's contempt for Bali. Moreover, according to the government's two-way split proposal, the capital of West Nusa Tenggara would not be Singaraja, but the geographically more central city of Mataram on Lombok, a prospect that had the Balinese fearing the loss of their discretionary powers. I Gusti Ketut Puja (who had been appointed governor just after the dissolution of the Japanese military occupation, was arrested by the Dutch forces, and subsequently founded and headed the Jakarta Hindu Bali Association) was fiercely opposed to the relocation of the provincial capital to Mataram, and announced that 'the ideal is to maintain the unity of Bali.' Such declarations notwithstanding, the representatives of Bali lacked the sort of political connections that Masyumi had to make their case before parliament.[13]

In terms of supporting the three-way split, the Balinese and Masyumi effectively shared a common stance, but their objectives were utterly different: for the former, the objective was the autonomy of the province of Bali, while for the latter it was the severing of Bali from West Nusa Tenggara.[14] The result of Masyumi's effort was that religious domains were reflected in administrative units, with Lombok and Sumbawa united as an Islamic territory, Bali as Hindu, and East Nusa Tenggara as Christian. The intertwining of religion with the new regional administrative system was a fait accompli that would exert a significant impact on Balinese society, for it meant that within the national state, the Hindu religion would be conclusively linked to Bali's territory, its government, and the identity of its residents.

Loss of unity

The cultural unity of which Oka spoke in the course of the regional administrative reform process was not a reality for Balinese society during the 1950s. If anything, its salient characteristic during this period was the growth of an extremely severe factionalism. Even after the collapse of the Japanese occupation, the maintenance of law and order remained the purview of the Japanese army. While the republicans elected the aforementioned Puja as governor, his authority was tenuous, and when Dutch forces landed in March with the former colonial administrator in tow, Puja was arrested and incarcerated. With the formation of the State of East Indonesia, the Council of Royal Families became the dominant political force in Bali. Paying lip service to democratization in theory, the State of East Indonesia set up an assembly in parallel with the Council of Royal Families and held elections in April 1947 and September 1948. In the first election, the council blocked the election of republicans to the assembly, as a result of which the assembly became a body that did nothing more than ratify the policies of the council. With its authority guaranteed by East Indonesia, the council secured for itself dictatorial political powers that brooked no interference from any other body (Agung 1985: 45–9; Robinson 1995: 117–22, 174).

Meanwhile, republican forces, which had been expanding their operations in Bali, had foreseen the Denpasar Conference as a pro-federation victory that would lead to the separation of Bali from the republic, and began marshaling their troops for armed confrontation. The battle that took place near Marga, a village in southern Tabanan, is recorded in Indonesian history books as the fiercest fight in Bali during the war for independence. It ended in utter defeat for the republicans and a great number of officers were killed, notably the commander Ngurah Rai, who had been entrusted by the republican army with leading the fight for independence on Bali. Most of the republicans' small cache of weapons was lost as well. For van Mook, who had chosen Malino and Denpasar as conference sites, the choices were intentional: by holding the conferences in Bali and South Sulawesi (which was also the location of a fierce independence movement), he hoped to showcase the success of pacification efforts to eliminate radical elements. The results of the Battle of Marga did an excellent job of validating his claim.

After the death of Ngurah Rai (today a national hero whose name adorns Bali's international airport), the independence movement was transformed into one of separate groups led by multiple commanders. The republican forces attempted to expand their support base by shifting tactics from armed struggle to political activities, but after the first Dutch military offensive they viewed the Linggajati Agreement as null and void, and resumed their struggle, which included the use of armed force. When a second ceasefire agreement was reached between the Republic of Indonesia and the government of the Netherlands, however, continuation of the independence struggle became problematic. In the agreement, the republic rejected the use of arms, a development met by the republican forces on Bali with shock and consternation. After the agreement, the republicans were treated as criminals disturbing the peace, making it easier for the police to crack down on them. Fully aware of the dangers they faced, Balinese republicans felt they had no choice but to fight on without the support of the republic. Republicans on Bali were thus forced to live out a profound contradiction engendered by Bali's fate as a border zone.[15]

Among the royal families that had accrued increasing power, the royal family of Gianyar had grown particularly strong. Anak Agung Gede Oka of the Gianyar royal family was a representative on the Council of Royal Families, and his older brother Anak Agung Gede Agung was the prime minister of East Indonesia; moreover, the latter's wife was the daughter of the East Indonesian president, Sukawati. In other words, the political power centers of East Indonesia and Bali overlapped one another and were monopolized by a small group of individuals closely linked by blood and marriage. This group took an extremely hard line against the armed struggle by the republicans, not only frequently requesting armed intervention by the Dutch forces but also pursuing their own campaign against the republican forces scattered in the mountains.[16] The result was a dramatic split among the republicans, and in May 1949 a large number agreed to surrender their arms. Those who continued to fight regarded this as the ultimate betrayal, causing a deep schism within the ranks of the combatants. At this time, it was discovered that republican forces had been infiltrated by police informants, and public support for the independence movement was also waning. Options had dramatically narrowed for the few remaining republican combatants.

Circumstances had evolved quickly after the second offensive by the Dutch against the republicans in December 1948. Support for independence enjoyed a rebound, and religious ceremonies and other events increasingly served as opportunities to advocate for independence. Some of the Balinese representatives at the East Indonesia assembly called for a merger with the republic, and some members began to engage in party activities in Bali. It was against this backdrop that the administrative framework inherited from the colonial era was abolished. Already, in March 1948, a law had been enacted transferring power from the Dutch administrator to the Council of Royal Families, and the controllers appointed for each autonomous region resigned and were replaced by Balinese (Schiller 1955: 252). However, a Dutch Resident remained in place at the top of the administrative hierarchy. It was not until March 1949 that the Resident relinquished his authority to the representative of the Council of Royal Families, and the colonial administrative framework of Bali and Lombok was no more (Robinson 1995: 177).

The establishment of the unitary Republic of Indonesia also saw the advent of the Bali Regional Assembly. Though republicans formed the nucleus of the assembly, the emergence of multiple leaders after the death of their commander Ngurah Rai, as well as the enmity fostered by the surrender of some, caused a dispersal of leadership among the republican faction. Moreover, the assembly included former members of the pro-Dutch faction. The enmity around the surrender issue extended even to the national army, to which the independence movement participants nominally belonged, fomenting a controversy about retirement guarantees.

The divided movement spawned several complexly intertwined cliques that made their influence felt in party memberships and created a structural element that aggravated partisan trends. Since the beginning of colonial rule, Balinese society had been subjected to a series of extremely heavy-handed political systems—the colonial government, the Japanese military occupation, and then the State of East Indonesia—but in 1950 the centralized political framework was dismantled. The Bali Regional Assembly, which was supposed to constitute a new political center, lacked adequate authority, nor did any politicians capable of exercising decisive leadership come to the fore.[17] This sudden power vacuum produced a dependence on various political forces that acted upon the government of the Republic of Indonesia. In other words, regional politics in Bali were affected by such factors as the expansion of party politics, the personal influence of Sukarno, and the stance of the military. Even as Bali's economic circumstances worsened, a scramble ensued for political support and advantage.

Violence and fear

The lack of social unity led to a breakdown in public order that afflicted Balinese society in the 1950s. Murder, arson, looting, theft, robbery, and beatings were all rife. Movements associated with religion were directly involved in efforts to resolve this dire situation. In 1955, the year of the first post-independence election, the chief of police explicitly acknowledged the increase in murders, stating that 'the public security situation is utterly unsatisfactory.'[18] Expressing grave concerns about the spread of violence, the chief declared that decisive action was called for. The crimes were not merely reckless, opportunistic acts, but were being committed by organized groups, primarily participants in the independence struggle. These groups had links to the Bali Regional Assembly, the police, the military, and political parties. Thus politics was a factor in the violence—a sign that Balinese society was threatened with a serious schism. Public order failed to improve even after the election; in a speech at the beginning of 1956, the governor of Nusa Tenggara province voiced his concerns about the situation. The Balinese did not enjoy a respite from violence and fear until 1958, when the arrest of the perpetrators was announced.

The practice of going from village to village procuring food and money was an extension of the activities of guerrillas during the independence struggle. Many participants had received military training from the Japanese and were familiar with the use of firearms. The progress through the villages of these groups, which were not averse to employing threats and extortion, filled the villagers with fear. Contributors to magazines told of feeling stress akin to 'an egg placed atop a sharp stone.' Coffee growers were afraid to tend their crops for fear of encountering these groups. People who refused to feed them when they came to their door had their houses burned down. Fraud was also rampant in the form of 'swindlers in hero's garb' who would gain the trust of their victims by posing as veterans of the independence movement, which fomented suspicion of movement participants in general.[19] The police, who perceived these groups to be especially prevalent in Bangli, Tabanan, Gianyar, and Badung, drew up a list of members based on information gathered from those arrested, and then arrested those individuals. Meanwhile, vigilante groups were being formed in southern Bali.[20]

For those who had participated in the independence movement, the 1950s were a time of disillusionment. True, independence had been achieved. But the collaborators in the colonial system, the enemy they meant to vanquish, had survived. These individuals, who had profited under the colonial regime and the State of East Indonesia, were now Bali Regional Assembly representatives, *punggawa* (administrative officials), and village heads. Revenge was at the root of the violence: tolerance for the presence of collaborators by the Bali Regional Assembly and the political parties was the impetus for the formation of organized groups.[21] Anxiety about their livelihoods further intensified the despair of independence movement veterans, who had been provided with no economic guarantees and were unable to live as they had envisioned. Exacerbating their frustration was the lack of respect shown to those who had contributed to the independence struggle.

Jajasan Kebaktian Pedjuang (JKP, Freedom Fighters Service Foundation) was formed in response to this situation to address the problems faced by movement participants. On January 14, 1951, Bali Regional Assembly leaders and thirty-five movement participants met in Denpasar to discuss the treatment of the veterans. They determined that, while the regional government had an obligation to support the participants, actual aid from the government was inadequate. A decision was then made to set up a fund with assistance from the central government and form an independent foundation. JKP was thus established on October 3. From 1952 onward, under a directive from the Bali Regional Assembly, JKP took charge of Bali-related duties on behalf of the Republic of Indonesia's Biro Reconstruksi Nasional (National Reconstruction Bureau)[22] (Pendit 1979a: 348).

The primary objective of JKP was to foster in veterans a spirit of independence and of service to the nation, and its activities centered around providing the veterans with material and emotional support. This specifically included monetary loans, job training, care of the injured, opportunities for treatment in Java when Balinese hospitals were inadequate, care of children who had lost their mothers, and the construction and operation of farms and pig-raising facilities. The foundation also strove to educate the veterans through lectures. Additionally, it built memorials to honor the achievements of those who had contributed to the independence struggle. Tombs and a monument dedicated to those who died in the struggle were erected in Marga, where Ngurah Rai was killed in battle.[23] In honoring a hero who had died too young, the monument came to symbolize the legitimacy of the independence movement and a call to prevent its disintegration.[24]

As part of the effort to educate and enlighten movement veterans, a social department established at JKP published a magazine to provide a forum for participants. The editor-in-chief of the magazine, *Dhamai* (which means 'peace'), was I Gusti Bagus Sugriwa.[25] He had been a member of the foundation's executive committee since its inception, and served as vice-chairman of the planning committee for the monument-building project that began in 1953 (Meidiary 1999: 61). JKP also took under its wing a support organization for students in the independence movement,[26] and together with Wedastera Suyasa and Nyoman Pendit, the leaders of this organization, Sugriwa was among the most prolific writers and critics of the 1950s.

Sugriwa belonged to BDL (discussed in Chapter 2) and also served as a representative of the Bali Regional Assembly in the Hindu recognition movement's dealings with the Religion Ministry, as will be described in Chapter 4. Thus he was a pivotal figure linking politics and religion in Bali. Born in Singaraja in 1900, almost the same year as Sukarno, he first attended a village school in Kubutambahan. From the age of sixteen, he was educated at a teacher-training institution in Singaraja. This type of school had first been established in Bali in 1914, so Sugriwa belonged to the earliest generation of teachers trained not in Java but in Bali. He was formally hired as a teacher's assistant at the village school in Jinengdalem in 1920, and for the duration of the colonial era made his living as a teacher, albeit with several changes in his place of employment. Though he lacked the opportunity to encounter the Dutch language directly, Sugriwa apparently learned Dutch through correspondence with a friend in Yogyakarta from the time he began teaching. In 1928 he was assigned as a teacher's assistant at the middle school in Kubutambahan, and was appointed principal in 1935. Indisputably a lower-level civil servant within the hierarchy of the colonial administration, Sugriwa became secretary of the Kubutambahan branch of BDL and an active contributor to *Djatajoe*, mostly in the form of essays on religious teachings or stories.

Sugriwa was one of the resistance fighters in the independence campaign who continued the struggle to the end, refusing to surrender, and joined the leadership of the Indonesian Independent People's Movement, which was formed with Cilik[27] as its representative on July 15, 1948. This movement engaged mainly in social actions such as making the rounds of villages, attempting to raise national consciousness, caring for the sick, and teaching people to read and write. Cilik was appointed head of JKP, and the foundation's activities thus had their antecedents in the independence struggle.

Sugriwa gave many lectures to the JKP membership. He warned about a jealousy- and hatred-driven decline in morality, called for the maintenance of a healthy spirituality, and made frequent use of religious ideology. In a lecture published in *Dhamai*, he had this to say about the 'fighters' and 'service' cited in JKP's name: first, the term 'fighter' had, in practice, taken on varied meanings, extending not only to participants in the independence movement but also to those who had fought for the Dutch, rebels who merely sowed chaos, and members of political parties. To JKP, however, 'fighters' were specifically those who had participated in the independence movement. Defining 'service' as an unwavering attitude toward God born of the merging of God and spirit, Sugriwa argued that a fighter was a body sustained by that attitude, for whom nothing was more essential than the unity of body and spirit.[28] He also stressed the meaning of service in the context of striving for social justice and avoiding factionalism. Sugriwa reaffirmed his hopes for a society built upon mutual cooperation, without sacrifice of the lives of others, and based on equitable justice in thought, word, and action. As he repeated his views in lectures in different parts of Bali, Sugriwa's idealistic stance came under attack. Critics said JKP's own activities were partisan in character, and that Sugriwa was laying exclusive claim to an extremely authoritarian view of culture and religion. However, this stance of seeking solutions to social problems in religion and morality originated, in fact, in the economic crisis and religious revival of the 1930s, to which Sugriwa was an heir.

Kreneng and its significance in the 1950s

Although Singaraja remained the official political center of Bali in the 1950s, as it had during the colonial era, Denpasar, the economic center, was expanding its political functions. On the east side of Denpasar, the Kreneng district, in particular, where the Bali Regional Assembly, educational institutions, and the national government-operated radio station were concentrated, was a strategic administrative zone. Today the site of a bemo minibus terminal, Kreneng was the dream location for construction of the new society of the 1950s, a stage on which religion, politics, education, and the media all played overlapping roles.[29]

In accordance with the East Indonesia Regional Administrative Law, which was promulgated on June 15, 1950, a Regional Administrative Law Implementation Committee consisting of representatives of the assembly, the royal families, and the political parties was established on August 7.[30] Based on the committee's deliberations, the East Indonesia Assembly was dissolved on September 20 and the Bali Regional Assembly formed on September 25.[31] The legal precedent cited for having a regional assembly under the republic was a law of the ostensibly defunct State of East Indonesia.[32] On this day, a regional assembly recognition ceremony took place at the Bali Hotel in Denpasar. As representative of the Assembly Chair Selection Committee, Sugriwa promptly appointed three committee members, and a process was approved for selecting the chair, in accordance with which an election was held. The result was the election of I Gusti Putu Merta, a key member of BDL and contributor of numerous articles to *Djatajoe*, including one detailing the Balinization dilemma. The assembly elected chairs of four departments in charge of actual administrative tasks, with Sugriwa designated as head of the General Affairs Department. On September 26, the assembly selected candidates for regional representative; Anak Agung Bagus Suteja of the Jembrana royal family and Cokorda Anom Putra of the Klungkung royal family were chosen. The central government in Jakarta picked Suteja, who, though a member of a royal family, had participated in the independence struggle. The establishment of a Swapraja Assembly Preparation Committee followed on November 16; thus even the former autonomous regions were to have their own assemblies.[33]

At the time of formation of the Bali Regional Assembly, which Pendit (1979a: 359) hailed as 'an extremely significant reform for the ordinary people of Bali,' its leadership was dominated by the republican faction led by Sugriwa. The core of the faction consisted of former members of BDL, as exemplified by the election of Merta as assembly chair. The newly formed assembly immediately passed five resolutions, all of which were demands made by BDL to the Council of Royal Families. The lower-level civil servants who had participated in the independence struggle now occupied center stage in Balinese politics. However, the Bali Regional Assembly itself was a product of compromise. The assembly's inauguration had not been accompanied by a new election of representatives, just a scramble among the parties for assembly seats. As mentioned above, the process by which the assembly was formed meant that it included former collaborators with the colonial government.

The Bali Regional Assembly building and the representatives' official residences were built in Kreneng, and it was stipulated that representatives must reside in Denpasar.[34] At the time these residences were sold by the government to the representatives, and even today many relatives of politicians of the 1950s continue to live in the district. The government-owned radio station, which was the primary source of information during that period, began broadcasting on November 9, 1950, from Jempiring Street in Kreneng, moving to Melati Street in the same district in 1953.[35] The reason for construction of the government residences and radio station in Kreneng was the presence of Dutch administrative and military facilities there. The conversion of the property of the former rulers into a strategic district for implementing the new era was itself a symbol of independence.

Kreneng also became home to the adjacent headquarters of Bali's two largest educational institutions: the Saraswati Foundation and the Dwijendra Education Foundation. The former, whose official name was the Saraswati People's Educational Institution, was founded on December 8, 1946. Saraswati was the successor to the educational movement Taman Siswa, which, as mentioned earlier, became active in Bali in the 1930s. Saraswati's leader, I Gusti Made Tamba, had studied with Taman Siswa in Madiun, beginning in 1934. From 1946 onward, Taman Siswa was treated as a threat and labeled a 'barbaric school,' so it was relaunched under a new name. During the East Indonesia era, even while subjected to various pressures and with its associates constantly under surveillance, the organization set up a People's Educational Council and began operating an educational institution. In 1949 it resolved to expand its educational activities, and at the same time formally adopted Saraswati, the name of the Hindu goddess of wisdom, as the title of its educational organization. In 1951 it received funding from the Bali Regional Assembly and began constructing a high school and other new educational facilities in Kreneng. Until 1959 Saraswati underwent an 'extremely enthusiastic period of development,' setting up a huge educational center covering everything from preschool to university-level classes, expanding its student population, and growing into one of Bali's most famous educational institutions (Pendit 1979b: 90).

Founded on January 28, 1953, the Dwijendra Education Foundation was an institution on par with Saraswati, with a focus on religious and cultural education. The foundation was named after Dang Hyang Dwijendra, a priest who was active during the Majapahit era. He traveled to Bali, Lombok, and Sumbawa; in Bali, where he was known as Pedanda Shakti Wawu Rauh or Dang Hyang Nirartha, he is considered the forefather of the Hindu priesthood. Visiting Bali during the reign of King Waturenggong, who unified the island and presided over a golden age, the priest was welcomed by the king, built many temples, conducted grand ceremonies, and brought prosperity to the land of Bali. Guided directly by the supreme god Sang Hyang Widi, he achieved enlightenment at Uluwatu Temple, where, according to legend, he became a god himself and departed this world (Parisada Hindu Dharma 1978: 40).

The Dwijendra Education Foundation was created by a group of individuals, including educators who belonged to the leadership of Saraswati and associates of the Bali Regional Assembly, led by Sugriwa, who believed in the importance of religious education. They formed a preparatory committee and launched the foundation after consultations with the royal families of Badung.[36] Other royal families outside Badung also cooperated in the establishment of the foundation and provided funding. Even in the 1950s, the royal families still retained tremendous influence in the religious sphere. Cilik, the JKP chair, and Shastri, an Indian who will be discussed later, were also involved from the preparatory stage. Initially the foundation borrowed classroom space from Saraswati and began providing middle-school education, then added a building next door to Saraswati and extended its activities into higher education. Today its operations range from preschool to university education (the university now has five faculties), but the emphasis of the entire institution is on religious education. In 1959 the foundation opened a school, Pendidikan Guru Agama Atas Hindu Bali, with the objective of providing the first training program for religious instructors in Bali. The head of the school was Sugriwa, who had served as adviser to the foundation since its inception. During the 1950s, meetings concerned with religion were held in the Dwijendra Education Foundation building, which became a gathering place for all entities with influence on religious issues (Panitia Catur Windu Yayasan Dwijendra 1985; Meidiary 1999: 53).

The central Indonesian government's Ministry of Education and Culture and the Religion Ministry had already decided in 1951 that religious education was obligatory in public schools.[37] At that point, however, the Religion Ministry lacked a department with jurisdiction over Hinduism, so there was no state apparatus for implementing Hindu education. As will be detailed in the next chapter, the Bali Regional Assembly responded to this situation by establishing an Autonomous Religion Bureau in 1953 and announcing that it would initiate religious education on its own, with the bureau in charge.[38] Textbooks were published that same year, and Sugriwa was one of the writers. In this manner, Hindu religious education got underway, but with local religious groups also engaging in their own educational activities there was as yet no unified stance on religious education. The unification of Hindu religious educational practices came after a Hindu department was established at the Religion Ministry.

Compared to the 1930s, which saw the publication of only a few magazines, notably *Bhawanagara* and *Djatajoe*, publishing in Bali took off in the 1950s, its rapid growth sustained in large part by books related to religion. Two bookstores opened in Denpasar during this period: Bali Mas on Gajah Mada Street to the west, and Perhatian to the east. The latter shifted its business focus to newspaper publishing and began issuing a newspaper affiliated with the Nationalist Party.[39] Its owner, I Ketut Nada, was an important Nationalist supporter, and his publishing company became a party stronghold in Denpasar. The other bookstore, Bali Mas, focused more on carrying religion-related publications. Patra, who had worked at the general store Dharma (known as Toko Kelontong after the bamboo baskets used by peddlers), had founded the bookstore in the late 1940s. At its peak it had more than fifty employees and branches in various parts of Bali. In 1955 these two bookstores were joined by a third on Gajah Mada Street, a Communist Party bookshop named Toko Buku Rakyat.

During the colonial era, printing was done in Java, but in the 1950s printing facilities were available in Bali. During the Japanese occupation, a print shop had been built next to Puputan Square at the eastern end of Gajah Mada Street to produce the *Bali Shimbun*, a newspaper published by the Yomiuri newspaper company.[40] Books and magazines published in Bali during the 1950s were printed here. The founder of Perhatian had been an employee at the print shop, which was where he learned the newspaper publishing trade. The 1955 elections triggered a dramatic increase in printed materials, particularly those carrying political slogans. Meanwhile, Bali Mas sold calendars first issued by BDL in the 1930s and focused on the printing and selling of religion-related works. It also served as Bali's general agent for Javanese publications, and became the exclusive agent for Balai Pustaka, the state-owned publisher. People associated with Saraswati and Dwijendra sought out religion-related books at Bali Mas. Its owner, Patra, took an interest in religious issues and had briefly taught at Dwijendra.

For Bali Mas, Sugriwa was one of the greatest writers around, and for Sugriwa, the owner of Bali Mas was the ideal reader because he informed Sugriwa about which of his works had proved popular and earned a following. The relationship between Sugriwa and Bali Mas also illuminates the state of the media in Denpasar at the time. Sugriwa produced a prodigious body of writings on religious matters during this period, much of it consisting of lectures that had been broadcast as part of a Cultural Course program on the government radio station, then printed and published by Bali Mas. Sugriwa not only lectured at Saraswati and Dwijendra, but also devoted his spare time to traveling around Bali to speak in various places. To Sugriwa, radio was an invaluable means of disseminating information, and publication of his lectures satisfied his insatiable desire to educate and enlighten people.

Associates of Bali Mas at the time confirm that the publication of religion-related books and calendars soared in the 1950s. Beratha, who left Bali Mas to open another bookstore in Denpasar that handled many religion-related works, attributed this to the fact that people were seeking vindication for their daily lives, and were able to gain familiarity with the holy scriptures because these books were written in the Indonesian alphabet, not Balinese script. Blessed by the presence of Sugriwa and many other writers, the publishers of the 1950s helped advance the free exchange of religious knowledge. In doing so, they were heirs to the thirst for legitimate knowledge and an understanding of religious practice that first became conspicuous in the 1920s and accelerated with BDL in the 1930s.

Sanglah as a center for new religious scholarship

Around 1958, when the province of Bali was established, the critical mass of influence in the religious sphere began to shift from the generation that had been active in Kreneng to a new generation whose activities were centered elsewhere, in the Sanglah district on the south side of Denpasar. Though Kreneng was the political center, Sanglah was the choice for construction of a government-owned hospital and a new institution of higher learning, Udayana University, which was built in 1958. In contrast to institutions like Saraswati and Dwijendra, which were founded by people who had lived through the colonial era and the independence struggle, this was a national university that lacked direct involvement with social conditions in Bali. The new generation of religious scholars that gathered at the university's Faculty of Letters was characterized by a shared experience of studying in India. People who had studied Sanskrit and Hinduism abroad acquired teaching positions at the university and, from there, expanded their influence in religious matters. Whereas Sugriwa's generation had been born in the 1890s and 1900s, those who had studied in India were born in the 1920s or later. A defining difference between the two generations was those who had personally experienced the independence struggle and those who had not. Embodying this difference was the elder statesman of the India students group, Ida Bagus Mantra, who had lost his older brother in the independence struggle but did not participate in it himself.

When Balinese scholars began seeking out direct contact with India, the epicenter of Hindu scholarship, it was a sign, one may argue, of a clear intention to free themselves from reliance on colonialist scholarship and acquire knowledge on their own. The Balinese themselves wanted to explore the Indian form of Hinduism at a remove from the Hindu scholarship of the colonial era, when a research framework set up in the nineteenth century had resulted in the introduction of laws and a caste system as part of the ruling structure established over Bali. Interest in India itself had been shared by Balinese scholars from the time of *Djatajoe*, stimulated by the influence of the Javanese nationalists' theosophical leanings. In his analysis of 'the theosophy that clung like a shadow to the intelligentsia of Java,' Tsuchiya (1982) traces the philosophical development of Javanese intellectuals who did not wish to follow the path of Western thought, and argues that theosophy was an ideal system of thought for overcoming the spiritual crisis of the West. The intellectuals regarded theosophy—with its emphasis on the mystical aspects of all religions, its treatment of the Bhagavad Gita as a holy scripture, and the pride of place it gave to Indian thought—as a clear manifestation of skepticism and criticism aimed at the modern Western view of humanity. According to Tsuchiya's analysis, a major reason for the Javanese intellectuals' acceptance of theosophy was that it was led by Westerners living in Java during the colonial era, and it was the most suitable framework within which to describe Javanese culture in a Western context. Together with the thought of Rabindranath Tagore, who visited Java and Bali in the 1920s (some years after receiving the Nobel Prize), theosophy was viewed by early-twentieth century Javanese intellectuals as offering an alternative worldview distinct from that of the West[41] (Tsuchiya 1982: 62–3, 146–51; cf. Sears 1996: 125–31).

Tamba, the leader of Saraswati who had studied with Taman Siswa, as mentioned earlier, felt an affinity for both theosophy and Tagore's thought, and headed for India. In 1954 he visited the school famously founded by Tagore in Santiniketan, outside Calcutta. He then traveled through India with Nyoman Pendit, who was studying at Santiniketan, and closely scrutinized several educational facilities. Tamba later related to Pendit his impressions of Santiniketan. He described being profoundly impressed by its educational system, which provided facilities extending from preschool through university, and said that he had subsequently expanded Saraswati's educational facilities (which had opened in 1952) with the Santiniketan system in mind. Tamba also made note of the simplicity of the educational spirit there, saying that seeing students and teachers studying together under a tree outdoors taught him that education is not just the transmission of knowledge but must provide an actual experience of living in society and in nature. He further asserted that within the larger trend of liberation of former colonies from the 1950s onward, he sensed that such educational practices did not reflect an idolization of the West, but were an Eastern, Asian form of education (Pendit 1979b: 152–7). Tamba did not merely travel to India, but also devoted himself to collecting and translating materials related to Indian studies.[42]

The number of scholars gathered at Udayana University who had studied in India was not large, nor was there any shared aspect of their experience abroad that would enable them to form a unified lineage. Not only did later students attend different institutions from that of Mantra, the first to study in India, but the circumstances of their decisions to study abroad were disparate and unrelated. Mantra studied at Santiniketan and took his degree in Sanskrit. Upon his return to Bali, he became a member of the Udayana University Faculty of Letters Establishment Committee, and later went on to become governor of Bali province. The next students to go to India were Ida Bagus Oka Punyatmaja and Cokorda Rai Sudharta. Oka studied Sanskrit in Nagpur and Varanasi from 1953 to 1958, and upon his return took a teaching position in the Udayana Faculty of Letters. Sudharta, too, studied at Nagpur and Varanasi from 1954 to 1957, then returned to Indonesia and began teaching at Gadjah Mada University in Yogyakarta. From 1958 to 1961 he studied again at Varanasi, then returned home and took a job at Udayana. These three were the only returning India scholars to teach in the Faculty of Letters at Udayana.[43]

The name 'India students group' was applied to this small group of returnees from abroad who were not only scholars but later rose to eminent positions in politics. A significant factor is that the generation of Suteja and Sugriwa viewed Mantra and others with enmity, as leaders of a younger generation that threatened their authority. The reason for this hostility was a difference in political stance. Mantra had been encouraged to go to India by Sukawati, president of the State of East Indonesia, and Oka and Sudharta by Ibu Gedong, the wife of I Gusti Bagus Oka.[44] Sugriwa and others therefore viewed the India students group as collaborators with the colonial government. In line with this perception, Tamba and Pendit, who had also been to India, were not treated as part of this group. The generational shift brought about by Mantra's ascendancy was a bitter pill to swallow for those who had participated in the independence struggle.

Despite their small numbers and the enmity of the independence struggle veterans, the India students group came together as a group that played a significant role in the institutionalization of Balinese religion. Their emblematic achievement was the compilation of the *Upadesa* (Parisada Hindu Dharma 1978). This book, which describes the fundamentals of Hinduism in the Indonesian language, is a comprehensive religious text that includes instructions on how to carry out ceremonies; it became the most definitive source of guidance for Hindus not only in Bali but throughout Indonesia. It served as a basic textbook, constantly referred to by Hindu religious educators, who also added to its content and revised its index, among other improvements. The book comprises seventeen chapters in a classical dialogue format through which the priest Rsi Dharmakerti, who speaks 'truths based on sacred knowledge gleaned from the Vedas,' provides teachings in response to questions from his disciple Sang Suyasa. Starting with the general question 'What is Hinduism?,' the text goes on to reveal 'truths' about God, holy scriptures, famous priests in history, the origins of temples, holy days, places of worship, ethics, ceremonies, and methods of prayer. It ends with instructions on the Tri Sandhya, which will be discussed below. It was the India students group that compiled what is arguably the most important text for Hindus in Indonesia. The members of the group all lived in Sanglah along Sudirman Street, which was lined with the residences provided to employees of Udayana University. They sequestered themselves together until they had finished the book.

Recognizing that the Vedic passages scattered through various Balinese texts were extremely fragmented, the basic stance of the India students group was to use the organized system of Hindu scholarship they had studied to systematize the religious knowledge of Bali. This was the premise according to which the *Upadesa* was created, as well as a point of emphasis by the group's members when they presented their work as that of scholars specializing in the teaching of Sanskrit at the university level. The group did not take the position that Indian scholarship represented legitimate Hinduism and that Balinese religious practices were a provincial variant; rather, they averred, their reference point was Bali, and they saw themselves as bringing something back from India that would be of use in organizing Balinese doctrine—not attempting to change Balinese religion through an infusion of knowledge from India.[45] Following on from the work of Sugriwa's generation, which had focused on translating Balinese texts into Indonesian with additional commentaries, the younger group's efforts offered a new approach—the analysis of Balinese texts with the aid of Sanskrit-based knowledge—to a body of religious knowledge that was in the process of democratization.

Shastri and advice from the diaspora

Several non-Balinese also made major contributions to the study of Sanskrit and Hinduism during the 1950s. One was Goris, who became an authority on Balinese studies after his assignment to the island by the colonial government. He remained in Bali in the 1950s, and was involved in the establishment of the Faculty of Letters at Udayana University and taught there. Based in Singaraja until 1958, Goris had taught Sanskrit to the India students group before their departure, but he did not participate directly in the development of religious education in Kreneng. There was, however, an Indian scholar of Sanskrit named Shastri, who worked with Tamba and Sugriwa and taught in Kreneng at Saraswati and Dwijendra. Today he is highly regarded as someone who contributed to the institutionalization of religious doctrine in Bali by introducing Sanskrit and Vedic teachings. Most notably he is the individual who devised the system of praying three times a day, known as the Tri Sandhya, a significant factor in the recognition of Balinese religion as an independent faith on par with other religions, such as Islam, that center around scriptures and prayer. Until the completion of Udayana University in 1958, Shastri's expertise had a tremendous impact on the effort to integrate Hindu-related scholarship and Balinese religion. However, assessments of his work do not always reflect the thinking articulated by Shastri himself. Moreover, his presence in Bali during this period was tied to political circumstances in India, and he was not directly involved with the religious situation in Bali per se.

Shastri was a university instructor who had taught Sanskrit in India during the final years of British rule. After receiving his education in Sanskrit at the Banaras Hindu University in Varanasi, he studied Hindu literature and taught Sanskrit at a university in Lahore, now part of Pakistan. He was there in 1947 when India achieved independence and the partition of India and Pakistan took place. From July to November that year he participated in the conflict on the pro-India side, but became a displaced person when that side lost. Thus Shastri was a victim of the partition, which produced massive numbers of fatalities and refugees. After visiting friends in India and seeking employment there without success, he left the country and entered Singapore through an acquaintance's assistance. He was offered a job in Medan, and so began his association with Indonesia. Moving from place to place, and after a sojourn in Yogyakarta, he eventually arrived in Bali, where he happened to make the acquaintance of a Sanskrit scholar from Poland, and the two of them began to examine the religious practices of Bali, in which they noted a resemblance to Hinduism. In 1950, as it became clear that Bali was on track to join the republic, Shastri began teaching at Saraswati and participated in the formation of the Dwijendra Foundation. He made his living in Bali as a teacher of Sanskrit and Hinduism.

Along with his teaching activities, Shastri played an important part in the movement, detailed in the next chapter, to get the Religion Ministry to officially recognize Hinduism as a religion. Together with Sugriwa, he met with the ministry's representatives to elucidate the position of Balinese religion in the context of Hinduism as a globally recognized faith. He also explained the relationship between Hinduism and Balinese religion to Sukarno himself. Shastri's most salient contributions to the negotiation process were his proposal of the Tri Sandhya and his interpretation of Sang Hyang Widi.[46] In response to the ministry's argument that Balinese religion lacked a clear object of worship, Sugriwa and the other Balinese representatives presented Sang Hyang Widi as the name of the god worshiped in Bali. However, they were met with the retort that this deity name did not appear in Sanskrit literature and was no more than the name of a local god; thus Balinese religion was not a descendant of Hinduism but merely a regional faith. Shastri was the one who prepared the rebuttal that the name could be interpreted as meaning 'he who is the only one, there being no other.' For the duration of negotiations with the Religion Ministry, which lasted until 1958, Shastri was the only person at Kreneng who organized the concepts of Balinese religion by introducing Sanskrit-based interpretations from a Hindu perspective.[47]

To those associated with religion in Bali, Shastri was an invaluable presence who served as a bridge between Indian Sanskrit scholarship and Balinese religion. Shastri himself, however, took a critical view of

Balinese religion. In his reminiscences, he states that his introduction of the Tri Sandhya was motivated by misgivings about religious practices in Bali, and not specifically by a desire to provide materials with which to persuade the Religion Ministry. In his eyes, the most outmoded aspect of Balinese religious customs was the authority wielded by the priests. Shastri was particularly skeptical of the central role played in all religious practices by holy water prepared by the priests. His sense was that Balinese religion was an undemocratic phenomenon in which ordinary people were oppressed by the priests' power. Hence he felt an antipathy toward such appellations as 'Religion of Holy Water' for the Balinese faith,[48] fearing that a name of this sort only reinforced the status of the priests. It was from this critical perspective that Shastri devised the new religious practice of the Tri Sandhya. His thinking was that chanting this prayer three times a day was sufficient to achieve the purposes of the faith, thereby liberating people from their dependence on the priests. This was an outright repudiation of the authority of the priests from the anti-ritualistic stance taken by Shastri.

However, Shastri appears to have felt some sympathy with Balinese religion. As someone who had become a refugee because he fought on the Hindu side during the partition of India and Pakistan, he could identify to a degree with Sugriwa and other Balinese activists who were struggling to get the Muslim-dominated Religion Ministry in Jakarta to recognize Hinduism. But Shastri was also concerned about the spread of Christianity and kept a particularly vigilant eye on the activities of Tisna in northern Bali. After stepping down from the editorship of *Djatajoe*, Tisna had continued to write novels at his library in Lovina. On July 6, 1944, during the Japanese occupation, he was arrested and incarcerated by the Japanese military and his library was burned down. In 1946 he renounced his right to succession as ruler of Buleleng and converted to Christianity. His faith was not a purely private matter; he engaged in evangelical activities and sent Balinese to a church in Surabaya. Even though he had renounced the throne, the fact that a member of a powerful royal family had converted to Christianity and was actively proselytizing was significant to Shastri, who acknowledged that he felt a duty to protect Hinduism from the spread of Christianity.

During the first half of the 1950s Shastri was not merely a teacher. He was also an object of veneration as a holy man who had come from India, the homeland of Hinduism. He was addressed by the title Pandit, meaning 'great teacher' or 'holy man,' and his portrait was painted.[49] However, his status in Bali was precarious. Engaged as he was in public—and, for that matter, political—activities, there was always the risk he would be expelled from Bali.[50] What is more, having come to Bali as a refugee, he would have no place to return to if he was expelled. Shastri was forever compelled to limit himself to the role of advisor, and he could not make public the criticisms he harbored toward Balinese religion. As more political power accrued to the India students group after 1958, Shastri's contribution gradually faded from view. Sugriwa transcribed the Tri Sandhya into Balinese script and it became holy scripture. Thus advice from the Indian diaspora was folded into Balinese religious doctrine. Though Shastri himself received accolades as a prominent contributor to religious reform, his status was always that of a supporting actor.

During the first ten years of Bali's participation in the Republic of Indonesia under the leadership of the lower-level civil servants who had first become active in the 1930s, the religious and political realms remained intertwined, and the priests and royal families, recognized anew, retained their authority. The renewal of Balinese society, promoted under the banner of religious morality, could not prevent the spread of factionalism brought about by political schisms, even as the democratization of religious knowledge proceeded apace, spurred by the rapid growth of education and publishing. Amid these circumstances, the only unifying cause shared by otherwise opposing forces was the movement for recognition of Hinduism as an official religion. This movement came to a close in 1958 with the establishment of Bali as a province under the regional administrative reforms and the beginnings of a generational shift among the religious activists. Ironically, the movement's opponent across the negotiating table had been the Religion Ministry, the central government of the same republic from which the republican faction in the border zone of Bali had refused to remain separate.

CHAPTER 4

Religion and the State

Hindus and the Religion Ministry

Based on the 1945 Constitution, as well as the Pancasila or Five Principles that constitute the national policy of the Republic of Indonesia—Principle 1 being 'belief in the one and only God'[1]—the Indonesian state today guarantees freedom of religion. At the same time, the significance of religious faith is accepted as a given and as the cornerstone of the nation. The Religion Ministry, the government entity responsible for systemically implementing this policy, was established on January 3, 1946, and began organizing the country's religious structure after the 1950 integration of the various states of the Federated States of Indonesia into the Republic of Indonesia. The Religion Ministry, which has its origins in the Religious Affairs Office established during the Japanese occupation of Indonesia, began its existence as a government agency rooted essentially in Islam. However, when the Lesser Sunda Islands (which belonged to East Indonesia, one of the Federated States) joined the republic, the ministry encountered a serious problem: Muslims were a minority in the region, and nowhere was this more so than on the island of Bali. The Bali Regional Assembly was deeply involved in religious issues; aligning itself with religious groups, it declared that religious practice on Bali consisted of a form of Hinduism and pressed for the establishment of a 'Hindu-Bali' department in the Religion Ministry. This movement for the official recognition of Hinduism, which grew during the 1950s, formed the structural basis for the religious order subsequently established on Bali. It also resulted in agreement by the Religion Ministry to set up a Hindu-Bali department and a pluralistic religious structure, even as it remained Islamo-centrist in outlook.

The struggle over whether Indonesia should be a secular nation-state or an Islamic state—an issue that had remained unresolved since the

Japanese occupation—subsided temporarily after the 1955 election, which secured the primacy of the Indonesian Nationalist Party and Sukarno, who sought to create a nation-state (Benda 1983, particularly pp. 189–90; Boland 1971). Meanwhile, as described in Chapter 3, regional separatist movements continued through the 1950s, and the establishment of a regional administrative system as part of the transition from a federation to a unitary republic was delayed until 1957. Thus progress in the negotiations between the ministry and the Bali Regional Assembly over recognition of Hinduism as an official religion was closely intertwined with the circumstances of nation-building in Indonesia as a whole.[2]

Amid the process of national unification into the Republic of Indonesia, the Religion Ministry convened a general conference in Yogyakarta from April 14 to 18, 1950, bringing together representatives of both the republic and the Federated States of Indonesia for the first time. From this point onward, the central ministry began setting up a structure under which to establish departments for each recognized religion and open branch offices in each regional administrative district. The decision was made that religious affairs belonged under the purview of the central government. Initially, separate departments were set up for Islam and Christianity only, and religious activities outside these two religions were defined as non-religious 'beliefs' (kepercayaan or aliran agama), which were administered collectively under another special department.[3]

The organization of the Religion Ministry brought with it a significant problem. Rather than ensuring religious freedom, it created a distinction between religions and beliefs, which resulted in the formation of a hierarchy among religious practices. The establishment of a separate department for a particular religion meant that the government recognized the religion as legitimate, and that it would provide funding and human resources in support of the religion's educational and other activities. This aspect was evident in the allotment of staff to the Lesser Sunda Islands. The Religious Education Section assigned one full-time employee to Bali, seven to Lombok, nine to Sumbawa, none to Sumba, one to Flores, and two to Timor, demonstrating a clear bias in favor of districts with many Muslim adherents.[4]

Meanwhile, even as religions collectively assigned to the department for 'other beliefs' received less support, they increasingly became objects of government scrutiny. Granted, a 1951 Religion Ministry directive decreeing the establishment of this department calls only for cooperation with and fostering of religious activities, and does not say anything about monitoring or surveillance. However, a 1952 decision by the Religion Minister[5] specified details on the activities of this department and declared that a primary objective of the department was to investigate religious activities in each region and obtain advance information on political activities that might pose a danger to the state system. It was this difference in the treatment of beliefs versus religions that turned the official recognition of religions (i.e. authorization of their own ministry departments) into a political issue. Groups, including the Bali Regional Assembly, criticized the ranking of religions as a form of discrimination against Indonesian citizens. They asserted that the Religion Ministry was dividing the citizenry into nobility and commoners according to their religion.[6]

In the face of these accusations, the Religion Ministry defended its position as follows. At the Religion Ministry general conference held in Semarang from January 27 to 31, 1954, the Religion Minister began his opening address by speaking about religious freedom and the involvement of the ministry in religious activities, making reference to the situation in 1953 when the official recognition of religions became an issue in Bali and elsewhere. The Minister went on to say that in accordance with the spirit of the Constitution, neither the government nor the Religion Ministry had the authority to recognize a particular religion, nor should the government involve itself in the internal affairs of individual religions. It was the government of the colonial era under the Dutch that had intervened in religious matters, and a policy of non-intervention was nothing less than a manifestation of the spirit of national independence. Religious freedom was already guaranteed under the Constitution, and there was no need for the Religion Ministry to recognize religions per se; its policies only concerned the recognition of religious groups or organizations. The Minister further brought up the issues of decolonization and national identity, expressing the view that the dispersion of religious affairs among the jurisdictions of different government offices during the colonial era was itself a sign of contempt and disdain for the spirit of the Indonesian people, and that the creation of a single unitary government office, the Religion Ministry, to handle religious affairs was a reflection of the spirit of independence.[7]

The Minister also presented a document stating that the Religion Ministry acknowledged all beliefs. The document stipulated that the ministry did not engage in the hierarchical ranking of religions; further, it was not a government agency for Islam but was intended to serve all religions in conformity with the law and to support, not interfere in, religions or beliefs. At the same time, the Minister issued a notification to all entities of the Religion Ministry throughout Indonesia reaffirming the role of the ministry to guarantee religious freedom and strictly prohibiting interference in the internal affairs of religions and the promotion of particular religions.[8]

At the beginning of the 1950s, statistics compiled by the Religion Ministry on Hinduism in the Lesser Sunda Islands were ambiguous at best. According to ministry figures, Bali had 1.7 million Hindu-Bali adherents, 80,000 Muslims, and 2000 Christians; Lombok had 50,000 Hindu-Bali adherents and 964,000 Muslims; and Sumba, Flores, and Timor respectively had 169,000, 500,000, and 550,000 people classified as Hindu-Bali. However, all the Hindu-Bali figures had the footnote 'Animism' appended to them; thus Hinduism and animism were treated as identical, with no clear distinction made between them in statistical categories. Animism was treated as synonymous with being a-religious and hence the status accorded to Hindus was extremely low. At the same time, the figures made it impossible to ignore the fact that Muslims were in the minority in this region, as mentioned earlier. This presented the Religion Ministry with practical dilemmas when setting up branch offices in the region. For example, should it permit a non-Muslim to run the department? Or, in the worst case, was it acceptable for Islam to be treated as the purview of just one department among others, and not as the dominant religion?[9]

Recognizing that Balinese Hindus constituted percentages of the populations of these islands (including Lombok) that could not be ignored—or, in the case of Bali, were the overwhelming majority—the Religion Ministry began to take steps to accord the Balinese religion a certain special status from the outset. In 1952 it recognized 'Hindu-Bali' as a religion (rather than a mere belief) that incorporated Hindu traditions. In 1953 it began using the term Agama Hindu-Bali (Hindu-Bali religion) in official documents. On October 1, 1953, the ministry opened a regional bureau in Singaraja, Bali, with jurisdiction over the Lesser Sunda Islands and assigned an officer in charge of Hindu-Bali affairs to the bureau. The officer was Ida Pedanda Gede Nganjung, who will be discussed later.[10] Additionally, the ministry had begun preparing for the establishment of a department for Hindu-Bali affairs separate from the 'other beliefs' department at its central headquarters.

Meanwhile, the ministry was putting pressure on the Bali Regional Assembly by raising the issue of Christianity in Bali in the name of protecting religious freedom. Christian mission activities in Bali had been suppressed for many years, from the colonial era through the Japanese occupation. Only with independence had it become possible to publicly discuss the status of Christianity. Balinese Christians appealed to the ministry bureau for assistance, citing the problems they faced due to the inseparability of religion and custom in Balinese society. For example, Christians ran their own churches, but were also expected to contribute money and labor to their village temples. Non-Christian Balinese argued that this was an obligation to the village, not to a religion, while the Christians viewed this demand as a form of extortion that imposed a double burden on them. Another conflict involved observances for the dead, for which there were strictly defined auspicious and inauspicious days according to Balinese custom. Christians felt that such constraints were coercively imposed on them. Ultimately, the Lesser Sunda Bureau of the Religion Ministry dispatched separate officers for Catholicism, Protestantism, and Hindu-Bali to the villages that sought assistance, where they presented compromise solutions to the various problems. At the same time, the ministry expressed the view that Balinese village customs sometimes infringed on the right of religious freedom espoused by the Indonesian nation and declared that Balinese Hindus and Christians must cooperate in the effort to protect religious freedom.[11]

Preparations for the opening of a new Hindu-Bali department at the Religion Ministry had begun in 1952, but had stalled when the Bali Regional Assembly established an Autonomous Religion Bureau, which will be described momentarily. At this point, the attitude of the Religion Ministry toward Hindu-Bali underwent a pronounced shift from a positive stance to a more detached one. The ministry now concentrated its efforts on clarifying and gathering information about Hindu-Bali religious activities. The long-unresolved question of Hindu-Bali's lack of a holy prophet or a holy book came to the fore again, and the ministry began focusing on collecting written materials about Hindu-Bali doctrine and compiling records and reports about the religion's core tenets, its modes of worship, its leadership structure, its role in local customs, and its differences from other religions.[12]

During the 1950s, with an invigorated publishing industry and the increasing democratization of religious knowledge, requests by the Religion Ministry for clarification on religious practices contributed significantly to the accelerated compilation of such knowledge. Far from ignoring the ministry's requests for information, activists in the religious recognition movement made positive efforts to respond. Interactions with the Religion Ministry overlapped with studies of religion undertaken in Bali itself, and the results of these efforts gave shape to the religious doctrines that prevail in Bali today. Moreover, negotiations between the Balinese and the Islamo-centrist Religion Ministry spurred attempts to find common ground between Balinese religious practices and the latter's monotheistic viewpoint. This resulted in the introduction into Bali of religious characteristics that would be viewed as legitimate by Muslims and hence by the Indonesian state.[13] A representative example is the interpretation of Sang Hyang Widi by Shastri, mentioned earlier, which introduced a monotheistic tinge into Balinese Hinduism.

Concurrent with its efforts to compile information on religious activities, the Religion Ministry began publishing articles about Hindu-Bali in its periodicals. Ministry publications included descriptions of Hindu-Bali under such headings as 'the foundations of the Hindu-Bali religion,' while acknowledging that a formal decision had not been made about certain aspects of Hindu-Bali.[14] The officer for Hindu-Bali at the Lesser Sunda Bureau of the ministry also contributed articles to an information bulletin published by the ministry. In his writings, the officer not only described the religion but mentioned the dissatisfaction over the government's failure to accord it legitimate status. In Bali itself, the bureau published a magazine with a regular column about Hindu-Bali, thus providing on an ongoing basis information about Hinduism alongside Islam and Christianity.[15]

Even as it continued detached observation, in 1955 the Religion Ministry exhibited a certain degree of consideration for Balinese religion in its policies. In that year a general election fell on the same day as Galungan, the most important religious day on the Balinese calendar. As the result of an agreement reached between the Religion Ministry and the governor of Nusa Tenggara, Galungan was formally declared a 'Balinese ethnic holiday' and the election day was shifted to a different date.[16]

Unifying the priesthood

Since the time of the State of East Indonesia, two groups of priests had been established in Singaraja: Paruman Para Pandita and Panti Agama Hindu-Bali. Ida Pedanda Made Kemenuh argued the need for a priest group before the Council of Royal Families in December 1947. In July 1948, his request was accepted and on January 9, 1949, the first group, Paruman Para Pandita, was organized. This group declared its primary objective to be the unification of religions and customs in Bali and Lombok, to which end it would bring together, and provide a venue for dialogue among priests from the heretofore separate Balinese traditions of Shiva and Buddha, thereby elevating the culture of Bali. The group opened branches in each autonomous region, thus establishing an organization that would link the priests in close proximity to the royal families. Gathering an assemblage of high-ranking priests, it held its first general conference from November 16 to 19, 1949. The heads of all the autonomous regions attended, and the president of the State of East Indonesia sent a letter of greeting (Diantari 1990: 83–4). If Paruman Para Pandita was a royalist group, the second group of priests, Panti

Agama Hindu-Bali, was an extension of the Bali Dharma Laksana (BDL), described in detail in Chapter 2, judging by its goals and participants (Subagiasta 1999: 118). This group was established in 1952 with the declared objectives of deepening religious knowledge, simplifying ceremonies, and eliminating customs inappropriate to the times.

There was some overlap in membership of the priest groups and the Lesser Sunda Bureau of the Religion Ministry. The head of Panti Agama Hindu-Bali was Gede Nganjung, who was appointed the officer for Hindu-Bali at the Lesser Sunda Bureau (although he died in 1955). Moreover, serving as his adviser in the priest group was Wayan Bhadra, Bali's representative intellectual, as mentioned in Chapter 2, who was recommended for the Hindu-Bali officer post then being planned at the central Religion Ministry. Although Bhadra ultimately declined the post, the ministry was highly cognizant of his presence. Kemenuh, the head of Paruman Para Pandita, also worked at the Lesser Sunda Bureau until 1963. This overlapping membership was a distinguishing characteristic of relationships among the Religion Ministry, the Bali Regional Assembly, and religious groups on the island of Bali. Even when the Bali Regional Assembly opposed the central Religion Ministry, the Lesser Sunda Bureau did not become a target of antagonism. Sugriwa, who headed negotiations with the ministry, belonged to Panti Agama Hindu-Bali as a former member of BDL, along with Nganjung (Subagiasta 1999: 115–16).

Though Kemenuh and Nganjung were priests, they had been educated and employed under the colonial administration and, like the republican faction of the Bali Regional Assembly, were inhabitants of 'another space.' Kemenuh, who was born in 1906, earned certification as an administrator in Denpasar and later as a tax collector in Surabaya. In 1922 he began working in the local colonial government office, served in the tax administration department from 1923, and from 1935 to 1950 worked for the native court. Until he became a priest in 1941, Nganjung, who was born in Buleleng in 1898, worked as a clerk in a local colonial government office, for Balai Pustaka, and for a regional bank.[17]

In addition to the priest groups, other religious groups that had been ongoing since the 1930s conducted group activities. The activities of Anandakusuma, who had been a core member of the Klungkung branch of BDL, are a representative example. A contributor of writings to both *Bhawanagara* and *Djatajoe*, he founded Trimurti in Klungkung in 1939.[18] In 1951 the group changed its name to the Hindu Council, and during the 1950s Anandakusuma published numerous works about religion. These various groups shared the basic objective of reforming religious practices and customs, and in that sense they continued a debate that had begun in the 1930s. However, the leaders of these groups were not unified in their stance on the name of the religion and unification of religious practices— the primary issues under negotiation with the Religion Ministry.[19] The ministry took the parallel activities of these groups as a sign of a religious schism, which put the Balinese side at a disadvantage in negotiations.

The Bali Autonomous Religion Bureau

Despite movement within the Religion Ministry toward official recognition of Hindu-Bali as a religion, antagonism between the ministry and the Bali Regional Assembly continued to grow, and the establishment of a separate Hindu-Bali department in the ministry became a political issue. Negotiations began in 1950. On December 28 that year, a ministry delegation visited Bali to ascertain the actual conditions of religion on the island. Sugriwa, who was in charge of negotiations in his capacity as general affairs officer for the Bali Regional Assembly, presented the following list of requests to the ministry: (1) expenses for ceremonies and repairs at Besakih Temple, (2) expenses for the translation of holy texts into modern language, (3) salaries for priests, and (4) establishment of a Hindu-Bali department of the Religion Ministry at the central and regional levels. A priest group conference held on June 10, 1951, resolved to petition the Religion Minister, members of the Bali Regional Assembly, and the governor of the Lesser Sunda province for the establishment of a Hindu-Bali department. Thus was born a configuration in which priest groups with the assembly at their core formed and adopted a confrontational stance against the Religion Ministry. In August that year the ministry replied to the assembly, announcing that it would defer the opening of a Hindu-Bali department, presenting a list of questions, and expressly declaring that priest salaries and temple operations fell outside the purview of the government.[20]

On November 14, 1952, a motion was made at the Bali Regional Assembly to form its own religion bureau. On February 14, 1953, tripartite talks opened with representatives from the Religion Ministry, the Bali regional government, and the Bali Regional Assembly. At this meeting the Religion Ministry made the following requests of the assembly: define the duties of the ministry toward the Hindu-Bali religion, select a candidate for an officer in charge of Hindu-Bali religion at the central ministry, and compile information on legal matters pertaining to religious customs toward the establishment of marriage law, inheritance law, and holidays. For its part, the ministry pledged to set up a new system, to heed the views of the Bali side, and to continue discussions in the future. However, on March 24, 1953, before it had responded to these requests, the Bali Regional Assembly deliberated on its 1952 motion and voted to open an Autonomous Religion Bureau entirely separate from the Religion Ministry.[21] From May 26 to 27 that same year, a general conference (Pasamuan Agung Daerah Bali) was held in Denpasar, with the participation of all Bali religious groups, not only the priest groups. This was the first general conference to be held with the participation of all Hindu religion-related groups in Bali.[22]

The Bali Regional Assembly submitted a letter of request to the Religion Ministry dated October 23, 1953, citing the constitutional guarantee of religious freedom and forcefully appealing to the ministry to recognize Balinese religious practices as a religion under the name 'Hindu-Bali religion.' The ministry replied in the name of the Religion Minister with a response reflecting the standpoint on recognition of religions described above.[23] In other words, it stated that recognition by the government was not accorded to religions per se but to religious groups, and that the establishment of a religion bureau had no legal grounds, thus rebuffing the request. The Religion Ministry viewed the Autonomous Religion Bureau as a sect and hence treated the problem as lying with the establishment of the group known as the Autonomous Religion Bureau, rather than with religion in general. The Bali side took this response as a sign of contempt toward the Hindu-Bali religion and did not acquiesce to the ministry's demand to abolish the bureau. To the contrary, it expanded the bureau from what had initially been a single office in Denpasar to branches in eight autonomous districts.[24]

With battle lines thus clearly drawn, negotiations reached a dead end. The first point of contention was a difference in interpretation of the conditions surrounding recognition. That is, while the Religion Ministry refused to recognize the Autonomous Religion Bureau, the Bali Regional Assembly declared the real problem to be the ministry's lack of a Hindu-Bali department, which it saw as evidence that the ministry did not recognize Balinese religion. A second source of conflict was a disagreement over the negotiation sequence. The ministry wanted to first put an officer for Balinese religion in place, then develop a new system framework to respond to subsequent requests from the Bali side. When Bhadra, the ministry's first choice, declined to take the position, the ministry asked the Balinese to recommend an alternate, but they could not agree on one candidate. The ministry took this as indicative of a schism among the adherents of Balinese religion and blamed the delay in appointing an officer on the lack of effort by the Balinese to resolve their differences. Meanwhile, the Bali Regional Assembly did not accept the order of priorities and viewed the ministry's failure to appoint a Balinese officer as yet another indication of its contemptuous attitude toward Bali.[25]

A third point of contention was a difference in the legal grounds cited by the two sides for jurisdiction over religious affairs under the apparatus of the state. The Religion Ministry demanded that the Bali Regional Assembly abolish the Autonomous Religion Bureau in accordance with the statutes of the Republic of Indonesia, which recognized the central government's authority over religious affairs. The Lesser Sunda Bureau of the ministry also conveyed to the central ministry its judgment that religious affairs fell under the purview of the central government and that the actions of the assembly deviated from the agreements reached at the tripartite talks.[26] For its part, the Bali Regional Assembly defended the establishment of the Autonomous Religion Bureau by citing a 1938 law by the Dutch colonial government that recognized the authority of the heads of autonomous regions, as well as 1950 Law No. 44, a regional administrative law of the East Indonesia era. The Pancasila and the

Constitution of the Republic of Indonesia were further cited as legal grounds for the guarantee of religious freedom.

The Bali Regional Assembly interpreted the 1938 law as stipulating that the head of an autonomous region had authority over matters of customary law. The regional administrative law of the State of East Indonesia, which, as discussed in Chapter 3, recognized the unique identity of individual regions and defined the authority of the central government, could be interpreted as recognizing a regional government's right to establish an Autonomous Religion Bureau because matters of custom or religion did not fall within the scope of the central government's authority. Vociferously stressing these legal grounds, the Bali Regional Assembly unanimously declared that 'religion belongs to the believer.' Thus the assembly and the Religion Ministry asserted their positions on jurisdiction over religious matters based on utterly different legal grounds. The fundamental cause of the dispute was a lack of unification between parallel regional administrative laws. Although the Religion Ministry made constant appeals to the central government to improve the legal structure, the situation remained unchanged until 1958, when a unitary regional administrative law was implemented, as mentioned earlier.

On June 25, 1953, the Bali Regional Assembly issued a document describing the establishment of the Autonomous Religion Bureau and providing details on its operations and functions.[27] Regarding operations, the assembly retained power over appointments and budgetary matters, and four levels of jurisdiction were defined, extending to the villages, with officers to be appointed in charge of each jurisdiction. Fifteen distinct functions of the bureau were itemized, including religious education, spiritual guidance, marriage, religious facilities, general religious life, religious holidays, ceremonies, fair implementation of customs, and publication of religion-related materials. Among these, in practice the bureau's primary functions were religious education and the distribution of religious information, and the promulgation of religious education centered around the Dwijendra Education Foundation (described in Chapter 3) was based on this document. However, the actual operation of the Autonomous Religion Bureau did not go smoothly. The Bali Regional Assembly applied to the Indonesian Ministry of Home Affairs (not the

Religion Ministry) for funding for the bureau, but the Ministry of Home Affairs turned down the request due to the opposition of the Religion Ministry and the bureau remained poorly funded.[28] Thus, whereas initial plans called for the installation of five officers, as of 1955 only two had been appointed.

A noteworthy aspect of the document is that its first article called for the broadest possible application of the first principle of the Pancasila, declaring that the purview of the Autonomous Religion Bureau included not only Hindu-Bali, but all religions under the 'one and only God.' Article 2 vowed that the bureau would protect religious freedom, and Article 3 that it would work toward the development of all religions, not only Hindu-Bali. Subsequent articles described the work of the bureau in terms of coordination among religions. The final article added the task of coordinating pilgrimages to Mecca, the most important undertaking for devotees of Islam. Though in practice the bureau lacked the organizational framework to carry out such duties, its commitment on paper reflects an idealization of the notion of the full implementation of religious freedom. The Autonomous Religion Bureau was not intended merely as a regional entity devoted to Balinese religion, but as a reflection of what the Bali Regional Assembly thought the Religion Ministry should be.

The conclusion of negotiations

Even as activism on the Bali side persisted with support from the network of Balinese in Java, relations between the Bali Regional Assembly and the Religion Ministry remained at a stalemate. A solution was not forthcoming until the middle of 1958, when tangible progress was made on the longstanding issue of regional administrative system reform. On June 26 that year, eight religious groups gathered and resolved to petition the Religion Ministry to treat Hindu-Bali on an equal footing with other religions, open a Hindu-Bali department, and permit the continuation of the Autonomous Religion Bureau.[29] The gathering also voted to dispatch a petitioning delegation to the ministry to ensure approval of the requests. The group was led by Bali Regional Assembly representative Suteja and chair Merta, and Nusa Tenggara Governor Oka. On June 29, the delegation met with President Sukarno, who was staying at the presidential palace in Tampaksiring, Bali, and conveyed the substance of their petition. The president expressed approval of their requests and promised that he would do his utmost to fulfill them. On July 12, after making offerings and praying for the success of their negotiations, the delegation was seen off to Jakarta by well-wishers in traditional dress. On July 25, the Religion Minister announced to the delegation that he had approved the opening of a Hindu-Bali department. The news was broadcast throughout Bali on July 28, after the return of the delegation to the island. At the same time, the Religion Minister visited Bali and spoke of the importance of further elevating religious devotion for the sake of the Balinese, the nation, and religious development.

From the Balinese standpoint, the negotiations had ended on a favorable note, bringing to a successful conclusion the long struggle with the central government. The Balinese had convinced the Religion Ministry to set up a Hindu-Bali department without abolishing the Autonomous Religion Bureau, which the ministry had wanted to eliminate first. A reading of the views of the Religion Minister indicates that he was concerned about the rise of separatist movements in other regions and feared that Bali's religious dispute could trigger such a movement. Having approved the establishment of a Hindu-Bali department in principle, the ministry wanted to avoid aggravating central-versus-regional conflicts through any further delays in establishing the department. The strategy chosen by the ministry at this stage was to first approve the Hindu-Bali department, then eventually absorb the Autonomous Religion Bureau into the ministry.[30]

On October 7, 1958, the Bali delegation hosted a gathering in Denpasar to celebrate the official recognition of Hindu-Bali, with representatives from the government, the Bali Regional Assembly, religious groups, the military, and the police in attendance. At this meeting it was affirmed that while the central government had accorded Hindu-Bali the same status as other religions, the development of Hindu-Bali depended on the adherents themselves, and the duties of the petitioning delegation were now complete. In January 1959 the central Religion Ministry formally opened a special department for Hindu-Bali, separate from those for Islam, Christianity, or other religions.[31]

Concurrent with the establishment of the Hindu-Bali department at the Religion Ministry, the organization of religion in Bali itself advanced to the next stage. Following the October 1958 gathering, a conference was held to study future directions to take in religious matters. At this conference, Oka, a member of the petitioning delegation, reviewed the history of negotiations and argued for the need to establish an entity that would decide all matters pertaining to Balinese religion. In response, a conference was immediately held (on October 12 in Bedugul) to set up a preparatory committee for establishing a body of Hindu representatives. The organizer was the Autonomous Religion Bureau, and participants included representatives of priest groups, religious groups, and the Hindu-Bali department of the Religion Ministry. Members of the preparatory committee were selected at the conference, with Ida Bagus Mantra as chair, Wedastera Suyasa as vice-chair, I Gusti Bagus Ngurah (a member of the Autonomous Religion Bureau) as adviser, and Pedanda Made Kemenuh, I Ketut Kandia, and Sugriwa (Sugriwa did not attend the Bali meeting because he was attending a conference in Jakarta).[32] Wedastera Suyasa, who founded the Hindu Bali Youth Alliance (a nationwide organization that extended across political party lines on religious issues), had supported the religious recognition movement from outside Bali. After being appointed vice-chair of the preparatory committee, he proceeded to Lombok, where, on October 20 and 21, he met with members of the Lombok Hindu community, described the events that had transpired, and asked for their understanding and cooperation in the establishment of a representative body.[33]

The preparatory committee opened a conference on February 21, 1959, at the Udayana University Faculty of Letters, and on February 23 announced the establishment of the representative body Parisada Dharma Hindu Bali. This organization later changed its name to Parisada Hindu Dharma and became a body purporting to represent Hindus throughout Indonesia. Inasmuch as it was created by a preparatory committee launched at a conference hosted by the Autonomous Religion Bureau, the founding of Parisada marked the conclusion of the religious recognition movement. From its inception, Parisada combined two identities: one as a representative body and one as a religious authority. Accordingly, it was divided into two sections: the *Sulinggih*, comprising eleven priests, and the *Walaka*, composed of twenty-two ordinary representatives. Decisions by the *Sulinggih* carried the highest authority on religious matters, and the chair of the *Sulinggih* also served as chair of the overall Parisada. At the top of the roster of *Sulinggih* members was Kemenuh, who had united the priest groups, but the appointed chair was Wayan Sideman, who had served in the military before becoming a priest. Thus, from the outset, Parisada could not ignore the wishes of the military.

The objectives and duties of Parisada articulated in its founding declaration were general in nature. Defined as an organization that would strive for the harmonious implementation of religious activities with the objective of improving the religious and societal consciousness of the Hindu-Bali community, it would hold meetings on a regular basis and a general conference every five years. Religious education, which had been the primary objective of the Autonomous Religion Bureau, was made uniform with the establishment of Parisada. On July 22, 1959, representatives of religious groups, the Religion Ministry, and Parisada gathered at a conference on religious education held at Dwijendra. At this meeting it was proposed that religious education be integrated under Parisada and the Religion Ministry. This signified the beginning of Hindu-related religious education incorporated into educational administration by the state (Subagiasta 1999: 92–3).

The Parisada first articulated its character and the nature of its activities at the regular meeting held from November 17 to 23, 1961, at Campuan near Ubud; here, Parisada adopted what was known as the Campuan Charter. Campuan is famed as the place in Bali where Dang Hyang Nirartha, considered the ancestor of Balinese priests, as mentioned earlier, first set foot. In adopting its charter at Campuan, Parisada was declaring itself the heir to the priestly tradition and laying claim to its status as a religious authority. The charter consists of sections on the religious order and the national order. Regarding the religious order, the charter presents documents that serve as its foundation and addresses issues that had been under study since the 1930s, such as cremation ceremonies and the standardization of Nyepi, the starting point of the calendar. Regarding the national order, the charter affirms that the religious order is based on the 'one and only God' and states unequivocally that Parisada is anti-colonialist, that it abides by the policies of the state, and that it is a representative body for the Hindu-Bali religion on a national scale. It further requests that the Religion Ministry immediately establish Hindu-Bali departments at ministry bureaus in regions with Balinese populations outside Bali itself, such as Lombok and Lampung.

The founding of Parisada was a clear sign of the change in generations mentioned in Chapter 3. Mantra, who had led the India students group and would be a highly influential voice in Balinese politics and culture, had become chair of the preparatory committee, while Sugriwa, who had been a central figure in the religious recognition movement, was relegated to the position of adviser. Although Sugriwa did not lose his standing straight away, the fact that the Bedugul conference was held in his absence was symbolic of the transition from one generation to the next. Shastri, too, refused to be involved with Parisada on the grounds that it was too politicized. The declaration of the founding of Parisada took place at the Udayana University Faculty of Letters, the stronghold of the new generation. In 1962 Sudharta, a member of the India students group, was appointed secretary-general of Parisada, and in 1963 he began serving concurrently as director of the Bali Provincial Bureau of the Religion Ministry. Publication of the *Upadesa*, the compilation of which would be a collective effort by members of the India students group, was decided upon at the Campuan meeting, and it was published in 1967.[34]

Even after the establishment of the Hindu-Bali department at the Religion Ministry, organizational problems remained. The Autonomous Religion Bureau had not been abolished, and continued a parallel existence with the Bali Provincial Bureau of the Religion Ministry. The bureau expressed its dissatisfaction with this situation and urged the central ministry to resolve it. Moreover, in 1960 the strategic commander of the armed forces voiced concerns about the potential adverse impact on public safety of having duplicate administrative apparatuses for religion at the central and regional levels, and asked the Religion Ministry to devise a solution.[35]

The problem was legally resolved by a 1962 decision by the Religion Minister that took effect on January 1, 1963.[36] The Religion Ministry had undergone an internal reorganization from 1960 to 1963, and as part of this the scope of activities by the department in charge of Hindu-Bali was further clarified. At this stage, the incorporation of Hindu-Bali into the apparatus of the state was more or less complete. The 1962 decision directly addressed the parallel operations of the ministry and the Autonomous Religion Bureau, stipulating that the ministry bureaus would be reorganized for the newly established province of Bali under the recent regional administrative reforms, and that the authority and property—everything from buildings to documents—of the Autonomous Religion Bureau would be transferred to the Bali Provincial Bureau. Besides dividing Bali into two jurisdictions, north and south, the ministry established the headquarters of its Bali Provincial Bureau at Denpasar, in keeping with the transfer of the provincial capital to Denpasar from Singaraja in 1960. It also established branches in each district of the province. While stating that it would be desirable for the directors of the Bali Provincial Bureau and its various branches to be Hindu-Bali adherents, it also made a point of saying that it would assign a Muslim as secretary-general of the bureau. The decision made clear that the director of the Bali Provincial Bureau of the Religion Ministry would be responsible not to the regional government but to the central ministry. At the same time, it stipulated that the Religion Ministry would provide the necessary funding for the bureau's operations. In point of fact, until 1965 the director of the Bali Provincial Bureau used the name of the Autonomous Religion Bureau; it was not until 1965 that the latter bureau truly ceased to exist.[37]

A lack of centripetal force

In the political environment of Bali in the 1950s, the religious recognition movement was a unique and exceptional phenomenon. As mentioned in Chapter 3, Balinese society was riven by factional strife so intense as to be irreparable. The sole arena in which the political forces aligned and various parties could unite was the religious recognition movement.

The membership of the petitioning delegation whose appeals to the president and the Religion Ministry brought the movement to a successful conclusion extended across party lines, and the fact that such an alliance was possible reflects its singular character.[38]

The leaders of the religious recognition movement did not by any means excuse themselves from the political arena. Sugriwa represented the Bali Regional Assembly, the primary platform for regional politics. Wedastera Suyasa, appointed vice-chair of the preparatory committee at the Bedugul conference and a passionate advocate of religious recognition, was a prominent Nationalist Party politician in Bali. Even while playing a leading role in party politics, he had called for all political forces to rally together in the religious recognition movement. Like Sugriwa, Suyasa had participated in the struggle for independence. In 1945 he had organized an anti-federation movement in the city of Singaraja and thereafter established links with republican forces in the mountain districts. In the early 1950s he worked with Pendit, as mentioned earlier, to provide relief for students who had fought in the independence campaign. He later left Bali and spent time in Makassar and Bandung, during which period he joined the Nationalist Party, and upon his return to Bali in 1957 he became a leading party activist (Lane 1972: 39 57).

While studying in Java, Suyasa led the Hindu Bali Youth Alliance, a Balinese student group that became active in the early 1950s and carried out actions opposing the notion of an Islamic state. In 1955 the group changed its name to a Sanskrit-derived appellation[39] but when Suyasa returned to Bali in 1957, the group reverted to its former name of Hindu Bali Youth Alliance. Supported not only by the chair of the Bali Regional Assembly, Merta (a member of the Nationalist Party), but also by assembly representative Suteja and by Sugriwa, the organization provided a base for unified action by disparate political forces. Suyasa himself encouraged anyone to join his group regardless of their party or other political affiliation. Thus, blessed with a broad base of support, the Hindu Bali Youth Alliance played a major role, in terms of both leadership and militancy, in the religious recognition movement (Lane 1972: 54–6).

Considering the structural fragmentation of the political sphere—in which many participants in the religious recognition movement were leading figures—the fact that the drive to gain official religious recognition brought all these forces together is testimony to the tremendous mobilizing power of the religious recognition issue. At the same time, however, the fact that the movement was ultimately unable to create political unity also demonstrates the relatively weak centripetal force of religious issues in the world of politics. Although the religious recognition movement had a clearly defined central versus regional character, it did not develop into a separatist movement like those that erupted in other regions of Indonesia during the 1950s. This is because the mobilizing power of the religious issues it addressed ultimately did not translate into political mobilization, and the movement ended without generating any enduring centripetal force.

The primary cause of the failure of the religious recognition movement to give rise to a political movement was the fact that it was the separation of religion from politics that enabled the movement to bring rival political forces together in the first place. As will be described in detail later, participants in the movement shared a consensus that religion must be kept separate from politics at the national level precisely because Muslims comprised the majority of the nation—and, in a representative parliamentary system, the majority rules and the minority loses. They further argued that it was the Islamic side that was politicizing religion, and criticized Islamic forces for using party politics to cement their political power. Members of the movement also shared a general sentiment that politics was an 'unclean' world that must be kept at a distance from religion. The struggle for religious recognition became a movement capable of bringing disparate forces together precisely because movement leaders explicitly declared that religion must remain independent of politics, which was tainted by the power and flow of money. By keeping politics at arm's length from the outset, the movement thus sought from its inception to avoid confrontation on the political level, even as its spokespeople framed it as a struggle with the central government. However, this also meant that an opportunity to unite the disparate political factions of Balinese society was lost, creating the conditions for unchecked conflict.[40]

A second cause of this failure was the process of arriving at what the religious recognition movement saw as a solution to the dispute. The prerequisite for negotiations stated by the Religion Ministry had been the abolition of the Autonomous Religion Bureau set up by the Bali Regional Assembly. But even before the Bali side could acquiesce to this demand, the ministry went ahead and approved the establishment of a Hindu-Bali department. The Bali side viewed this as a victory and gave its blessing to the decision in a lavish ceremony. Thus the struggle was resolved before the movement could achieve the sort of peak momentum that could spark a mobilization of political forces. In this respect, the approach taken by the Religion Ministry was accurate: other than the sore point of the Autonomous Religion Bureau, the Hindu-Bali religion itself did not pose any serious political threat. What really worried the central government was its potential for development into a separatist movement.

Finally, the Bali side never had the political means to raise a regional issue to the central government level, and thus lacked the wherewithal to generate a political movement out of its religious concerns. The Bali Regional Assembly made efforts to expand the network of Balinese, particularly in Java. Puja, head of the Jakarta Hindu Bali Association[41] and an ardent speaker on behalf of the religious recognition movement (as well as the issue of a new, separate province of Bali), attempted to organize a network for the performance of traditional Balinese ceremonies.[42] As with Suyasa's Hindu Bali Youth Alliance, these activities in Java provided an opportunity for diverse political forces to work together. However, Bali still lacked the direct political connections through which it might make its case to the Indonesian parliament as the Islamic Masyumi Party did in regard to the regional administrative reform issue, as described in Chapter 3. Certainly, it appeared as if the Bali side had achieved religious recognition through the successful efforts of its petitioning delegation. However, the delegation met only with Sukarno himself, and depended on the president's leadership for its political success. This reliance on a petitioning approach itself testifies to the dearth of other political means available to the Balinese.

Sukarno, whose own mother was Balinese and who maintained a palace on the island, had a strong personal attachment to Bali. As Indonesia's first president and the leading exponent of a secular nationalist state (not an Islamic state) based on the Pancasila, Sukarno had no reason to reject the Hindu-Bali position, based as it was on allegiance to the Pancasila and the 1945 Constitution. Moreover, the Hindu issue was linked to efforts then under debate to establish a national history, and thereby a narrative for national unity. The Majapahit kingdom, to which the Balinese considered themselves the true heirs, occupied a place of prominence in the formation of an official history of Indonesia.

This official history of Indonesia emerged from a sort of inverted projection of the imperial perceptions of the colonial era. The legendary golden age of the Majapahit kingdom acquired the substantiality of fact in the early twentieth century. When the colonial government destroyed a Balinese palace in Lombok during a military campaign in 1894, a philologist accompanying the troops found conclusive evidence in the form of a document, known today as the *Desawarnana*, which dates back to the Majapahit era (Robson 1995). As translations became available in the early twentieth century, the narrative that emerged of a king's journey through the realm proved pleasing to the colonial government, for it became clear that the Majapahit sphere of influence corresponded approximately with the expanding territorial acquisitions of the colonizers. This evidence of the geographical parameters of the golden age was viewed as historical justification for the region's unification under the colonial government. It was at this time that an official history of the Dutch East Indies took shape. History textbooks written for local schools carried maps of the colonial territories that framed the government as the successor to a great empire.

Ironically, the same history that gave such satisfaction to the colonial government was welcomed with equal ardor by the nationalists led by Sukarno, for in it they saw a history of their own heroic ancestors. The maps illustrating this official history were to them proof of the indubitable existence of 'our land' before the colonial era and, above all, proof that Indonesia was not something invented by the colonial rulers; though it had, tragically, fallen temporarily into the hands of Westerners, 'our land' could be reclaimed by 'us.' The maps graphically depicted the unity and substantiality of the territory that would belong to the new nation yet to be born (Reid 1979; Supomo 1979). Nobody embraced this vision of

Indonesia as the reincarnation of Majapahit or devoted himself to the construction of a national community that would not splinter into separate ethnic groups more fervently than Muhammad Yamin, right-hand man to Sukarno. Yamin wrote a biography of Gajah Mada (a leader of the Majapahit kingdom), studied the apparatus of the state of Majapahit, and in 1957 hosted a seminar on the national history at Gajah Mada University in Yogyakarta at which Mantra, who had returned home from India, also spoke and stressed the importance of having an official history.[43] While the entity promoting this history was no longer the colonial government but the new nation-state, both of these mutually opposing forces sought to be legitimized by the mantle of monarchy. For Sukarno, whose first priority was national unification, there was no reason to exclude the Hindu element.

Last rebellion, or perpetuation of the kingship concept

In 1958 in Bali the status of the administrative units known as swapraja changed from their previous designation as daerah istimewa (special districts) to that of swatantra (ordinary administrative units). As a result, the royal families lost their legal standing as the heads of each swapraja (even though the territorial boundaries of their former kingdoms were retained), and in their place the district assemblies became the highest decision-making bodies. Meanwhile, authority over religious matters was transferred from the royal families to Parisada, which was founded during this same period. In practice, however, the royals had retained a powerful voice in the religious sphere throughout the 1950s, and this shift in religious authority did not go smoothly.

From a political perspective, the administrative reform appears to have been cosmetic at best. The royal families had formally lost their privileged status in the political arena with the founding of a unitary Indonesia. As we saw in Chapter 3, the signs of decline of the royal families, who had expanded their authority during the East Indonesia era, manifested in the offensive by the republicans after the second military campaign. In March 1949, the province of Bali and Lombok, an administrative unit that was a holdover from the colonial era, was abolished, and Anak Agung Gede Oka of the Gianyar royal family inherited the position formerly occupied by the Dutch governor. When a provisional executive organization was established in May 1950, Oka became committee chair; however, the royal families did not dominate the committee. This organization, which was entrusted with full authority to represent the Balinese region to its ruling entities (i.e. the State of East Indonesia and the Federated States of Indonesia), consisted of five members, but the only royal member was Oka.[44]

With the beginning of the era of independence, the word 'feudal' became a political pejorative synonymous with 'the enemy'—and while there were royals like Suteja who participated in the independence struggle, the term was generally directed at the royal families. Formed under republican leadership, the Bali Regional Assembly took increasingly concrete steps to deprive the royal families of their status. One of the first five statutes approved by the assembly abolished the rules prohibiting marriage between members of royal families and commoners.[45] Here the assembly declared an end to the caste system, which had been introduced by the colonial government as described in Chapter 1, and nullified the privileges of the royal families as holders of the highest-ranking titles. Then, in 1952, representatives of the Lesser Sunda regional governments met and adopted a resolution calling for repeal of the 1938 law that guaranteed the status of the heads of the autonomous region (i.e. the royal families). In 1955 the governor of Nusa Tenggara province bemoaned the fact that the status of the royals as heads of the swapraja had remained legally protected even into the 1950s due to the retention of regional administrative laws from the East Indonesia era, expressing his frustration that this system, which violated the wishes of the people as well as the laws of the Republic of Indonesia, remained in place solely because of a failure to abolish it.

Notwithstanding the overt intentions of the Bali Regional Assembly to negate the political status of the royal families, its stance in relation to the royals was extremely dualistic insofar as it had no choice but to recognize their authority in the area of religion. This was because the 1938 law, mentioned above, was also cited as one of the legal precedents for demanding religious autonomy for Bali from the Religion Ministry. Moreover, at the first general conference on religion held in Bali in 1953, royal family representatives were not only invited, but declared to be 'the past and present executors and protectors of religion,' thus affirming their status at the center of the religious sphere.[46] Ultimately, it was the royal family that had the mandate to perform religious ceremonies for the entire swapraja—its former kingdom—and to have the final say on matters of custom and tradition.

By the time the Unitary Regional Administrative Law came into effect, consensus was rapidly building for abolition of the swapraja. On October 19, 1957, the Minister of Home Affairs visited Denpasar and gave an explanation of the Unitary Regional Administrative Law. In his talk he touched on the issue of status at the secondary level, declaring that the question of whether to perpetuate the swapraja leadership was up to the people of each region to decide. Prior to this, on February 22, the Buleleng Swapraja Provisional Assembly had disavowed the status of the royal family and had voted to become an ordinary secondary-level administrative unit, and presented a petition to this effect to the Minister of Home Affairs dated July 24. On August 13, the Tabanan assembly passed a similar resolution. After the Minister of Home Affairs had delivered his explanation, resolutions were passed in succession by the assemblies of various districts.[47] By the end of 1957, it was virtually assured that all royal families in Bali would lose their previous status. The justification offered for these resolutions by the assemblies was the need to abolish the feudal system and colonialism through democracy. The Buleleng assembly further called for the liberation of West Irian as part of the same struggle for democracy and declared its support for that struggle.[48]

The abolition of the swapraja did not, however, go smoothly. The royal family of Gianyar, which had profited the most from the colonial system within the political framework of the State of East Indonesia, clung to its special district status and attempted to mount a fierce resistance against passage of a resolution by the district assembly. On November 11, 1957, the Gianyar Swapraja Provisional Assembly convened a session to deliberate on a resolution to petition the Indonesian government for conversion to a swatantra on the grounds that this was the will of the people, who wished to see the fulfillment of the 'revolution' and the end of a feudal system that violated the spirit of the Pancasila. The meeting, which had thirteen participants—seven from the Nationalist Party, five from the Socialist Party, and one from the Communist Party—was a tumultuous affair. A group of more than 100 people shouting anti-petition slogans surrounded the assembly hall in the morning, even before the meeting was to start at ten o'clock. A nationalist newspaper reporting on the scene declared that the mob consisted entirely of supporters in the employ of Anak Agung Gede Agung, head of the Gianyar royal family, and that all were former collaborators with the Dutch government. Anak Agung Gede Agung belonged to the Socialist Party, and the socialist legislators attending the session opposed the petition—the earlier statement by the Minister of Home Affairs notwithstanding—on the grounds that status issues at the secondary level should not be decided by the region in question, but by the central government. Their supporters responded with loud cheers, while the nationalists harshly criticized the entire gamut of behavior by the socialists, saying that the interference of outsiders with the work of the assembly constituted a negation of democracy through violence.

The upheaval of the assembly spread to the villages, dividing them into two opposing camps. Anak Agung Gede Oka, the younger brother of Anak Agung Gede Agung, made the rounds of relatives of the royal family in the district, held secret meetings with allies among the district's power brokers, and sought to secure their allegiance to the royal family and perpetuation of its authority. He also dispatched popular dancers to far-flung villages to perform mask dramas extolling the significance of the royal family. It is also said that people were pressed to sign written pledges of loyalty to the royals, accompanied by threats that their homes would be burned down if they did not comply. On the other side, the nationalists and their allies on this issue, the communists, also circulated petitions in the villages calling for the abolition of the swapraja. While the Nationalist Party asserted that it did not force people to repudiate the royal family, the fact is that both sides made loyalty to the royals the primary point of their campaigns, resulting in an increasingly overtly partisan confrontation.

The Socialist Party in Gianyar threatened to split over this issue.[49] Even party supporters voiced misgivings over the behavior of the royal family. Party members in the villages castigated the movement against the petition as a self-serving action by party members close to the royal family who profited directly from their connection to the royals. A Socialist Party member from one village contributed an article to a newspaper calling for a 'return to the correct path,' saying that it was incomprehensible that the party would oppose elimination of the feudal system when, of all parties, the Socialist Party should be pursuing just such a course under its mandate to defend the interests of the people. On November 19, the village of Mas passed a resolution opposing the special district status that preserved the authority of the royal family, despite the fact that the village was a Socialist Party stronghold.[50]

Resorting as they did to intimidation, the actions of the Gianyar royal family represented a heavy-handed effort to protect its vested interests and resembled the brutal acts the same royals had allegedly committed against the republicans. But the problem of the retention of royal status as head of the swapraja was an intractable one that extended far beyond the self-interest of the royals. First of all, the district assemblies were at a loss to deal with the real source of the royal family's power in each district. Because the government was unable to guarantee the livelihoods of officials at the village level, from the village head down, these officials depended on the royals for a certain amount of income from usage rights to royal lands. This arrangement still remained in place.[51] The question of how to ensure the livelihoods of local officials had been a concern since immediately after the formation of the Bali Regional Assembly, and in 1953 the assembly formulated a policy to solve the problem: officials would receive a monthly salary with the amount to be determined according to the population under the jurisdiction of the official. The central government approved the assembly's proposal and earmarked a budget for Lesser Sunda province, but the budget was never implemented and the payment of official salaries remained in limbo. In his speech at a ceremony commemorating the end of the East Indonesia system with promulgation of the regional administrative reform in 1958, Suteja acknowledged that this problem remained unresolved and expressed his concern about it.[52]

The authority of the royal families was also a persistent, inextricable component of the political sphere because the political parties made use of the mobilizing power the royals had at their disposal. In the 1955 election, Bali was one of the few regions in which the Socialist Party gained seats, and a primary factor in its success was the participation of royals as party members—the Gianyar Socialist Party being a case in point. In Suteja's home district of Jembrana, even the Communist Party at one point announced a strategy to use the influence of the royal family. Furthermore, the Nationalist Party, which had taken the initiative in pressing for the elimination of the feudal system, could not ignore the mobilizing power of the royals when it sought to expand its support base, and welcomed the support of prominent royal families in such districts as Klungkung and Karangasem. The ultimate weapon for the royals was their religious authority, and the royal family of Gianyar exploited this authority for political purposes. When the royals attacked their arch-rival, the Nationalist Party, they did so by branding it the enemy of religion and the caste system. The nationalist rebuttal was that, far from belittling religion, the party included prominent priests among its members.[53]

This situation, in which the royal families retained their religious authority as redefined during the colonial era despite having lost their legal status, was ameliorated by the founding of Parisada. The preparatory committee members attending the conference that created Parisada included representatives not only of religious groups, but also of the secondary-level administrative units that were now designated as swatantra and of the Autonomous Religion Bureau branches set up in each such unit. By taking over the religious functions of the royal families while maintaining the formality of participation by the former kingdoms, Parisada emerged as a new religious authority in Bali. The biographers of Ida Bagus Mantra view the 'loss of the protectors of the Hindu-Bali religion' as the most pressing reason for the founding of Parisada (Tim Peneliti Jurusan Sejarah Fakultas Sastra 1998: 169–70).

The establishment of Parisada gave rise to two defining characteristics of the religious environment in Bali from that point on. First, even as the royal families lost their authority, the concept of kingship persisted in the religious sphere. Second, a new, inseparable relationship was formed between religion and the province of Bali, composed as it was of districts based on the former kingdoms. In this way, religion became intertwined with what was supposed to be a secular administrative apparatus. As we will learn in more detail in Chapter 5, a system emerged under which Parisada took over roles previously performed by the royal priests—the governor of Bali province, for example, now served as the executor of ceremonies at Besakih Temple, which the Council of Royal Families had controlled since the great earthquake of 1917.

Monotheism and pluralism

The issue of official recognition for the Hindu-Bali religion indeed generated a confrontation between regional interests and the central government, as the Religion Ministry had feared. Yet the recognition process highlighted the reality that minority religions had no choice but to position themselves within the framework of the Pancasila. This latter aspect revealed itself nowhere more clearly than in the character of the Autonomous Religion Bureau, which was established by a resolution of the Bali Regional Assembly. The avowed purpose of the bureau was not to protect the Hindu-Bali religion but to maintain the first principle of the Pancasila and the right to religious freedom espoused by the Constitution. The citing of the Pancasila and the 1945 Constitution of the republic, in addition to 1950 Law No. 44 promulgated by the State of East Indonesia as grounds for establishment of the Autonomous Religion Bureau, appears extremely eclectic in its approach. However, this very eclecticism reflects the anguish of Balinese legislators and religious leaders over the position of Balinese society and its minority religion within the Indonesian state during the first half of the 1950s.

Sugriwa, who represented the Bali Regional Assembly in negotiations with the Religion Ministry, explained in his own words why it was necessary to create the Autonomous Religion Bureau. The first, most concrete reason he gave was the need for a new religious system centered around education. Specifically, he cited the need to decipher and distribute to the common people an intelligible version of the religious texts that had been monopolized by the priesthood, an undertaking that would require adequate funding and an organization that could handle the task. Sugriwa articulated his convictions on this issue from the time of his writings for *Djatajoe*. However, the Religion Ministry rejected the institution of such a system, a stance that Sugriwa took to be proof that the ministry had no intention of modifying its Islamo-centrism, even in its dealings with regions like Bali, where Muslims were the minority.

Sugriwa went on to warn of the meaninglessness and danger of the position of the Religion Ministry if it did, indeed, adopt an Islamo-centrist posture where Bali was concerned. It was absurd, he argued, for the ministry to function as an office of the government in Bali if it existed only to serve the Muslim minority. Moreover, if the Religion Ministry set up regional branches in its role as a government entity, this would be tantamount to a proselytizing agency of Islam borrowing the name of the government to extend its reach into Bali at the village level. In short, Sugriwa believed that if the Balinese let the Religion Ministry have its way, it would be equivalent to acquiescing to their own Islamization.

Sugriwa also went public with emotional denunciations of the Religion Ministry in his capacity as negotiator. According to Sugriwa, his accruing frustrations—at the ministry's refusal to respond to Balinese demands at the negotiating table, the lack of respect it displayed toward the Hindu-Bali religion, and, indeed, its refusal to even recognize Hindu-Bali as a religion—spurred the Bali Regional Assembly's resolve to take the 'decisive action' that culminated in the creation of Bali's own Autonomous Religion Bureau. Furthermore, as mentioned earlier, the ministry assigned priority to the installation of a Hindu-Bali officer, and when the candidate selection process became bogged down, Sugriwa harshly criticized the ministry for what he perceived as a declaration that the Bali side had no adequate candidates. Such statements, he claimed, clearly betrayed a contemptuous attitude identical to that of the colonial government's belief that 'natives' were insufficiently qualified or talented. Brandishing a list of Bali's most prominent religious intellectuals, Sugriwa publicly expressed his indignation on this point. His reaction no doubt reflected both a pride in his religion and an ethnically based antagonism toward Java.

Instigators of the religious recognition movement, like Sugriwa and Suyasa, saw the issue from a broader perspective than that of mere confrontation with the Religion Ministry. Spurring their arguments was a dispute in progress on the national level during the first half of 1953, concurrent with the Bali Regional Assembly's decision to create an Autonomous Religion Bureau and the convening of a general conference on religious matters. The controversy came to a head with a speech by Sukarno in Amuntai, South Kalimantan, that reignited the debate over whether the Indonesian state should be based on the Pancasila or on Islam. Arguing for a national state, the president was fiercely condemned by Islamic forces. Sukarno warned that if Indonesians established a state based on Islam, islands with non-Muslim populations would secede from Indonesia, and West Irian would avoid joining the republic. Therefore, Sukarno argued, 'the state we want is a national state consisting of all Indonesia' (Feith and Castles 1970: 164–70).[54]

With acceptance of the Pancasila and its legitimacy still less than assured, and the possibility of victory by the Islamic parties in the upcoming general election, Sugriwa and Suyasa were sensitive to the ramifications of this controversy as they continued issuing statements. There were two central themes to the numerous declarations they made: the relationship between religion and politics, and support for the Pancasila. Concerning the former, Sugriwa's greatest fear was that deliberations on religious issues in the political arena would result in a victory for Islamic forces in the name of the democratic process. If Islamic parties secured a parliamentary majority, it was conceivable, he believed, that legislation changing the Republic of Indonesia into an Islamic state could be adopted by majority vote. The Balinese representatives constantly reiterated that religion was something that belonged to adherents, not to the state. On the one hand, this conviction derived from the struggle over jurisdiction in religious matters between central and regional forces, but it was also rooted in the conviction that politics and religion must be kept separate. And, as noted earlier, this argument was one reason why the unification of political forces under the religious recognition movement did not carry over into the world of real politics.

Sugriwa's apprehensions fueled a growing sense of crisis on his part over the future of Balinese culture. If the Islamic forces in the majority did, indeed, emerge victorious, the constitutional guarantee of religious freedom would be legally voided. In that event, everyone in Indonesia would have to convert to Islam, the temples of Bali would be turned into mosques, and the performing arts of Bali, so closely linked to its religion, would disappear. For these very reasons, Sugriwa asserted, religion must not be politicized; it must not become a subject of debate in a political arena where the majority rules. His conclusion was that the status of religion must be recognized not in the political arena, but on the basis of a consensus to abide by the Constitution and the first principle of the Pancasila.[55]

Suyasa, too, affirmed the necessity of separating religion from politics, but his argument extended to the relationship between religion and the state. A distinction must be made, he declared, between a state based on a single religion and a state based on the first principle of the Pancasila. The former state would give rise to a majority faction and a minority faction, while the latter state would recognize all religions as equally legitimate before the one and only God. Precisely because of this difference, religion must be removed from issues of politics or the state. Religious issues were spiritual, not political, concerns. Suyasa went on to castigate politicians for using religion as a means to gain power, and attacked the Religion Ministry as well. His critique of the ministry was that it should not behave like a government agency created for the purpose of fomenting distinctions between majorities and minorities. In making an issue of the recognition of religions, he maintained, the ministry had already overstepped its authority and demonstrated a lack of respect for religion.

Suyasa's attacks on the ministry grew even more vehement. At his urging, the Hindu Bali Youth Alliance held a conference from July 28 to 31, 1957. The fifth such conference (it had taken place annually from 1950 to 1953), the 1957 gathering had 'Hindu-Bali religion and struggle' as its first agenda item. At the concluding general session, Suyasa, who was serving as chair, acknowledged that the establishment of the Autonomous Religion Bureau had certainly been a cause of conflict with the Religion Ministry, but argued that this was a consequence of the ministry's own narrow-mindedness and its predisposition to politicize religion. He went on to say that if the Religion Ministry was to continue to exist, it must do so not as a Ministry of Islam, or of Christianity, or of Hinduism, but as a Religion Ministry for the Republic of Indonesia, and that meant accepting the Pancasila as its foundation. Therefore, Suyasa declared, the Religion

Ministry that repeatedly claimed religion as the purview of the central government, even as it announced its readiness to open a Hindu-Bali department, would best be abolished altogether.[56] Thus, while Sugriwa recognized a role for the state in religious matters, Suyasa rejected the notion out of hand.

Regarding their second theme, the Pancasila, both men argued forcefully that it was the foundation of the state. Sugriwa went so far as to declare that it would be better to revert to a colonial state than to let the nation become an Islamic state. His point was that colonial rule was only a physical form of domination, whereas an Islamic state would seek dominion even over the soul. Sugriwa escalated his warnings by showing a poster allegedly found on walls in Aceh with this message: 'We love our president, but we love our nation more. We love our nation, but we love our religion more. That is because Islam is holy.' If such sentiments carried the day, Sugriwa warned, the nation would inevitably split into an Islamic Indonesia, a Christian Indonesia, and a Hindu Indonesia. For just this reason, he said, the president was correct when he called, in his speech, for a state having as its foundation the entire Indonesian people.[57]

Sugriwa's heightened concerns stemmed not only from the debate over a choice between Islam or the Pancasila as the basis of the state, but also from the reality of what would occur if these two entities merged together. What was the Pancasila as perceived by Islam? Above all, how did Islam interpret the first principle? The 'one and only God' referred to only one God, not two or three. If this 'one and only God' was interpreted as inferring an absolute legitimacy based on exclusion—the belief that 'there is no other'—was it not inconceivable to Islam that it referred to any God other than the God of Islam?[58] Or might Islam, with its majority status, simply slide its God into the position of 'the one and only God' without even consciously addressing this issue? If that occurred, the Pancasila could well be co-opted as just another part of the teachings of Islam. The result would be a superimposing of Islamic identity on the national identity that the Pancasila purported to uphold, at which time the minority would lose its position and the majority would reveal its true nature as a force of violence and tyranny.

151

Here Sugriwa grappled with a fundamental problem. If one were to forbid such a 'slide' and declare that the 'one and only God' was not the God of Islam per se, then what or who exactly was the 'one and only God'? And what relationship did a specific religion like Islam or Hinduism have to faith in the 'one and only God' espoused by the Pancasila? Sugriwa's thoughts on the latter question were as follows. Islam did not contain the Pancasila; rather, the Pancasila occupied a higher position before which all religions were equal. Islam and Hinduism were equals regardless of the number of adherents, and it was the 'one and only God' who ensured this equality. Therefore, even if Hindu-Bali adherents embraced a monotheistic definition of their religion, that God did not occupy the position of the 'one and only God.' It was not permissible to project a God worshipped by a specific religion onto the 'one and only God'; such a projection would instantly lead to exclusion and the breakdown of equality. In that case, however, another question arose: what or who exactly was the 'one and only God'? Faced with this thorny ontological question, Sugriwa chose to evade it by resorting to an expedient definition: the 'one and only God,' he declared, was suci ('the holy').

These arguments by Sugriwa and Suyasa, among others, were met with a number of counterarguments. First of all, it was said, their fears that the nation would become an Islamic state were excessive and untenable. Islam's teachings did not advocate coercive religious conversion; Islam did not disparage other cultures and certainly did not make light of the Pancasila. Islam did not reject the rich cultural diversity of Indonesia and, indeed, was itself one of the elements sustaining that diversity. In this light, the rebuttal went, the claim—exemplified by Sukarno's speech—that many regions would secede from Indonesia if it became an Islam-based state itself served only to abet separatist tendencies. Moreover, critics added, the tenor of Sugriwa's argument betrayed an undercurrent of belief that Hinduism was a legitimate religion precisely because Hindu culture was indigenous to Indonesia, whereas Islam was an import from abroad. But if Islam was an import, they countered, so was Hinduism; hence, it was wrong to proclaim the latter as the only purely indigenous faith.

Critics also prepared an adroit rebuttal to Sugriwa's understanding of the 'one and only God.' Rather than address the definition of the concept head-on, they applied a form of reverse rhetoric: if no specific God could be said to meet the definition of the 'one and only God,' who were the beneficiaries of this conclusion? None other, they argued, than our ultimate adversaries, the atheists and anti-religionists. In other words, the understanding of the 'one and only God' not as a specific God but as an abstract concept like 'the holy' was an empty definition veering perilously close to atheism. For this very reason, critics maintained, any discussion of the 'one and only God' must be preceded by the rejection of the groundless fears of Islamization that provoked spurious confrontations; adoption of a confrontational posture in anticipation of majority rule was, in fact, a form of anti-democratic behavior, and Sugriwa and Suyasa were clearly in thrall to these very impulses.[59]

Sugriwa and Suyasa did not retreat from their positions in the face of these counterarguments. However much their fears might be branded as excessive, Islamization remained in their eyes a very real and concrete threat. The Hindu religious recognition movement was, in one sense, a struggle to achieve an institutional solution to these emotional fears, and the only viable political position for the struggle relied on the support of Sukarno and protection of the Pancasila.

From the process of institutionalization of Hinduism during the 1950s, a paradoxical situation emerged in which religious pluralism became a reality even as allegiance was maintained to the 'one and only God' of the Pancasila, and religion was institutionalized at the state level amid calls for the separation of religion and politics. The ultimate symbol of this paradox was the Autonomous Religion Bureau, which had triggered the confrontation with the Religion Ministry but in the end was incorporated into the national government as a Hindu representative body. Thus the separation of religion and politics did not necessarily entail the secularization of the state.

The year 1958 saw the establishment of Parisada and an institutional framework for ensuring the status of the Hindu religion in the still-young Republic of Indonesia. At the same time, the new generation involved in the founding of Parisada took over the reins from the previous generation, which had sought to rebuild Balinese society through the establishment of religious institutions, first as lower-level civil servants during the colonial era and then, after the struggle for independence, as republican legislators. However, the new generation was no more successful in resolving outstanding deficiencies in the unification of Balinese society. With Sukarno's institution of guided democracy, there were no new elections after 1955; without an electoral outlet, inter-party strife only grew more intense, and the rifts in society continued to widen even at the village level. These rifts were abruptly closed in the most brutal way—a failed coup in September 1965 led to widespread massacres of people associated with the Communist Party. In the process of restoring social order in the wake of the massacres, the discourse around religion took on a new significance, and a reorganization of religious institutions began.

CHAPTER 5

The Spirit of the New Order

Participation in the national unification of the Republic of Indonesia did not improve the livelihood of the Balinese, as the poverty experienced during the 1930s persisted into the 1950s. People could not secure adequate supplies of rice, so dependence on infusions of rice from the central government was the norm. Staple foods were increasingly adulterated with fillers, and reports of widespread malnutrition became common. As Bali entered the 1960s, infestations of mice and insects exacerbated the problems, and in 1963 the situation grew even more dire. In March and May of that year, Mount Agung erupted, causing the deaths of 1500 people and severe malnutrition in about 10,000 others, and creating about 75,000 refugees (Robinson 1995: 239). Then, in 1965, political violence surpassed natural disasters in claiming a colossal number of lives.

On September 30, in what came to be known as the 'September 30 Incident,' soldiers imprisoned or killed several high ranking generals in Jakarta. The Partai Komunis Indonesia, or PKI (Communist Party of Indonesia), was subsequently identified as having a hand in the incident, triggering the massacres of those alleged as being affiliated with the party throughout Indonesia. The island of Bali ranked alongside Central and Eastern Java as the regions with the most killings. From the end of November through December 1965, a campaign of organized murder was waged; suspects were hauled away in trucks and shot or stabbed to death, and their bodies were dumped in rivers or the ocean or buried in mass graves. It is estimated that between 80,000 and 130,000 Balinese—approximately 5 percent of the island's population at the time—were killed in this campaign.

These events led to the first regime change in Indonesia since it had gained its independence. General Suharto, commander of the army's Strategic Reserve Command, which asserted its control over the chaotic conditions that followed the September 30 Incident, succeeded Sukarno as president, thereby beginning a 'New Order' that signified the end of the Sukarno era. In Bali, religion played a prominent role in the transition from the outbreak of violence to the establishment of the New Order. In its public appeal for moral behavior, religion served as the most concrete means of actualizing the state's call to preserve order.

Through the direct involvement of the Bali provincial government after the founding of Parisada, Besakih Temple became the headquarters of the Hindu religion in Bali, and thereby the symbolic center of religious activity under the new regime. At the same time, it was at this temple that mass rites were held for the vast numbers of dead. Starting in the 1960s and continuing into the 1990s, Besakih Temple was the site of large-scale ceremonies that grew even bigger over time. The same period saw a rewriting of Balinese cosmology in which the island of Bali came to represent a symbolic space with Besakih Temple at its center. The ultimate purpose of the ceremonies was for every citizen to be anointed with holy water created in the temple's primary ritual, thereby uniting the individual with the cosmos. The creation of a holy water 'conduit' with Besakih Temple at its center completed the bureaucratization of religious ceremonies that had begun in the wake of the 1917 earthquake.

The main focus of this chapter is the institutionalization of religion under the Suharto regime, beginning with the purification of the dead, through the revival of the old Balinese kingdoms with the provincial governor at the helm and Parisada priests wielding religious authority.

Circumstances of a bloodbath

Let us examine the situation in Bali in the aftermath of the September 30 Incident. Immediately following events in Jakarta, the concerns of the Bali provincial government and army were limited to maintaining order. Beginning October 9, several announcements were made in the name of the provincial governor or regional military commander, including the decision to prohibit the posting of leaflets, unauthorized assembly, patrols by armed groups, and other such inflammatory activities. On October 13, the district heads were summoned to Denpasar, where the regional commander spoke to them about the September 30 Incident and affirmed the implementation of systemic reinforcements to maintain public order. Additionally, measures such as rice donations and increased monitoring of distribution networks were announced to stabilize the prices of goods, particularly rice; this was a significant factor in preserving the peace as the price of rice had soared. Moreover, security measures were enhanced in all districts. For example, in Badung, the arrival of a cruise ship at Benoa Harbor on October 22 prompted leaders of political groups and the police force to gather and reach consensus on security measures; this was based on the assumption that the steps taken by the provincial government for this purpose were insufficient.[1]

Denunciations of the Jakarta incident and calls to root out its causes began to grow louder in November. The perception that this was no mere incident, but rather an organized movement to overthrow the established order, was becoming widespread throughout Indonesia, and the focus was shifting to the specific question of whether such a movement had actually been planned and instigated, and, if so, by whom. On November 1 a fact-finding group was formed to determine the facts and root out those associated with a movement that called itself the 'September 30 Movement.' Activities by student groups and labor unions were declared 'frozen,' and an order demanding lists of the names of members of the PKI and affiliated organizations was issued. A ban was placed on activities by PKI-related groups, ethnic Chinese groups, and certain newspapers and other communications media, and the army began monitoring communications facilities and television stations. This series of announcements reflected measures that had already been taken by the central government; however, the actual implementation of the measures indicated a coalescing of shared assumptions regarding the targets of the offensive. On November 3 the provincial government and army held a joint meeting, after which they announced the reinforcement of security measures against arson and other destructive acts, a strict ban on bearing arms, and a nightly curfew from 11:00 p.m. to 4:00 a.m.

The entity that initiated the purge was none other than the army, which had been privy to the September 30 Incident. On November 4 the regional military commander declared that clear evidence had been found that the September 30 Movement had also been plotting actions in Bali. According to this claim, the perpetrators had been meeting in secret since August, and had planned to order an operation by certain units of government troops on the evening of October 1. The report was specific in identifying which units had planned to seize control of which positions. As in other regions, the objective of the movement had been to kill certain military leaders, and specific details about these assassination targets were provided in the report, which concluded by declaring that Suharto's announcement that the post-incident situation was under control at 9:00 p.m. on September 30 had foiled the plot. Several days after the report was issued, the army declared that the presence of the September 30 Movement in Bali was an incontrovertible fact, and the location where the movement participants allegedly held their final meeting was made public. The army then began arresting suspected movement participants, carried out an internal purge, and implemented harsh measures to deal with the movement's aftereffects. It was also announced that 'cleansing' would be pursued both inside and outside the army, and the cooperation of the public was enlisted in this endeavor.[2]

Accompanying these revelations of the movement's presence in Bali were increasingly loud cries for condemnation. The PKI was blamed as the instigator behind the movement. The theory of PKI involvement had found its way to Bali after the September 30 Incident, as had reports of attacks on the PKI in Java, beginning with an appeal to the president by the Islamic group Nahdatul Ulama to smash the party. However, in Bali the incident was still being referred to as a counter-revolutionary movement, as there had been no overt attacks on the PKI. Denunciations of the PKI began in earnest on Heroes' Day (November 10), which was celebrated in honor of those who had fought in the war for independence. The Nationalist Party, which organized the commemorative ceremony, was joined by other parties and various political groups in supporting a petition that asserted that the PKI was undeniably involved in the September 30 Movement and calling for its eradication. The petition was submitted to the president and various government and military agencies. At the ceremony, the regional military commander declared that 'sentiment runs high among the people of Bali for the eradication of the movement; if the order is given, they will surely act at any time' and, from that day on, notices of withdrawals from the PKI and its affiliated groups began appearing in newspapers. The organizations posting such notices ranged across a broad spectrum, from factory labor unions to village youth groups.[3]

Denunciations of the PKI included attacks on provincial representative Suteja, a veteran of the independence movement who had enjoyed Sukarno's wholehearted support. Suteja had never joined the PKI, but he did support its activities and was said to be close to its leaders. Resolutions demanding his resignation from the post of provincial representative were submitted by political parties, the Bali Regional Assembly, educational institutions, and regional administrative agencies. The day after Heroes' Day, Suteja left for Jakarta with other members of the provincial government and, on November 18, the Minister of Home Affairs announced that governmental authority had been transferred from the provincial representative to the army.[4]

In mid-November a number of reports of clashes with PKI-related groups that resulted in fatalities began appearing, and mass slaughter appears to have begun around November 30. Troops with orders to 'eradicate' the September 30 Movement, who had already been active in Java, landed in Bali on December 7 and 8. The Strategic Reserve Command, including Suharto, also arrived in Bali on December 8. Upon landing at the airport, Suharto told reporters, 'We have come to see the situation in detail and directly support all measures necessary to utterly destroy the power and will of the counter-revolutionary movement known as the September 30 Movement.'[5] A newspaper article reported that local villagers, who associated the troops with their red berets, had heard of their exploits in Java, and although they had initially been somewhat fearful, the 'friendly demeanor' of the troops eventually won them over.

A shift toward the restoration of order did not begin until the end of December. On December 18, Nationalist Party leader Merta, who also served as Bali Regional Assembly chair, was appointed the new provincial governor; this was made public on December 25. That same day, the regional commander announced that 90 percent of the counter-revolutionary forces had been wiped out, remarking that from that point on, the focus would be on restoring order. Discussions began on the specifics of recovery, such as assistance for rebuilding destroyed houses. The new governor issued an appeal calling for a halt to violence on December 30. Deviating from the norm of providing government documents exclusively in Indonesian, the appeal was also translated into Balinese and published in various newspapers. On the same day, the regional commander also issued an appeal for people to cease engaging in partisan, emotional actions and to obey the directives of the government and the military.

Efforts to restore order became more pronounced in January 1966. In a New Year greetings speech, the regional military commander made it clear that he wanted New Year's Day to symbolize a turning point from chaos to recovery. In fact, the military units that appeared to have directed the massacre ended their operations after a little more than three weeks and withdrew from Bali at the beginning of January. Since late December, banquets honoring the troops had been held in various districts, not only by the army, but also by district administrators, police, and political organizations. At each banquet, the commanding officers voiced their gratitude to local citizens for cooperating in the operations. At a farewell banquet in Tabanan, Colonel Edhie declared that should trouble ever arise in Bali, his troops could be there within three hours.

The provincial governor held a farewell dinner for the troops at the Bali Hotel on the night of January 13. He expressed his thanks and praised the Balinese who had collaborated in the operation as having emulated the sacrificial spirit of *puputan*, which had been displayed by those who had fought against the Dutch.[6] The monitoring of governance at the village level and the rooting out of movement sympathizers continued as part of efforts to reorganize the administrative apparatus. Meanwhile, concrete measures aimed at restoration were launched, including an attempt to secure transportation by requiring the registration of usable vehicles belonging to public agencies. On January 19, just before the beginning of Galungan (the holiday celebrating the return of ancestral spirits), the nightly curfew was lifted and, on January 25, the army issued a declaration of public safety.[7]

It is clear that the massacre developed in an organized manner over two months after the initial incident in Jakarta. Geoffrey Robinson (1995) has squarely addressed this fact and analyzed the process that led to the mass killings as follows.[8] The primary factor that brought the slaughter in Bali to a peak in December 1965 was the arrival of military units engaged in operations with the objective of physically dismantling the old order in the name of 'restoring public security' on the island. However, a 'kill or be killed' mindset had already taken hold, with ordinary people irrevocably caught up in the bloodbath. The perception that the PKI was responsible for the September 30 Incident and was itself the enemy of the social order had spread. Based on denunciations and accusations, a sharp line was drawn between those who were and those who were not associated with the PKI, and hit lists of collaborators were drawn up. This established a clearly defined target, and the whole of society was driven into a state where neutrality was impossible and one could not easily disavow a connection with the enemy. It was at this point that the army stepped in and provided the specific means and methods by which to deal with the target. Along with military tactics that actually produced fatalities for strategic purposes, verbal propaganda that justified murder and encouraged collective action was a significant factor in the massacre (Robinson 1995: 293).

Discipline under God

Among the discourses that played a role in the massacre, religion was one of the most crucial. The accusation that the communists were blasphemers provided justification for targeting the PKI for eradication. Blasphemy specifically meant violation of the first principle of the Pancasila, belief in the 'one and only God,' and, by extension, a fundamental subversion of the Indonesian state. For this very reason, consensus could be achieved around the idea of exterminating the PKI. The PKI was not solely responsible for the economic and social problems of the day, and it had not engaged in overtly anti-religious activities or any other behavior that could be construed as 'destroying the cosmic order'; nonetheless, the communists were denounced as blasphemers of religion.[9] In a speech in Jakarta in late December 1965, Suharto said, 'According to evidence and statements, planners and leaders of the counter-revolutionary September

30 Movement were planning to eliminate the Pancasila, the underlying principles of the nation, and thereby purge faith in God from this land of Indonesia.'[10]

On October 3, immediately after the September 30 Incident, priests and other religious leaders in Bali issued a condemnation of the incident. While they did not directly attack the PKI, they were unequivocal in making a connection between religion and the social order. They declared that enemies of the revolution were the most savage enemies of religion and therefore must be eradicated on every level. Here the term 'revolution' included the war for independence and the subsequent nation-building process; the implication was that religion was essential for the establishment of order and morality in the nation, and spiritual development was indispensable for material development. The September 30 Incident was considered a challenge to the revolution, and thus an attack on the religious order. It was also said that the incident had failed because it did not take the power of God into account, an after-the-fact assertion identifying God with the established order.[11]

As previously described, the relationship between religion and state order, along with policies on the administration of religion, became systematized from the time of the establishment of the Religion Ministry. Conditions in the religion-related departments were a concrete reflection of the state's administrative stance toward religion. Just prior to September 30, 1965, this stance was clearly articulated in the conventional format of a presidential decision (Presidential Decision No. 1). This law stipulated that, in light of the objective of restricting religious activities that threatened the security of the nation or the achievements of the revolution for independence, any activities deviating from basic religious objectives would be subject to restriction in public. The law further cited the necessity of protecting legitimate religions (as defined by the Religion Ministry) from deviant religious activities. To make the meaning of the law clear, it was amended with a clause defining 'legitimate religions.' Reaffirming the 'one and only God' precept of the first principle of the Pancasila, and that legitimate religions could not be treated independent of the 1945 Constitution, the law specifically listed six faiths as 'religions followed by the people of Indonesia: Islam, Protestantism, Buddhism,

The Spirit of the New Order

Catholicism, Hinduism, and Confucianism.'[12] The list was based on the historical process by which these religions were propagated in Indonesia, an explanation of which followed the definition of what constituted a religion. Legitimate religions were to be protected under the Constitution, with no government-imposed restrictions on their activities. Other religions were subject to government guidance, the nature of which was further specified by this law.[13] Due to the perceived association of the PKI with the September 30 Incident, Confucianism was later removed from the list of legitimate religions due to its Chinese origins, leaving the number of official religions of Indonesia as five.

The massacre instilled extreme fear in the hearts of people and came to be associated with the acronym G30S-PKI, a combination of G30S (for Gerakan 30 September, the September 30 Movement) and PKI. Even after the eradication of the PKI, Suharto skillfully and relentlessly exploited this fear by frequently warning that the PKI's destructive plots might yet flare up again. In this regard, religion, as a criterion for identifying enemies of the state, transformed into something akin to an absolute precondition for citizenship. To be non-religious was impermissible, as religion moved beyond its role of maintaining peace and public order to one of serving as an instrument to instill discipline in the citizenry. On an entirely different level from the organizational relationship between religious groups and the government, religion proved to be the perfect means to maintain order among the populace and became an all-encompassing presence in the lives of Indonesians. The name of one's religious affiliation was required on residential certificates, and it was not unusual for people to volunteer the name of their religion when introducing themselves. Religion was now an essential part of identity and came to embody the spirit of the New Order.

In Bali the discourse around religion began to acquire greater significance as the massacres came to an end in early 1966. Amid the ongoing attempts to assign responsibility for the September 30 Incident, the importance of religion was repeatedly mentioned. At an inquiry into the incident, Sukarmen, a Javanese who had served as regional military commander at the time of the incident and was later appointed provincial governor of Bali, was asked whether rumors that the PKI would have turned temples into pigsties if it had won were true. He replied that he had not heard of such rumors, but that temple construction was always being delayed by interference from the PKI. When addressing a Catholic group in September 1967, Sukarmen spoke of the importance of the Pancasila spirit and declared that religion was a bulwark against the communist threat. Likewise, Merta, the new governor of Bali, never missed an opportunity to stress the crucial role played by religion. At a temple purification ceremony in Payangan village, he stated that before the incident, numerous actions had been undertaken with disregard for religion and God, and that it was essential to prevent their recurrence. Religion, he asserted, was the linchpin of the nation, and the Pancasila and Constitution that guaranteed freedom of religion must be vigorously protected. When speaking to non-Hindus, in consideration of their status as minority groups in Bali, Merta never failed to add something about the importance of interreligious cooperation predicated on freedom of religion.

The speeches of Bali's political leaders resonated closely with those of Suharto. Speaking in Jakarta in late November 1967, at the opening ceremony of an interfaith conference in which Parisada also participated, Suharto declared that it was the duty of the state to ensure freedom of religion, and that religion played a major role in maintaining and improving peace and security under the New Order. He also announced that state agencies had ample evidence proving that G30S-PKI remnants were plotting to provoke religious followers so as to deepen rifts between religions and ethnic groups. Interfaith conflict could be exploited by the communists; for this very reason, harmonious relations between religions was crucial, and the 1945 Constitution and the Pancasila, which provided the foundation for those relations, must be faithfully observed.[14]

The significance of religion formulated in political speeches began to permeate religious ceremonies attended by the public at large. These ceremonies gave new physical form to what had previously been a strictly political discourse. Parisada, with the consent of the provincial governor, issued a call for walikrama alit (purification ceremonies) to be held in every village on January 22, 1966; this date happened to fall during the first Galungan to take place since the September 30 Incident (which provided the occasion for lifting the curfew) and coincided with the new moon. The written instructions provided details on the type and content of offerings to be made. They also clearly stated that the purpose of the ceremonies was to greet Galungan with spiritually purified hearts in the wake of the 'physical slaughter' of those associated with the September 30 Incident.[15] Sudharta, a member of the India students group who was secretary-general of Parisada at the time, wrote a series of essays urging people to 'shed themselves' of the incident; these essays were subsequently published in the newspaper.

In 1967 conscious efforts to appropriate Galungan became even more conspicuous. The Bali Provincial Bureau of the Religion Ministry issued a joint proclamation with the cultural affairs administrator requesting that villagers collectively hold prayers, lectures on religious doctrine under the guidance of Parisada, and performances of classical dances with the aim of gaining a deeper understanding of religion and culture. The bureau called on people to pray for God's help during Galungan in the successful realization of the policies of the new government. This appeal was accompanied by specific instructions: houses and streets should be cleaned, every household should put up the bamboo decorations known as *penjor*, gambling and drinking liquor were prohibited, and young people should engage in recreational activities that promoted physical exercise, health, and the arts. Religious ceremonies had clearly come to be viewed as an opportunity to instill discipline in the public. Each of Bali's district governments responded to the Religion Ministry's policy directives. For example, Jembrana established a Galungan Implementation Committee that called for the wearing of formal attire on March 29, the day of Galungan, and the holding of prayers at *pura puseh* (village temples) with the regional administrator in attendance. The year 1967 also marked the first special event celebrating Galungan at the Bali Beach Hotel.[16]

One specific activity that served to entrench religion's enhanced political role under the New Order at the village level was a religious education campaign launched by the Religion Ministry and Parisada. They implemented a scheduled course of periodical religious instruction in each village, lectured on religious teachings to priests, elementary schoolteachers, and the general public, and rehearsed songs to be sung at religious ceremonies. Initiated with the aim of lending spiritual support[17] to victims of the Mount Agung eruption, the campaign began in Karangasem, the district most severely affected. After the massacre, the instruction course spread throughout Bali, with districts seemingly vying with one another to hold the course as frequently as possible.[18] With so many requests for the course, a shortage of instructors became problematic, and seven instructors divided into two teams were reportedly unable to meet demand throughout Bali. In addition to the course, song contests were held on occasions such as Independence Day and Galungan.

The Religion Ministry and Parisada focused the campaign on elementary schoolteachers in the villages and made an effort to place instructors specializing in religion in each school. Reports stated that in Karangasem, where the campaign was launched early, religious instructors had been placed in every elementary school by February 1968, while at the end of 1967, in the district of Gianyar, seventy-two religious instructors for grade schools had completed coursework, and another sixty-seven were still in training.[19] The education received by these teachers clearly reflected the role that the government anticipated for religion. For example, a large-scale, three-week 'Basic course in Hinduism' for elementary instructors was held at Jagatnatha Temple in Denpasar in November 1967. In a speech at the closing ceremony, a representative of the provincial governor declared that when the PKI had been active, it had constantly interfered with or threatened religious activities in order to foment conflict with other political parties; however, religion was an 'absolutely indispensable element' in the nurturing of morality and spirituality under the New Order, for which reason the government was giving top priority to religious education. In the speech that followed, Mantra reiterated this point—that attention to religion in accordance with the needs of the New Order was essential—and that expanding religious education via religious schools was important. I Gusti Agung Gede Putra, head of the South Bali sub-bureau of the Religion Ministry, announced that by the end of 1967, there would be at least one religious instructor in every elementary school, and declared that courses of the same type would continue.[20]

The Indonesianization of Hinduism

With the opening of the Hindu-Bali department at the Religion Ministry and the promulgation of the aforementioned 1965 Presidential Decision No. 1, which defined Indonesia's official religions, it became an irrevocable fact that Hinduism was not only a local tradition in Bali, but also one of the religions of the nation. What might be called the Indonesianization of Hinduism, in the sense that it was now a state-recognized faith with systemic and legal backing, also had its equivalent in another phenomenon: the emigration of Balinese from the island. The poverty that had persisted since the 1950s, coupled with the damage caused by the volcanic eruptions, had turned large numbers of Balinese into refugees within their own country. They relocated to and settled in places such as Sulawesi and Sumatra, and the population of Balinese living outside of Bali soared. Because religion was an inextricable part of the Balinese lifestyle, intense interest was sparked not only in the emigrants, but also in the Balinese who remained on the island. However, from the standpoint of Islam or other majority religions in the emigrants' new places of residence, they were heretics and a potential threat. Meanwhile, circumstances in Bali from 1965 onward caused further troubles for the Balinese emigrants. As the locale of mass killings in the wake of the September 30 Incident, Bali acquired a reputation as a communist hotbed, arousing suspicions that communists might be hidden among the emigrants.

The Indonesianization of Hinduism in the political sphere grew more pronounced during the period following the September 30 Incident. The bedrock for the political structure of the New Order was provided by Golkar, an organization of 'functional groups.' The Sekretariat Bersama Golongan Karya (Sekber Golkar, Joint Secretariat of Functional Groups) had been formed at the behest of the army in the early 1960s to counter the expanding organizational activities of the PKI. When a return to party politics stalled with Sukarno's declaration of guided democracy, Golkar emerged as the political arm of the army and was hurriedly reorganized in the wake of the September 30 Incident. Abandoning its pre-1965 status as an entity coexisting in parallel with party memberships, it redefined itself as a 'pure' functional group organization and expelled the Sukarno faction that remained active at the leadership level. By the end of 1967, the majority of its executives, from committee chairs down, had been replaced with members of the army, and its identity as the political arm of the New Order had grown increasingly pronounced. In late June 1968, it became known that several Hindu religious groups had joined Sekber Golkar and, on July 23, Parisada and the Indonesia Hindu Youth Alliance announced their formal participation.[21] Both of these groups held large conferences in 1968 in which they openly espoused their positions as members of Golkar.

The Indonesia Hindu Youth Alliance, which was born from a post-1966 reorganization of the Hindu Bali Youth Alliance led by Suyasa, held a nationwide conference from June 30 to July 5, 1968, in Tampaksiring, where the Balinese presidential palace was located. Hosted by Anak Agung Gede Oka of the Gianyar royal family, which was responsible for maintaining the palace, the conference was attended by representatives of religious groups, as well as representatives of the Bali Regional Assembly and provincial, district, and other administrative entities. President Suharto and a representative of the Majelis Permusyaratan Rakyat Sementara, or MPRS (Provisional People's Consultative Assembly) sent written speeches. The stated theme of the conference was national and regional development, which was a fully fledged endorsement of the Suharto era's new political goal of development.

In one of the opening speeches, based on his discussions with Hindu adherents during his travels throughout the country, Suyasa declared that he estimated there were as many as ten million Hindus in Indonesia. Although it is difficult to judge the veracity of this figure, it reflected a recognition of the increase both in Balinese emigrants and in Hindu converts outside Bali after the September 30 Incident. In the wake of the incident, conversions to official religions proliferated as people sought to avoid the taint of association with the communists (cf. Lyon 1977).

Complaints that Parisada suffered from organizational insufficiencies were voiced at the conference, which concluded with the adoption of an Oath of Tampaksiring, which vowed contributions to the 'Pancasila Order,' as the New Order was called. A copy of the oath signed by twenty-four regional groups was delivered to representatives of the army, administrative entities, the Bali Regional Assembly, and Parisada.

Sukowati, leader of Sekber Golkar, rushed from Jakarta to be present at the closing ceremony and the recitation of the oath.[22]

From December 2 to 5, 1968, Parisada also held a general conference.[23] At the time of its founding in 1959, Parisada had decided to hold such a gathering, with participation by all branches, every five years. This was changed to every four years at the first general conference in 1964, so the 1968 meeting was the second to be held. The results of these first and second conferences, occurring as they did before and after the September 30 Incident, bring into sharp relief the changes in Parisada's character over this period. A particularly salient shift was in the organization's response to the issue of Indonesianization.

Participants in the 1968 conference included not only the representatives of Parisada's regional branches, but also those of all the administrative agencies in Bali province. The theme was 'Hinduism and the Five-Year Plan,' which was a direct response to the Five-Year Plan announced by the new government. Similar to the Indonesia Hindu Youth Alliance conference, Suharto sent a speech to be read at the opening ceremony. He began by declaring that it was the ideal time to hold a conference on this theme, and went on to expound the need for selfless effort by the entire nation to achieve development and the importance of a spiritual attitude conducive to religious life in accordance with the Pancasila. He concluded by saying, 'Religion is vital to the people of Indonesia because the dream of independence can only be realized through a combination of both spiritual and material attainment.'[24]

With thirty-five branches throughout Indonesia at this time, Parisada asserted its own qualifications as a member of Golkar. First, it resolved the dispute over religious names that had endured since the 1950s. Rejecting 'Hindu Bali' and 'Hindu Dharma,' it settled on 'Hindu,' effectively removing the semblance of Bali from the name. Furthermore, in joining Golkar, Parisada stressed its qualifications as a functional group, not a mass political organization; this signified that Parisada as a group would not join forces with any specific political entity other than Golkar. Moreover, it asserted that the primary challenge for Parisada as a member of Golkar was one of reorganization; it must adopt an organizational framework that conformed to the administrative apparatus of the state. In response to the attitude articulated by the Parisada representatives, Sukowati, who was attending the conference, welcomed Parisada into Golkar and declared that in signing on to the policies of Golkar, the region of Bali had become a 'cornerstone of the Pancasila.'

Within Parisada, there were also arguments against joining Golkar, which, even as an organization of functional groups and not a political party, was clearly on the verge of becoming a political entity of consequence.[25] As described earlier, the fact that various political forces could overcome factional differences and work together in the religious recognition movement during the era of political parties in the 1950s was largely due to the separation of religion and politics. Parisada itself had separate representatives for the priests and the secular membership, but the head of the organization was the priests' representative, who feared that political affiliation would weaken his authority. Despite the assertion that joining Golkar did not make Parisada part of a political party, opponents could only view it as a clear move toward participation in the state political structure. Some also feared that membership in Golkar would be tantamount to banning political activity by Parisada members.[26] Mantra, the central figure of Parisada, was allegedly of the view that Hindus, as a minority, needed the protection of Golkar. In addition to this, the existence of emigrant Balinese was a practical factor in the increasingly intimate relationship between religion and the New Order, as well as in the expulsion of those opposing membership in Golkar. With its close links to the army and police, Golkar was able to obstruct the issuing of construction permits for temples.[27] Amid the crisis described earlier, Balinese emigrants saw lack of access to temples as the loss of a lifeline. Particularly in times of crisis, the construction of a temple was a matter of life or death to them.

Whatever negotiations transpired between Golkar and Parisada, the general conference at which Parisada decided to join Golkar was the occasion for Parisada to make a public declaration of its Indonesianization. In an interview with a Jakarta radio station, a Parisada representative announced that the group had completed its purge of extremists who violated the Pancasila, and that the holding of the conference at that time accorded with the nation's desire for the advancement of the New Order. He further declared that Hinduism was no longer something exclusive to

Bali, citing as proof a national Galungan ceremony to be held in Jakarta with the Religion Minister attending. This was the first state-level Galungan, and similar ceremonies were also held in Yogyakarta and Surabaya.

The shadows of the dead

By the mid-1960s in Bali, the struggle for independence, volcanic eruptions, and massacres had resulted in vast numbers of dead, and carrying out burial rites for the deceased posed a tremendous challenge for Balinese society. Parisada and the provincial government dealt with the problem by holding ceremonies at Besakih Temple. By the 1950s, the organization responsible for maintaining Besakih had become unstable, and this situation persisted after the establishment of Bali province and Parisada.

Since the founding of the unitary Republic of Indonesia, the Bali Regional Assembly had inherited authority over the operation of Besakih from the Council of Royal Families. In 1951 the assembly sent a letter to the governor of Lesser Sunda province regarding the operation of Besakih.[28] The letter acknowledged the fact that Besakih represented all of Balinese society and served as the center of faith for the Balinese people, but stated that although the assembly had taken over the administration of the temple from the royal families, it could not manage its operations alone. Therefore it requested financial support from the government. The assembly recognized that it lacked both the administrative framework and the economic wherewithal to manage the temple. It was precisely for this reason that assistance with the operating expenses for Besakih headed the list of requests submitted to the Religion Ministry by Sugriwa, as mentioned in Chapter 4. In practice, management of the Bhatara Turun Kabeh ceremony held at the temple with the participation of all the royal families, which had still been the responsibility of the Council of Royal Families in 1947, was rotated among the royal families of Gianyar, Karangasem, and Klungkung in the 1950s. The assembly's assertion of administrative authority over Besakih notwithstanding, it had to depend on some royal families to carry out the ceremonies (Stuart-Fox 2002: 313–14).[29]

171

Besakih is not simply one temple, but a complex of many temples. Stuart-Fox (2002: 67), who has researched Besakih, categorized a total of eighty-six temples at Besakih into three groups: (1) twenty-two public temples, (2) fifty-three descent group temples, and (3) eleven regional or other temples. Ceremonies may be held separately at individual temples, but some simultaneously involve several temples. Various groups conduct the ceremonies, including villages and descent groups in the Besakih area, descent groups from outside the area, and Parisada. Bhatara Turun Kabeh is a ritual that symbolizes the unity of Besakih in the sense that all the gods of the public temples gather there at this time. At the ceremony, the name of which means 'the gods descend together,' objects representing all the gods of the twenty-two public temples are greeted at Penataran Agung, the temple at the center of Besakih.

Besides Bhatara Turun Kabeh, a cyclical ritual held once a year, there are two great ceremonies, Panca Walikrama and Ekadasa Rudra. The former was introduced in 1933, as mentioned in Chapter 2, and then held again in 1960.[30] The latter first took place in 1963. The 1960 Panca Walikrama ceremony was the first major ritual held after independence and is said to have enjoyed a level of interest heightened by the founding of the province of Bali in 1958. It was also the first ceremony hosted by the provincial government and Parisada since they succeeded the Bali Regional Assembly as administrators of Besakih (Stuart-Fox 2002: 330–1). The fact that the ceremony was held two years after the founding of Parisada might suggest that the newly established religious order prepared the event, but no direct connection was actually formed between the birth of Parisada and the 1960 ceremony. If anything, the prevailing view is that the impetus for the ceremony is to be found in the social unrest provoked by a 'millennial kingdom' movement of sorts that had arisen in Java in the early 1950s. According to I Nyoman Wijaya, a historian who has described these events in light of newly unearthed documents, an incident came to light in 1959 that involved Besakih and a prophecy that the priest Sabda Palon, who served under the last Majapahit king, would return 500 years later and restore the realm of Shiva and Buddha.[31]

Counting from the fall of the kingdom, which was said to have occurred in 1478, 500 years later would bring us to 1978. A man named Ejang Gusti

Haji, from Blitar in East Java, was obsessed with the prophecy and began preparing for its fulfillment in the early 1950s. Telling his followers that he had been gifted with the power to make a *tumbal*, an object of magical power that was required for the restoration of the kingdom, Haji began collecting materials for the *tumbal* in Bali. According to the prophecy, the kingdom was to be restored in Bali, from which it must extend its domain to Java. He created a *tumbal* that included soil from the famous temples of Besakih, Pejeng, and Gunung Kawi, a dagger known as a *kris* that symbolized spiritual power, and a photograph of a young Balinese girl frequently sent to foreign countries. The *tumbal* also contained a map of the territory of the kingdom to come, which included seven mountains, among them not only Bali's Mount Agung but also a peak in northern Australia. Mountains, of course, were symbols of the power of the kingdom.

In 1959 this activity came under intense scrutiny due to a complaint lodged by Anandakusuma, an active member of the Klungkung chapter of BDL who had continued to publish numerous books and engage in religious activities well into the 1950s. On March 21, 1959, the day of Kuningan (a religious ceremony following Galungan), Anandakusuma visited Besakih with some colleagues to offer prayers. As he began praying before Penataran Agung, he noticed that something had been buried behind the altar, with a marker placed atop it. Being a member of the provincial legislature, Anandakusuma sent a letter to the governor dated July 15, 1959, reporting what he had seen at Besakih and inquiring whether the provincial government was aware of this fact. The letter gets straight to the point, beginning as follows: 'While offering continual prayers, including appeals for fair weather amid the torrential rain, I discovered something unusual.' It goes on to request clarification as to who placed the marker and for what purpose, and what lay buried beneath it. Upon receiving the letter, the provincial government launched an investigation and learned that a *tumbal* had been buried there in secret on October 17, 1958. The object was dug up on November 1, 1959, and returned to Haji. The provincial government followed up by convening a meeting about the incident on November 25 and disclosed it to the public via the newspaper on December 10.

Once made public, the fact that a *tumbal* had been buried in Bali's most sacred precinct sparked widespread anxiety, which was accompanied by growing distrust of the government. It became clear that Haji had close relations with the director of the Bali Provincial Bureau of the Religion Ministry, the Karangasem royal family, the chairman of the Karangasem District Assembly, military personnel, and other key government officials, primarily in Karangasem, and that he had buried the object in a private ritual held with these individuals. Distrust was further exacerbated by the fact that the government divulged this incident sometime after the object had been dug up. Fearing a deterioration of public order, the military authorized the financing of a religious ceremony by the provincial government, which resulted in the Panca Walikrama of 1960, according to Wijaya's account. Stuart-Fox (2002: 329–33) also mentions this incident and explains the holding of the Ekadasa Rudra in 1963 as arising from an awareness of Ekadasa Rudra's existence during the preparations for the 1960 ceremony and perceptions that it must be held following the Panca Walikrama.[32]

Cooperative relations between Parisada and the provincial government notwithstanding, leadership roles were far from defined when it came to actually carrying out the 1960 and 1963 ceremonies, and it would be a stretch to say that a system for implementing the ceremonies was in place. It was Bali's provincial representative Suteja who organized the executive committee for both ceremonies, and the provincial government provided the funding.[33] In an appointment notice for the executive committee, Suteja wrote that the governor could not avoid the obligations of leadership in customs and religious practices as undertaken by past leaders. The regional military commander, who wielded tremendous authority, served as patron of the ceremonies, while Suteja served as supervisor. Whatever process the preparations for the ceremonies entailed, the provincial government insisted that it be democratic; in other words, the ceremonies were to be carried out not by the feudal royal families but by Parisada, an organization representing Hindu adherents, in cooperation with the government. In fact, however, the position of chairman of the executive committee was delegated to the Dewa Agung (king) of the Klungkung royal family.

It appears that neither the Dewa Agung nor Suteja enjoyed cordial relations with Parisada. Suteja viewed Mantra, Parisada's leader, with enmity, while the Dewa Agung distanced himself from the organization, which he viewed as a dogmatic group that promoted a rationalized version of the religion based on Indian thought.[34] Indeed, Klungkung was the district most resistant to Parisada influence. The Dewa Agung himself had been directly involved in the Panca Walikrama of 1933 and enjoyed a mythical reputation as Bali's most legitimate ruler. When the Dutch attacked the Klungkung palace in 1908, the Dewa Agung, then a child prince, was shot in the foot, yet was 'miraculously' discovered alive amid a pile of corpses. Well into the 1950s, this ruler, lame in one leg, was spoken of as a longtime anti-colonialist and viewed as someone with mystical powers.[35] Still, whatever his mystique at the time, the Dewa Agung did not have the funds to carry out the ceremonies, while the provincial government and the military did. Testimony by at least one participant in the ceremonies jointly conducted by these actors describes a disorganized chain of command and chaotic on-site conditions. The Klungkung royal family and the provincial government each had their own separate chain of command, resulting in a jumble of conflicting orders at the ceremony site. One altar might be adorned with too many offerings, while another did not have enough.[36] Adding to the confusion at the Ekadasa Rudra was the eruption of Mount Agung, which occurred just before the ceremony and, at one point, threatened to bury the temple in lava.

Unlike the Panca Walikrama, which had been held in 1933, no records have been found about the implementation of the Ekadasa Rudra, even though the ceremony was mentioned in documents. In addition, no one had any memory of it; therefore, it was essentially a new ceremony. The primary rationale for holding the Ekadasa Rudra was its designation as a ritual to be performed once every 100 years. Yet 1963 was not a centennial year, and reasons other than the calendar were thus given for holding it. These reasons included that the ceremony had not been held for several centuries, and that Balinese society needed purification after experiencing the upheavals of colonial rule and the war for independence. The specific objects of purification were the dead who had not yet received proper rites. Regarding rites for the dead, the governor issued a public notice commonly referred to as the *instraksi ngaben* (instructions on cremation).[37] This constituted a directive to carry out ceremonies suitable for the dead throughout Bali so as not to *ngeletehin jagat* (desecrate the world) in advance of a major ceremony. A government-issued order with respect to rites for the dead was unprecedented, but it established a routine according to which every district of Bali performed cremation rites ahead of each grand ceremony held at Besakih. On October 21, 1961, Parisada convened a meeting at which it endorsed the content of this directive and resolved that the provincial government would carry out the symbolic cleansing of the dead (Parisada Hindu Dharma 1970: 5). The provincial government used its administrative channels to disseminate the directive and send teams out to the villages to provide guidance. Implementation of the Ekadasa Rudra depended on whether the cremation order was scrupulously observed throughout Bali.[38]

The primary target of the cremation directive was the existence of the dead who had been buried without any rites. It was a general custom to bury the dead with the intention of holding a large-scale ceremony at a later date, but during the impoverished years of the 1950s, it had been difficult for people to conduct these large rites. In view of this situation, the directive recommended holding *pengabenan irit* (economical ceremonies); it stipulated that small-scale rites were sufficient and provided concrete suggestions for economizing (e.g. by holding collective ceremonies). It also urged people to economize as much as possible by reconsidering the most expensive customs, notably providing guests with food and cigarettes.[39] The directive went on to define conditions for identifying the dead who would have no effect on the Ekadasa Rudra. In addition to stipulating how to deal with the non-Hindu dead, it classified the Hindu dead into different types, proposed ritual methods appropriate to each type, established deadlines for holding ceremonies, and indicated how to deal with those who died just before a ceremony took place. It also mentioned the 'heroes' who died in the war for independence, affirming that they were buried in suitable locations in accordance with the 'will of the people' and did not pose an impediment to the Ekadasa Rudra.[40]

The performance of rites for the dead throughout the island of Bali in response to the cremation directive was a highly significant event. The directive established a system under which decisions made by Parisada were carried out throughout Bali via the administrative channels of the provincial government, heightened the central role of Besakih Temple, and enabled the government to involve itself in matters related to death, a concern shared by all people. It also clearly established, for the first time, a policy of participation by all Balinese in temple operations, as the royal families had originally proposed when they asked the colonial government to restore Besakih after it was damaged in the 1917 earthquake, as described in Chapter 1. Moreover, the government's recommendation of simplified ceremonies paved the way for people to conduct cremation rites as soon as someone died. The idealization of large-scale rituals stemmed from the perception that ceremonies must reflect the social position related to a person's title, and that the cremation ceremony was the ultimate opportunity to demonstrate status and honor. The leveling of cremation, with its intimate connection to status and honor, had been a major point of contention since the days of Surya Kanta, as mentioned earlier. The cremation directive provided a degree of resolution of this issue and accelerated the trend toward simplification of such rituals. In effect, the directive initiated both a strengthening of government authority and the democratization of religious ceremonies.

If the issue of how to deal with the dead appeared at least somewhat resolved in 1963, it resurfaced in particularly cruel fashion with the massacres of 1965. How were the Balinese to care for the souls of so many murder victims? In early 1966, Parisada and the provincial government began devising concrete measures to address this problem. On February 26 a joint meeting was convened to discuss what sort of rites to hold for murder victims. The participants included members of the Parisada priesthood and representatives of the provincial government, the Hindu department of the Bali Provincial Bureau in the Religion Ministry, and Parisada branches in Bali. They agreed to hold a purification ceremony with a ritual sacrifice, Tawur Agung, at Besakih at the same time as the Bhatara Turun Kabeh on April 20. The government, the military, and Parisada collaborated in carrying out the ceremony, which was performed by eleven priests from Bali and one from Lombok. An article publicizing the ceremony, which it described as having 'the objective of preserving the spirit of all of Indonesia, particularly Bali,' called for all Hindus on Bali to cooperate in making the ceremony a success and requested that those who could not gather at Besakih instead offer prayers from their own villages.[41]

The policy that the provincial government would handle ceremonies for the dead who were victims of political violence had been established ever since the 1961 meeting when Parisada endorsed the cremation directive. However, the 1966 decision also contained a pronounced element of concern for public order. On the grounds that the provincial government had already carried out such a ceremony, the provincial government prohibited privately conducted ceremonies for the political dead. Its concern was that private rites provided opportunities for the recurrence of violence for reasons such as revenge. A notice issued on September 16 stated that there were 'signs of erroneous use' of ceremonies for the dead, and that since the government had conducted a ceremony, there was no need for individuals to hold them. Yet an addendum was attached to the effect that rites for the dead were ultimately a matter pertaining to individuals and village society, and that the freedom to conduct ceremonies must be guaranteed. However, this addendum was clearly for administrative purposes, stating as it did that (1) ceremonies must be in keeping with religious objectives; (2) ceremonies to be held for those involved in violent incidents must be reported to the administrative office specified by the provincial governor or district governor and permission obtained; and (3) punitive measures would be taken if religious ceremonies were held for any other purpose.[42]

Another meeting to determine how to deal with the dead was convened on June 28, 1967. Representatives from the provincial government, the Religion Ministry, and Parisada participated, and the heads and leading priests of each district reported on the status of ceremonies for the dead related to the September 30 Movement. The result was the issuance of a new notice under the name of the provincial governor. It reaffirmed that a ceremony for the dead had been conducted at Besakih Temple on April 20, 1966, that the ceremony had included offerings of sacrifices and holy water, and that the performance of this ceremony rendered further rites for the dead unnecessary. Furthermore, an attached addendum clarified that while individual families still retained the right to perform ceremonies for the dead, such ceremonies would be prohibited for the time being 'due to psychological, political, and security concerns.'[43] The fact that a notice was issued more than a year-and-a-half after the massacres indicates that the fear engendered by the shadows of the dead continued to grip Balinese society. Moreover, the government exploited this fear to reinforce its administrative authority.

Along with rites for the dead, ordinary purification ceremonies were also held in a number of districts after the massacres. In the Tabanan district, a Panca Walikrama ceremony was held on June 23, 1966, in Tabanan city, followed by a malasti ceremony that began on June 25. The latter event involves a procession in which objects symbolizing gods are borne from Luhur Temple, at the foot of Mount Batukau in northern Tabanan, to Tanah Lot, a temple facing the ocean at the southern tip of the district, then back to Luhur, after which the gods are seen off with a sacrificial offering. The purpose of this massive ceremony, which involves the entire Tabanan district, is to *penyapsap jagat* (purify the land). An article describing the ceremony specifically identified the target of purification as the PKI, which had destroyed the cosmic order.[44] The malasti had been conducted twice before, once after the 1917 earthquake and once after the 1950 independence struggle, each time with the objective of restoring order through symbolic purification. Performance of the malasti was also discussed at the meeting of February 26, 1966, when it was decided to hold a ceremony for the dead at Besakih and the government recommended the conduct of purification rituals in all districts. Though differing from the Tabanan event in both scale and procedure, similar ceremonies were held in Badung, Tampaksiring, and Gianyar.

Symbols of the New Order

The process of repairing the damage sustained at Besakih Temple during the eruption of Mount Agung continued even after the September 30 Incident. The restoration plan had been announced on September 14, 1965, just a few days before the incident. The repairs took place amid a shift to a new system of governance at Besakih Temple, as the provincial government and Parisada worked together to institute changes in the temple's administration in the aftermath of the incident. On August 10, 1967, the government formally transferred administrative authority over Besakih Temple to Parisada, which had established an agency, Prawartaka Pura Besakih, for that purpose.[45] The provincial governorship also changed hands, from the Balinese Merta to the Javanese Sukarmen, who was not a Hindu. The fact that the governor could no longer exercise authority over Besakih Temple was a direct incentive for the formation of the administrative agency. However, the transfer of authority did not represent a severing of ties between the provincial government and the temple. If anything, it could be viewed as a reinforcement of civil authority over Besakih Temple by establishing a dual structure comprising both government and Parisada members. The vice-governor of the province served as a representative of the administrative agency, and the government continued to manage civil funding for the temple.

The restoration plan divided the repair work into stages, thereby establishing the sequence in which the numerous structures of the Besakih Temple complex would be repaired or rebuilt. Plans called for the soliciting of donations from Hindus outside Bali as well, thereby using the restoration project to cement Besakih's status as the primary temple of Hinduism throughout Indonesia, not only in Bali.[46] Work only got underway once the aftereffects of the September 30 Incident had subsided. At a conference held at Besakih Temple from July 25 to 27, 1966, discussions took place regarding how to make the project more efficient and how to secure funding. It was decided to resurvey the rice paddies belonging to Besakih Temple in the regencies of Karangasem, Klungkung, Gianyar, and Bangli, to build a rice storehouse at Besakih Temple to collect the harvest from these properties, and to issue a renewed appeal to Hindus outside Bali to participate in the restoration project.[47] The actual work did not begin until the following year. A groundbreaking ceremony was held on February 25, 1967, the day of a full moon, and repairs of Penataran Agung and other major structures began with the aim of completing them in time for the Bhatara Turun Kabeh ceremony in April. Regarding the mobilization of labor, the committee emphasized that it was abiding by the 'traditional' methods used for Besakih Temple, noting that the current project constituted only a partial restoration and that 125 structures in all were in need of repairs.[48] On April 25, the day of Bhatara Turun Kabeh, a small purification ceremony was held for structures on which work had been completed at that point.[49]

Repairs to the major structures did not end until well into 1968. The Bhatara Turun Kabeh that year, preparations for which began on April 1 and which reached its climax on April 13, was viewed as the first large-scale ceremony to take place since the September 30 Incident. This event put an end to the uncertainty over leadership that had arisen with the ceremonies of 1963, and made manifest the establishment of authority over Besakih Temple by the provincial government and Parisada. The Dewa Agung of the Klungkung royal family died after the incident and there were no successors with the mythical powers attributed to him. A representative of the provincial governor and the various regency heads led the ceremony executive committee that had been formed, while the regional military commander served as an adviser, as in the 1963 ceremonies. Clarification of the leadership framework also meant that methods of procuring funds were firmly established for the first time. While the provision of funds was to be voluntary, procedures for submitting donations were defined for each class of society. The written directives clearly articulated the intention of setting up a society-wide mobilization system for the purpose of carrying out ceremonies at Besakih.[50]

The Bhatara Turun Kabeh ceremony drew many participants from both outside and inside Bali and was deemed a success. The representative from the Hindu department of the Bali Provincial Bureau declared that, as a gathering of the gods of all the temples, the Bhatara Turun Kabeh also signified the unity of Bali and helped ensure the safety and security of Balinese society. Mantra noted the significance of the ceremony's performance upon completion of Penataran Agung, stating that with its long history, Besakih Temple itself embodied the promise of spiritual and material prosperity to come. Delivering greetings on the occasion of the joint prayer, the regional military commander warned of the danger of schisms along religious and ethnic lines, asserted that unity would overcome these differences, and called for people to 'participate in development together with President Suharto.'[51]

Suharto himself certainly did not overlook the strategic political value of the restoration of Besakih. From November 23 to 27, 1967, the new president paid an official visit to both Bali and Lombok for the first time since the cessation of the massacres. It was a large delegation, with five cabinet ministers in tow. Suharto disembarked at the airport wearing a gray civil servant uniform, not a military one. He was greeted by a Balinese dance troupe and a welcoming ceremony by the military before proceeding to Denpasar, where he spoke at another ceremony held in the central plaza. At this event, titled 'Rally of supporters of the New Order in Bali province' (peng-ORBAan), Suharto declared that the national order had recovered from the destruction and fear engendered by G30S-PKI, and proclaimed the restoration of allegiance to the 1945 Constitution and the Pancasila (in other words, the building of a state predicated on freedom of religion and belief in the 'one and only God'). In addition to appealing for cooperation with his government, he declared that he wished to use the opportunity to listen to the Balinese people, and he expressed his thanks for their 'voluntary' organizing of the rally. Finally, he asserted that development must advance on the spiritual level, as well as the material level, and that religious education was key to this effort. In his welcoming statement, the provincial governor professed his full support for Suharto's proclamation.

Besides meetings with government representatives and the provincial House of Representatives, Suharto's visit included inspection tours of two showpieces of development in Bali under the New Order: the airport and the Bali Beach Hotel. Construction of the hotel had begun with money from war reparations paid by the Japanese government, and it had been near completion and ready for operation during the Sukarno era. However, rumors of PKI connections among the employees prevented it from opening for business until 1967. Suharto was also provided an opportunity to meet with farmers and, together with former provincial governor Merta and the head of the Tabanan regency, he attended the opening ceremony for a canal in Tabanan that had been under construction since the Sukarno era. During his visit, Suharto stayed at the presidential palace built by Sukarno in Tampaksiring, a formal demonstration of the change in the nation's ruler.

After visiting Lombok, Suharto and his entourage landed once more at Bali's airport on their return journey. There they took in a presentation on the airport improvement project, and then headed for Besakih to inspect the restoration work. People lined the route to cheer the motorcade, and Suharto was greeted at the temple with a gamelan performance and people garbed in ceremonial dress. Suharto himself donned traditional Balinese-style attire, including a headdress and a *kris*, while the priests performed a ceremony of welcome for a person of high rank. Under clear skies, Suharto stood at the head of the row of dignitaries in attendance, including the provincial governor and regency head, and offered a prayer. Photographs of Suharto in Balinese attire subsequently graced the front pages of newspapers, with captions noting that the president had not only viewed firsthand the contributions of the Balinese people to the New Order but had also prayed with them. The welcoming ceremonies continued when Suharto's party returned to the presidential palace, with a variety of performances including a Legong dance by an ensemble from Peliatan. In a closing speech, Suharto announced that he had told the provincial governor that he was satisfied that recovery was progressing smoothly on both the spiritual and material fronts, that he was happy that he had been able to pray together with the Balinese people, and that, in so doing, he had been able to realize the first principle of the Pancasila. Moreover, he viewed the progress in restoration of the temple through the efforts of the provincial government as emblematic of recovery; he declared, 'For the sake of spiritual development, the government must work with the people to reinforce the status of the temple,' and pledged to work for the recovery of the Karangasem regency, which had particularly suffered from the volcanic eruption.[52] Thus Besakih and its restoration were treated as symbols of the New Order.

Expansion of rituals

Of the twenty-two public temples at Besakih according to Stuart-Fox's (2002) aforementioned categorization, the Parisada administrative agency deemed eighteen (excluding four temples associated with descent groups) as falling within its jurisdiction. Despite the fact that customary villages[53] in the Besakih area had traditionally managed these temples and continue to do so today, Parisada asserted its authority so as to highlight the public status of Besakih Temple.[54] Taking the standard Bhatara Turun Kabeh ceremony as an example, funding generally entailed the provincial government paying half of all expenses, with the remaining half divided between the regencies in proportion to their financial wherewithal (Stuart-Fox 2002: 219–28, 251–6, 316–17). The provincial government and Parisada also sought to improve the environment of Besakih Temple and its surroundings. In 1974 they designated Bali temples, including Besakih, as Tempat Ibadah (Places of Worship), which they earmarked for maintenance. They also stressed that the temples were significant not only as places of worship but also as tourist destinations.[55] Then, in 1977, it was decided to prepare a master plan to preserve and develop Besakih Temple and set forth the manner and timing under which the temple and its environs would be maintained.[56] In all such cases, the initiative began with Parisada, which would assert the need for a decision that would then be acknowledged and decreed by the provincial governor.[57]

In committing itself to maintenance of the temple and environs, the administrative agency had a primary objective to hold the Ekadasa Rudra in 1979—which was 1900 in Bali's lunar calendar. A consensus had been reached to conduct the ceremony in that year because it was the only year in a century to end in double zeroes. The administrative agency and Parisada as a whole worked assiduously on preparations. Conducting a comprehensive analysis of texts in the possession of the priesthood and traveling to the Netherlands to examine texts taken there during the colonial era, they settled on procedures for the ceremony. Motivated by his firsthand impressions of the 1963 event, I Gusti Agung Gede Putra, who had left his position as head of the South Bali sub-bureau of the Religion Ministry to direct the administrative agency, dealt not only with the substance of the ceremony but also its logistics, resolving such critical systemic issues as the procurement and allotment of labor power and materials. On March 28, the last day of the century on the lunar calendar, sacrificial offerings of numerous animals were carried out, among them creatures such as scorpions and crocodiles that had never been used in other ceremonies. President Suharto was present at the climax of this once-in-a-century event, which was deemed a success upon its conclusion (Parisada Hindu Dharma Pusat 1981).

With its achievement of this grand ceremony in 1979, Balinese society truly entered a new century. The development of the island's tourist industry, which was a priority among the national projects of Suharto's New Order, gained further momentum with the launch of high-volume air transport. Meanwhile, the New Order itself benefited from the financial stability provided by rising petroleum prices in the wake of the 1973–74 oil crisis. After remaining mired in poverty since the 1930s, Balinese society was finally taking off. At the helm, and providing a pivotal figure in the implementation of the Ekadasa Rudra, was Mantra, who had been appointed provincial governor in 1978. Mantra, who had occupied a top position at the Ministry of Education and Culture in Jakarta for ten years, returned to Bali to assume the governorship. The appointment of a Balinese to the post redefined the governor's position of authority in relation to Besakih Temple. The presence of a governor who had served in Jakarta, combined with Bali's status as a model region for tourism development, clearly helped reinforce the relationship between the province and the central government, a bond that had depended on Sukarno's good graces in the 1950s. Against this backdrop, a massive ceremony accomplished through the concerted efforts of Balinese society and Hindus throughout Indonesia drew the world's attention to the 'traditional world' of Bali.

Surprisingly, the 1979 Ekadasa Rudra, supposedly carried out to perfection, was later declared insufficient by Parisada, which announced that it had been unable to enact other requisite ceremonies and would have to do so in the future. The upshot was that three ceremonies were held concurrently with the 1993 Bhatara Turun Kabeh: the Candi Narmada, Panca Walikrama ring Danu, and Tri Bhuwana. These were followed by the Eka Bhuwana in 1996. The Candi Narmada and Panca Walikrama ring Danu were both associated with rivers, with the former held at Batu Klotok Beach in Klungkung and dedicated to the ocean deity Sang Hyang Samudra, and the latter at Lake Batur and dedicated to the lake deity Bhatari Danu. Both were described as purification ceremonies that should take place before the Ekadasa Rudra (Supartha 1993: 48).

Tri Bhuwana, which means 'Three Worlds,' is a ceremony of offerings to each of the three vertically aligned upper, middle, and lower worlds of the universe, while Eka Bhuwana presents an offering to the one world; both are supposed to occur after the Ekadasa Rudra. However, none of these ceremonies were performed around 1979, which saw the observance of the Ekadasa Rudra alone.

According to Parisada's explanation, the organization had been aware of these additional ceremonies in 1979. However, it had been unable to determine the proper types of offerings or the configurations of these ceremonies from the texts available at the time, and hence had put off their implementation. However, on the occasion of the 1989 Panca Walikrama,[58] arguments were made that those ceremonies, too, ought to be carried out. To determine whether it was actually feasible to do so, Parisada began re-examining existing texts related to the Ekadasa Rudra and searching anew for other texts. By the time of the sixth general conference of Parisada in 1991, it had been determined that these ceremonies were indeed doable, but it was decided to postpone them until after the 1992 general election. Immediately after the election, the Bali branch of Parisada passed a final proposal that was accepted by the provincial governor, and a decision issued in the governor's name declared that the ceremonies would be held in 1993.[59]

The written decision under the governor's imprimatur called for the formation of an executive committee, citing as precedent the law pertaining to regional administrative authority in effect since the founding of Bali province in 1958. Although Parisada had made the decisions about the implementation and configuration of the ceremonies, the actual executor was clearly the provincial government, which also furnished a reserve fund for the purpose. This was ultimately not spent, because funds amassed from other sources proved more than sufficient. Nonetheless, the provincial government then came to serve as administrator of all funds associated with Besakih Temple, including surpluses. Compulsory donations were levied on all civil servants of the Hindu faith, as well as on village families via the regency offices. Adding donations from individuals, schools, labor unions, companies, and tourism-related businesses, the sum total of funds secured for the ceremonies was considerable.[60]

The 1993 ceremonies represented one format for the successful functioning of a ceremony implementation system using the administrative apparatus of the provincial government. The ceremonies were conducted by central and local-level executive committees. The Central Committee stipulated by the provincial governor's decision was divided into fifteen sections with a total of 172 members, including a custodial supervisor, seven controllers, five executives (including the executive general), three secretaries, and two accountants. Serving as custodial supervisor was the provincial governor; the controllers consisted of the heads of Parisada's central office and Bali bureau, the regent of Klungkung, the head of the Religion Ministry's Hindu department, the regency head, the chairman of the Majelis Pembina Lembaga Adat (Customary Entities Development Committee), and the Religion Ministry bureau head at the regency level. The composition of the controllers signified a cooperative relationship among four institutions: Parisada, the provincial government, the Religion Ministry, and the Customary Entities Development Committee.[61] As indicated by the appointment to the committee of representatives from the Religion Ministry and the Parisada central office, these ceremonies were treated as not only being for the Balinese but for Hindus throughout Indonesia.

The Customary Entities Development Committee, an organization founded in 1979 with the objective of reinforcing the activities of the customary villages (Kagami 2000: 122–4), became actively involved in ceremonies at Besakih from the 1989 Panca Walikrama onward. Serving as executive general was the provincial government's secretary-general, a post directly below the governorship in which was concentrated all real power in the local political sphere. The other executives were representatives of the aforementioned four institutions, while a member of the provincial government was selected as chief accountant.[62] Unlike in the 1960s, there were no military personnel on the committee.

The Local Committee was formed at Besakih Temple and was run by the villages that handled the day-to-day operation of Besakih. Although the relationship between the Central and Local committees was outwardly one of harmonious cooperation, in practice the ceremonies themselves did not follow local custom, but rather the text-based configuration devised by Parisada. Hence, the Local Committee was compelled to abide by the dictates of the Central Committee.

The personal enthusiasm and commitment displayed by Cokorda Raka Krishna, who served as chairman of the Ceremony Subcommittee of the Executive Committee, helped bring the ceremonies of 1993 and 1996 to fruition. Assigned to the Bali Provincial Bureau of the Religion Ministry, he had been a student at Hindu Dharma University, a religious institution, when the head of the Besakih Temple administrative agency taught there, and had subsequently become involved in the ceremonies at Besakih Temple.[63] If the Sanglah-based India students group comprised the first generation of Parisada, then this represented a passing of the torch in relation to the management of Besakih Temple's ceremonies to a second generation that had received its religious education in Bali. At the meeting that took place in Campuan in 1961 soon after the founding of Parisada, it was resolved to establish an institution of higher learning to nurture religious leaders. Hindu Dharma University was that institution; opened in 1963, it received official accreditation from the Ministry of Education and Culture the following year. After completion of the campus, Parisada frequently held its meetings there in the 1990s.[64]

Religious ceremonies in Bali are composed of a series of stages. In the great ceremonies at Besakih Temple, specific offerings are made at each stage, with different priests officiating; the types of music and dance performed also vary from stage to stage. All tasks performed during the course of the 1993 ceremonies, from the preparatory stage onward, were allotted by the Central Committee to work crews organized by regency.[65] In other words, administrative units served as the basis for division of labor at the ceremonies. The Central Committee made overall determinations of the tasks associated with the ceremonies, from the preparation of offerings (the primary task at the preparatory stage) to the dispatching of musical and dance troupes over the duration of the ceremonies,[66] allocating them among the regencies with due consideration to their relative distance from Besakih Temple so as to prevent any disproportionate burdens.[67] At the same time, there were also customary work groups organized for each temple in the Besakih complex. These were afforded autonomous status directly under Bali province, with members to be mobilized from the regencies in the event of labor shortages.

The Central Committee also appointed the priests in charge of each stage of the ceremonies. The Parisada branches at the regency level prepared lists of priests in each regency, based on which the Central Committee evaluated the qualifications of each priest. The first step was to distinguish between priests who followed Hindu procedures in carrying out the ceremonies and those who followed Buddhist procedures, because, in the view of the committee, one or the other approach was appropriate for different ceremonies. However, the fundamental criterion for these evaluations was the ability of the priest, a paramount question being whether he had ever officiated at the highest level of ceremonies. The family lineage of the priest and the status of his wife were also factors. A priest was disqualified if his lineage had been interrupted three times, and it was also considered important that a priest's wife belonged to the priestly class. The Central Committee identified priests meeting these conditions and assigned them to the various stages of the ceremonies. In this manner, the committee constructed a system capable of supplying adequate human, as well as material, resources for large-scale ceremonies of this sort.

The scale of the 1993 ceremonies exceeded that of the 1979 event. The first prayer at Besakih Temple took place on December 10, 1992, immediately after the government's announcement of the start of the ceremonies. The final stage heralding their conclusion ended on May 4, 1993. As with the Ekadasa Rudra, the ceremonial climax came on the day before Nyepi, the start of the New Year on the Balinese calendar. On March 20, the procession to Klotok Beach began, and the offerings that formed the centerpiece of each ceremony were held on the same day, March 21, for both the Candi Narmada and Panca Walikrama ring Danu. The symbols of the gods were received at Besakih Temple upon their return from the procession, the Tri Bhuwana offering took place on March 23, and Nyepi was celebrated on March 24, the day of the new moon. The Bhatara Turun Kabeh was held on the day of the next full moon, April 7. With multiple ceremonies to perform, the entire series of events took more than five months and used seventeen different altars for offerings, well over the nine used for the 1979 ceremony.[68] There had clearly been a substantial expansion in the scale of ceremonies in Bali (cf. Sudibya 1996).

Completed cosmology—recreation of a kingship world

What made the expansion of ceremonies possible was the fact that the public rituals at Besakih Temple had no precedent in custom. Precisely because of this lack of precedent, the government was free to use its administrative apparatus to mobilize material and human resources in the presentation of ceremonies that took the form of grand spectacles. Even if a number of the ceremonial stages were rooted in custom, the Ekadasa Rudra and the ceremonies of 1993 were rituals reconstructed from written documents. Procedures for the 1993 ceremonies were approved by Parisada on the basis of review and revision of texts found by a group led by Krishna.[69]

A prerequisite for the text-based configuration of a ceremony is the presence of a group to read the texts and an authorized system to approve their interpretation. Such a text interpretation system was central to the process of systematizing Balinese religion described thus far. As mentioned in Chapter 2, the impetus for the establishment of the first library was the performance of ceremonies at Besakih Temple, and the establishment of textual interpretation authority was inextricably linked to the actual ceremonies and the framework for their implementation. The institutions that reproduced the authority of the priests as text interpreters did not fade away, but rather persisted after independence. Negotiations with the Religion Ministry in the 1950s reinforced this textualism, and the advent of the India students group further amplified the authority attributed to texts. Then, with the loss of legal status by the royal families, authority over textual interpretation became concentrated in the hands of Parisada. In the 1960 and 1963 ceremonies, when the Dewa Agung still retained his mythical personal power, authority was not yet exclusive to Parisada. After 1965, however, it was consolidated under the *Sulinggih*, the organization of Parisada priests, and this reality was no longer subject to dispute from any quarter by the time of the ceremonies of 1979 and 1993. There were no more royal families or organizations capable of asserting public authority to compete with Parisada, which was now in a position to screen the qualifications of Hindu priests throughout Indonesia. Underpinning Parisada's religious authority was the fact that it was an entity officially recognized by the state.

The fundamental tool that made possible the actual enactment of ceremonies constructed on the basis of texts were the manuals. The Central Committee prepared the manuals based on the approved general outline of the ceremonies. The ceremonial stages were named and arranged in sequence with listings of the appropriate offerings, priests, dances, and music, and the names of those in charge of each category, as well as the task allocation. The total offerings and requisite labor force for the ceremonies were calculated from the manuals and allocated among the regency work crews at the preparatory stage. The manuals also showed how to calculate the amount of food to be provided to those who came to work at Besakih Temple. A bureaucratic entity such as the provincial government was able to carry out these ceremonies because a system was in place for dividing the tasks required for their enactment according to the manuals.[70]

The manuals for personal use, entitled *Yasa Kerti*, were also prepared and distributed through government channels. In the context of religious ceremonies, the title means 'participation'; *budi pekerti*, a term that combines *kerti* with the word *budi* (reason or wisdom; introduced in Chapter 2), is used as a name for moral education courses in schools. The personal manuals outlined ritual procedures, explained their meaning, described how to receive holy water, and gave instructions on how to carry out ceremonies in one's own home or village in concert with those at Besakih Temple. The guidelines were intended for Hindus throughout Indonesia, not just in Bali. The manuals also described the manners and moral conduct to be observed by participants in the ceremonies. Instructions on how a good Hindu should participate in these ceremonies were presented as religious doctrine, with admonishments to maintain pure thought, speech, and conduct while carrying out sacred rituals, as well as to make material or monetary contributions to the ceremony to the best of one's ability.[71] Thus the eminently modern dissemination technology represented by the manuals was pivotal not only to the enactment of these massive ceremonies but also to the participation of large numbers of people.

One major ambition motivating Krishna and his team of ceremony architects was a desire to complete a cosmology centered on Besakih Temple. The grand ceremonies were a physical manifestation of Bali as a symbolic space with the Besakih Temple complex at its center. The offerings that formed the centerpiece of each ceremony were made in specific directions, and this directionality defined the relationship between the ritual, the cosmology, and the physical space of Bali itself. The Ekadasa Rudra and the similarly configured Candi Narmada involved the center and eight horizontal directions: north, south, east, west, northeast, southeast, northwest, and southwest. The Panca Walikrama had four directions (north, south, east, and west), as well as the center, while the Tri Bhuwana entailed offerings to the three vertical worlds. At the end came the Eka Bhuwana, which presented an offering to just one location at the center. In this manner, offerings were completed to all the worlds in both the horizontal and vertical directions, with the final, single offering representing the completion of the cosmos.

This cosmology, with Bali conceived as its symbolic space, is known as Padma Bhuwana: the world (bhuwana) in the form of a lotus flower (padma). The horizontal space extending in eight directions is superimposed on actual locations in Bali, with Besakih Temple at the center. This concept was officially formulated after the completion of the Eka Bhuwana. On September 3, 1996, the *Sulinggih* from all of Bali and the Parisada central office gathered at Besakih Temple and adopted a declaration.[72] The statement affirmed that 'Besakih Temple is the center of religious ceremonies for the Hindu faithful' and, furthermore, that 'Besakih Temple is the center of the world represented as a lotus flower, that is, the essence (*sari*) of Padma Bhuwana. For this very reason, Besakih Temple is the center that cleanses, or sanctifies (*menyucikan*) all the things of this world' (Parisada Hindu Dharma Indonesia Pusat 1996: 124–6).

This directionality affords a multilayered plurality of meanings. Each direction has a corresponding deity, color, sound, and weapon to provide the world with divine protection. The directions, with their manifold meanings, factor prominently in offerings, in the mantras intoned by priests, and in symbolic representations disseminated among the populace. Mountains or hills are also associated with each direction, thus superimposing this directionality on the physical space of Bali. Each mountain or hill has a temple, and the gods from these temples participate in the major ceremonies at Besakih Temple. Specifically, sacred objects representing the gods visit Besakih Temple, where they are met with a respectful reception. This part of the ceremony takes place at the end of malasti, the ritual in which the gods from Besakih leave the temple and are borne in a procession to the beach. When the Besakih Temple gods return from the procession and re-enter the temple, the visiting gods enter the center of the temple together and are enshrined there. This ceremony gives physical form to the unity of the Besakih Temple gods with the gods representing the directions of the cosmos—and thus to the concept of Padma Bhuwana.[73]

It is common for a large central temple to welcome gods from peripheral temples, so the ceremony for this purpose at Besakih Temple was not exceptional. In this regard, the ceremony welcoming the gods could be viewed as a practice rooted in custom. However, the notion of temples representing the eight directions became entrenched only with the formulation of the Padma Bhuwana cosmology in the 1990s.

Mountains and water formed the criteria for recognition of the temples constituting Padma Bhuwana. As dwelling places of the gods, mountains and bodies of water were fundamental to the establishment of the symbolic order given form by temple ceremonies. Geographically speaking, Besakih Temple is by no means at the center of Bali, but some distance to the east. The village of Taro, closer to the geographical center of the island, was originally chosen as the location of the most central temple in Bali. However, this place was considered unsuitable as a ceremonial center due to its lack of mountains and water; the center, it was said, therefore had to be moved to its present location at the foot of Mount Agung. The Besakih declaration of 1996 was the final stage in the process of reconstructing the Padma Bhuwana concept. Moreover, the establishment of the new concept was accompanied by the incorporation into ceremonies at Besakih Temple of the ritual in which the gods of temples in the eight directions gathered at Besakih. In this way, the space comprising the island of Bali was configured as a single symbolic world with Besakih Temple as its center (Figure 5.1) (Agastia 1996: 19–26).

Mount Batur

Mount Beratan
(Puncak Mangu)

Mount Agung
(Besakih Temple)

Mount Batukaru ———— Besakih Temple ———— Mount Lempuyang

Uluwatu

Goa Lawah

Mount Andakasa

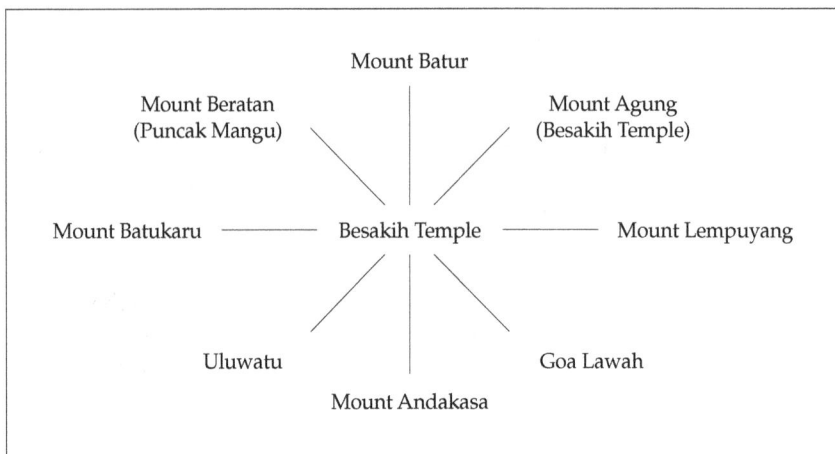

Figure 5.1 Padma Bhuwana (Agastia 1996: 19–21)

With its central status thus augmented, Besakih Temple made it possible to establish a clearly defined conduit for the distribution of holy water. The holy water prepared in religious ceremonies is disbursed among the leaders of customary villages, who bring it back to their communities to sprinkle along village boundaries and distribute among individual households. Each household then sprinkles the water on the boundary of its own property; in this manner, holy water bestows its blessings on all the land belonging to all the customary villages in Bali. The cremation directive that was promulgated at the time of the 1963 Ekadasa Rudra is also incorporated as a formal requirement for ceremonies at Besakih Temple today. Holy water is prepared in a special ritual conducted about one month before the ceremony, distributed to each participant, and sprinkled at sites where rites for the dead are to be performed.[74] The holy water removes impurities, so the personal manual stipulates special procedures for burying those who die after its distribution. By the 1990s it was broadly understood in Balinese society that cremation rites were to be carried out before the distribution of holy water. Thus the customary village leaders must visit Besakih Temple for holy water at least twice when major ceremonies take place: once to receive the holy water for cremation rites and once during the ceremony itself. The manual specifies the days, times, and places for receiving holy water, as well as the offerings that must be prepared for the occasion.

The rivers that are the source of holy water are a paramount symbol in Bali of the hierarchical order of society and the universe. The kingdoms controlled the order represented by the flow of watercourses by administering temples at the headwaters and mouths of rivers. The 1993 ceremonies gave form to this order by holding concurrent ceremonies at a lake, which represented the source of a river, and the ocean, which represented its mouth. Moreover, the malasti ceremony of the former kingdoms (now regencies), in which the symbol of a god is carried from a river's source to its mouth and back again, was enacted at the same time as the ceremonies at Besakih Temple. This, too, successfully positioned the latter as the pinnacle of all ceremonies performed in various locales.[75]

The configuration of these ceremonies as the concrete embodiment of a now-completed cosmology suggests a return to the old kingship order by Balinese society. In the relationship between the provincial government and the *Sulinggih* of Parisada, one can see traces of the relationship between the royal families and the priesthood in the days of the kingdoms. The status of these two authorities as 'natural' executors of the ceremonies and as administrators of the conduit between holy water and every individual in Bali represents a return to the kingship era (cf. Schulte Nordholt 1991). It is officially recognized that democracy is at most a general principle, that Indonesian Hindus approve this dual authority, and that it is as their representatives that the two authorities direct these ceremonies. Hindu doctrine is cited to justify the role of the provincial government, ostensibly a secular administrative entity, as an executor of religious rituals. It is assumed that *guru wisesa* (holders of power) will serve as *sang mayadnya* (executors of ceremonies) and particularly as *yajamana* (conductors of the sacrificial offerings that form the core of those ceremonies). Only someone at the highest level of power may enact the rituals at Besakih Temple, which constitute the highest level of offerings. Today that level is represented by none other than the provincial government. In this way, the ceremonies link Balinese cosmology to the ruling structure, and public consensus that this is a natural tradition is achieved through its legitimization in religious teachings.

The relationship between the *guru wisesa* and the *yajamana* was made explicit during the 1967 Bhatara Turun Kabeh ceremony. The provincial governor began espousing this doctrine after the consolidation of governmental power under the New Order and the death of the Dewa Agung. With the complete extinction of the influence of the one remaining royal personage capable of opposing the governor, the doctrine became official policy. In his opening speech before the ceremony, the governor touched on the relationship between religion and the provincial government in Bali. While noting that it would not involve itself in all aspects of religion, he specifically identified the provincial government as the *guru wisesa* and declared that the government could not disassociate itself from religion. The governor had made a similar declaration about the relationship of religion and the provincial government on the occasion of the Nyepi ceremony that preceded the Bhatara Turun Kabeh. At that time, he asserted that the spread of Hinduism throughout Indonesia necessitated the maintenance of Hindu institutions, in view of which 'the Bali provincial government cannot separate itself from Besakih Temple, the center of Hindu religious activities.'[76] The regional administrative reform of 1958 that made the island of Bali an autonomous province and recognized the former kingdoms as regencies made the relationship between Bali province and Hinduism explicit, and paved the way for a system of implementing ceremonies using the administrative apparatus of the provincial government. In short, what made the reinterpretation of 'traditional' doctrine possible was regional administrative reform at the national level that had no connection with religion at all. The Bali provincial government, with the governor at the helm, declared itself the *guru wisesa*, claiming that the holder of political power and the executor of ceremonies were now essentially one and the same in Bali, thus asserting its authority to carry out ceremonies at Besakih Temple.

This religious world with its kingship cosmology is defined as ultimately coexisting with the state. Employing the concept of Dharma in the sense of the proper order of things and the duties concomitant with that order, religion (Dharma Agama) and the state (Dharma Negara) observe parallel Dharmas in their respective domains. This way of thinking, referred to as Dwi Dharma, was put forward at the Campuan meeting that launched Parisada. In its call for the cultivation of Hindu adherents to the foundations of family and harmony, Parisada postulated two Dharmas as a methodology for guiding the faithful. Given that people residing in Indonesia live under the protection of the Indonesian government, and that the moral principles underpinning the state are contained in the Pancasila, the Dharma of the state therefore means that Hindus, as part of the nation of Indonesia, have a duty to follow the Pancasila to the utmost in their daily lives. Included in this Dharma are contributions to the nation's development and participation in the electoral process. Meanwhile, the Dharma of religion consists of obeying the holy scriptures and following the teachings of the religion. In the ancient doctrine of Dharma, the secular and the religious merge together, and national development and unity are promoted within the framework of religion (cf. Supartha 1995).[77]

The 1990s thus saw the creation of a grand cosmology and, with it, the participation of large numbers of people as worshippers at Besakih Temple, or as members of the labor force recruited to carry out large-scale ceremonies. However, the manner in which these participants viewed the cosmology and its moral principles necessarily varied from individual to individual. The fact that funds accrued to the extent that massive ceremonies could be successfully conducted, with money left over, must be acknowledged as indicative of the high degree of consensus and participatory zeal exhibited by the Balinese toward these events. However, the period of the 1990s was also when Balinese tourism was reaching a peak and a kind of money worship was taking hold, as manifested in purchases of cars and houses and the flaunting of other forms of material vanity. Hence it is difficult to argue that cosmology or morality prompted people's interest in religious ceremonies more directly than motivations of a more personal nature. In the 1930s efforts by lower-level civil servants in Bali had directly related to conditions caused by the Great Depression, and the passionate engagement in religious activities by Sugriwa and his colleagues in the 1950s was spurred by concerns about poverty and social reform. But the phenomenon of burgeoning sales of religious texts seen in the 1950s did not occur in the 1990s. Newspapers posted the names of donors and the amounts donated, as well as the steady increase in those amounts as ceremonies approached, which demonstrates that the big ceremonies now constituted a new opportunity for displays of conspicuous consumption and prestige.[78] Donating to the Besakih Temple ceremonies had become a means of showing off one's economic power.

Up to the end of the nineteenth century, when the kingdoms were still characterized by fluidity, the royal families at their center used grand ceremonies to quell competition from their highly autonomous satellites. The form taken by the symbolic universe of these kingdoms was fundamentally different from that of the grand ceremonies of the late twentieth century. The ceremonies enacted by the state administrative apparatus were, if anything, heirs to the formula of the ceremonies that the royal families, as redefined by the colonial government, conducted at Besakih Temple upon its recovery from the damage inflicted by the 1917 earthquake. The return to a kingship order was reproduced in a bureaucratic system. The procedures employed to enact the great ceremonies that reflected the completed cosmology, too, were very much of the twentieth century. Numerous modern technologies sustained these ceremonies: printing presses to mass produce manuals, telephone communications between central and local committees, automobiles, and transceivers to coordinate the progress of long-distance processions. Just as the Panca Walikrama of 1933 was made possible by a bridge built by the colonial government, previously nonexistent technologies enabled the enactment of large-scale ceremonies. These eminently twentieth-century-style events presented a sophisticated cosmology as the recreation of a kingship world that dated back before the nineteenth century.

Part III

Hinduism and the Global State

CHAPTER 6

Disintegration: Hinduism and the Pluralization of Values

Peradah, a Hindu youth organization in Indonesia, published statistics on the Hindu population and the number of priests and temples in each province in 1999. The Indonesian government also prepared statistics for each religion, including the Hindu population, by province. Comparing these two sets of statistics, item by item, reveals a substantial disparity in the reported percentage of the nation's total Hindu population residing in Bali province. The Peradah data gives a total Hindu population of 11,051,241, of which 2,842,317, or 25.7 percent, are in Bali. The government statistics for 2001, however, give 3,651,939 as the total Hindu population, of which 2,751,828, or 75.4 percent, were Hindus in Bali. The disparity derives from Peradah's estimation of the total Hindu population as more than three times that of the government's statistics. I am not equipped to compare the respective methods by which these figures were calculated, so will not attempt to address the question of why this gap in perceptions of the total Hindu population arose. The essential point is that Peradah's figure is significant because it represents a prevailing perception among Hindus themselves—that Indonesian Hindus outside Bali outnumber those in Bali. Rejection of Bali-centrism among Indonesian Hindus is based on this perception of the actual status of Hinduism in their country.

In the past, Hinduism in Indonesia had been concentrated on the island of Bali, as indicated by government statistics, and the institutionalization of Hinduism under the state order was predicated on this fact. Up to the present day, moreover, studies of Bali have always associated Hinduism with the identity of the Balinese and have discussed the religion from that standpoint. Even studies that have examined the circumstances of the Balinese people from international perspectives have not questioned the link between Hinduism and Balinese identity (Connor and Vickers 2003:

166–7). The data presented by Peradah drastically alter that assumption. The phenomena I would like to address at the outset of this chapter are the deterritorialization from Bali of Indonesian Hinduism, which first became salient in the mid-1980s, and the accompanying emergence of a critique against Bali-centrism within the Hindu population. The 1980s saw the development of an informal network among Hindus throughout Indonesia and the emergence of criticism of the Hindu order under the state, the institutionalization of which had been predicated on it being limited to the domain of Balinese people in Bali. The causes and consequences of this shift are issues that cannot be ignored in any consideration of Hinduism in Indonesia today.

The 'channel' of religion

Hinduism throughout Indonesia came under the purview of state governance with its official recognition by the Religion Ministry and the establishment of a Hindu representative body, Parisada Hindu Dharma. Then, as mentioned in Chapter 5, Parisada joined Golkar, a political party that increasingly took on the character of a regime support group after the establishment of the Suharto regime. In this sense, then, the Indonesianization of Hinduism and its concomitant deterritorialization from Bali had already begun. However, Parisada was still headquartered in Denpasar and the Parisada organizations in other parts of Indonesia functioned as no more than branches under Bali's jurisdiction. In various parts of Indonesia, people who considered themselves Hindu were not mutually connected with one another via local branches of Parisada; rather, the authority to speak about Hinduism was exclusive to Balinese living in Bali. The statistics publicized by Peradah, however, indicated that this arrangement was already a thing of the past.

The perception that Balinese no longer held a majority among Hindus in Indonesia took on concrete ramifications in an upheaval that occurred in 2001—a schism within Parisada on its home turf, Bali. The mid-1980s had seen the beginnings of Hindu organizations on a nationwide level and, with them, the birth of Peradah, a youth organization that linked

Hindus throughout the country. Prior to this, the only Hindu group besides Parisada had been Prajaniti, which belonged to the political arm of Golkar. The impetus for the Parisada schism in Bali was the activity of Pemuda Hindu, a youth group that had split off when Peradah was formed and then reorganized in 2000. This, too, was a nationwide organization, and it proceeded to mobilize Hindus throughout Indonesia to demand the reform of Parisada. Some forces in Bali that opposed this movement ignored the general consensus within Parisada and launched a new Parisada.

Pemuda Hindu, particularly its Bali branch, was characterized by a social orientation and mobilizing ability unprecedented in the history of Hinduism in Indonesia. The group was explicit in its espousal of a social role for religion. It became known for movements related to land issues in Karangasem in 1989 and Badung in 1996, as well as for its success as an outside mediator in the fierce confrontation between Golkar and the Indonesian Democratic Party of Struggle in Singaraja from 1996 to 1999. It also engaged in activities associated with the independence struggle in East Timor. Balinese who had settled in East Timor were subjected to threats and violence, and 768 households had fled back to Bali by 1999. The provincial governor of Bali urged them to move once again to a different district of East Timor, but those who had endured terror there wanted to remain in Bali permanently. Unable to return to their home villages, these families had no place to go, and Pemuda Hindu protested the governor's proposal on their behalf. With donations, the group then purchased land in West Bali and built a new village. Pemuda Hindu organized autonomous work teams to carry out these diverse activities.

The unifying theme of activities by Pemuda Hindu was the achievement of a civil society. Indeed, no place in Bali reverberated with the words 'civil society' more loudly than the Pemuda Hindu office on Diponegoro Street, a north–south thoroughfare in downtown Denpasar. The lawyers, journalists, teachers, and students who gathered there vigorously debated the possibilities for 'civil society,' using the English term.[1] Their approach to link Hinduism with civil society was embodied in the concept of gerakan social jalur agama (social movements through the channel of religion). Social movements may be conducted with specific objectives in mind, but their activities inevitably remain limited to people associated with or interested in those objectives. In the Hindu-majority society of Bali, arousing a sense of brotherhood by appealing to the common ground of religion was a means of calling attention to social problems shared by everyone. Members of Pemuda Hindu believed that by using the 'channel' of religion, they could gain a broader understanding of the significance of their endeavors among the public.[2]

The avowed objective of Pemuda Hindu in seeking the reform of Parisada was 'democratic Hinduism,' which derived from the group's concern with realizing a civil society. The aim was to transform Parisada into a more open organization by expanding rights of representation to people who had previously been denied a voice at Parisada conferences. Pemuda Hindu succeeded in mobilizing groups with utterly disparate attributes, ranging from religious entities with a worldwide presence like Sai Baba and Hare Krishna devotees to local Balinese title groups. The criticisms leveled by these groups also varied in character, from personal circumstances to views about communities, the state, or history. Pemuda Hindu demanded that Parisada take up these diverse issues for consideration instead of dismissing them out of hand, a point of contention that led to the schism.

In this chapter, I do not wish to focus solely on the fact that groups with the word 'Hindu' in their name engaged in advocacy for civil society or democracy, nor do I intend to cite the activities of Pemuda Hindu as indicative of a reformation of Indonesian Hinduism, even if such advocacy was a discourse emblematic of the era of reformasi (reform) that followed the collapse of the Suharto regime in 1998. Further, I am not interested in arguing that certain religious groups have increased their political influence since emerging from their politically powerless state during the Suharto era. Instead, I want to examine the pluralization of values in the Hindu sphere that progressed to the point of causing a schism in Parisada. In actuality, Pemuda Hindu's activities alone would not have caused that schism, and the movement spread as widely as it did only because of the participation of numerous groups. Further, these groups did not unequivocally support the program of civil society and democratic Hinduism promoted by Pemuda Hindu. If anything, many groups espoused mutually contradictory demands and differing reasons for joining the movement initiated by Pemuda Hindu. As I clarify later, these groups' demands originated in such stances as criticism of the religious governance exercised jointly by Parisada and the state, criticism of communities in Bali, historical perceptions that dated back to the colonial era, and postcolonial perspectives that sought to overcome those perceptions. Though these groups joined together in response to a call for democratic Hinduism, they were a highly disparate agglomeration. Indeed, the reality is that Indonesian Hinduism is an arena that incorporates these disparate elements.

A Hindu framework that admits the participation of multiple groups espousing diverse values is by definition a discontinuous structure. Indonesian Hinduism extends across differences in class, living environment, and ethnicity—elite versus subaltern, urban versus rural, Balinese versus non-Balinese—for which reason 'Hindu' cannot be treated as a singular concept. The term can simultaneously refer to individual adherents, community practices, the policies of the state, groups, activists, and the religion that extends around the globe. The democratic Hinduism that advocates the attainment of a civil society is merely one element of Hinduism. In this sense, Hinduism in Indonesia is a sphere in which new relations are being formed as debate swirls around existing relationships among individuals, communities, state, law, and morality, while the boundaries separating them undergo redefinition.

In examining the pluralization of Hindu values in this chapter, I first look at how Hinduism came to be organized on a national scale, and then elucidate the facts about the Bali-centrism critique that emerged during this process. Next, I consider how the Bali Parisada schism occurred and identify the issues that triggered it. I also examine the backgrounds of the groups that endorsed the call for democratic Hinduism, as well as the demands they put forward. By focusing on two examples, I intend to illustrate the internal discontinuities of the democratic Hindu movement, with individual groups so disparate in character as to be mutually opposed. Finally, I focus on the reality of Hinduism as it incorporates these discontinuous elements and contemplate the state of its pluralizing values.

Deterritorialization and co-optation by the state

As I have mentioned, Balinese had been moving off the island since the era of the kingdoms, but during the colonial period, emigration to the cities of Java increased for work and study purposes. This was accompanied by the formation of mutual support groups among the emigrants. When Indonesia became a nation-state, Balinese society became a target of emigration policy by the government of the republic because the island had the highest population density in the country. This led to the growth of communities built by Balinese emigrants on other islands, particularly Sulawesi and Sumatra. One reason they were compelled to emigrate concerned Balinese society itself. Bali was unable to extricate itself from poverty until the 1970s, when the tourist industry began to thrive under the auspices of state-sponsored development. Poor living conditions were exacerbated by earthquakes and other natural disasters such as the 1963 eruption of Mount Agung, which devastated the east side of the island. Additionally, the population of non-Balinese Hindu Indonesians was growing, particularly after the massacres of 1965. With the expansion of Hinduism, Parisada expanded its jurisdiction to the point where Aceh is the only province today that does not have a regional Parisada branch (cf. Suryadinata et al. 2003).

The organization of Hindus scattered across the islands began to take concrete form in the mid-1980s in response to calls from the government. In September 1983, Keluarga Besar Mahasiswa Hindu Dharma, an association of Hindu Dharma students at Gadjah Mada University in Yogyakarta, hosted a seminar to celebrate the Balinese holiday of Galungan. The outcome was a resolution calling for the formation of a nationwide organization. This movement was linked to debate in the Majelis Permusyawaratan Rakyat, or MPR (People's Consultative Assembly), over a law on organisasi kemasyarakatan (public organizations), which was promulgated in 1985. Preparations began immediately, with a letter of intent sent on October 5, 1983, to Hindu leaders, primarily Parisada representatives throughout the country, calling on them to launch such an organization. The letter elaborated on the necessity of forming an organization in light of the MPR decision, which stated that it was essential to the nation's development to enhance the role of public organizations in various fields, to which end, it would be 'necessary to achieve and maintain a stable balance among organizations.'[3] Thus the MPR decision explicitly addressed the lack of a social organization by Hindus on the national level in contrast to the Islamic presence.[4]

The letter of intent began with a statement recognizing that Hindus living outside Bali now exceeded the number of Hindus in Bali. Of the two sets of statistics introduced at the beginning of this chapter, the figures compiled by the Hindus were thus taken as a given from the outset. The assertion of a need for a nationwide public organization was predicated on the following perception of the situation at that time. Hindu organizations, including Parisada, continued to be headquartered in Bali and retained a leadership structure in which only Balinese Hindus could participate. Parisada, moreover, functioned as a religious authority, so that even Bali lacked what could be called a true social organization. Also, while Hindus in various locales outside Bali had formed organizations that engaged in social activities, these groups were isolated and not in contact with one another. If this state of mutual isolation persisted, it would be impossible to nurture a generation of leaders with a national perspective, and Hindu organizational capacity would remain minimal. The result, clearly, would be the inability of Hindus to participate in decisions made by the MPR or, for that matter, in any forum for debate at the national level. Therefore, the letter concluded, there was no time to waste in forming a nationwide social organization of Hindus.

As a result of the circulation of the letter of intent, a preparatory meeting for the launch of an organization was held in Kaliurang, Yogyakarta, drawing 125 participants over two days, November 19 and 20, 1983. Participants included three representatives from each city in Java and Bali, and one representative per city elsewhere. A taskforce was formed to decide on the leadership, rules, and action policies of the organization. The new entity was named Perhimpunan Pemuda Hindu Indonesia (Indonesian Hindu Youth Association), officially abbreviated as the aforementioned Peradah, a name associated with the priest Peradah, a famous historical figure. The meeting had already secured the government's approval, and several government figures participated as advisors: Ida Bagus Mantra, the governor of Bali; Gde Puja, representing the Hindu department of the Religion Ministry, and Gusti Putu Raka, representing the Bali Regional Assembly.

The organization was defined as a religious group based on Hindu precepts, and observed both the religious order defined by the Pancasila and the national order. Applying Hindu terms, these two orders were referred to as Dharma Agama and Dharma Negara respectively, as I mentioned in Chapter 5. The juxtaposition of the two orders was a concept that had been articulated in the 1961 Campuan Charter, which clarified Parisada's character as both a representative body and a religious authority. The concept was further reinforced in 1984, when a Parisada priests' conference formally endorsed the Pancasila as the 'base (asas) of the nation.'[5] At the fifth general conference of Parisada in 1986, a resolution was passed affirming the importance of 'socializing and culturizing' the guidelines[6] established by the government for the purpose of disseminating the Pancasila. Parisada's official endorsement of the Pancasila thus occurred in parallel with the founding of Peradah (Parisada Hindu Dharma se Indonesia 1986: 31). Concerning its relationship to Parisada as a group, Peradah affirmed that while recognizing Parisada's religious authority, it would retain complete independence in its activities as an organization in the social sphere.

On March 10 and 11, 1984, coinciding with Nyepi, the Hindu New Year, Peradah representatives from various locales again gathered at the place where the preparatory meeting had been held, this time for a general conference or Maha Sabha, the same appellation used by Parisada for its meeting. The occasion marked the birth of the first nationwide social organization in the history of Hinduism in Indonesia. March 11 was the date when Sukarno had handed the reins of power to Suharto in 1966, effectively the birthday of the New Order. Peradah welcomed the opportunity to commemorate its founding on a day that represented a new point of departure for the New Order, which looked to the Pancasila and the 1945 Constitution for its authority. Thus, from the outset, Peradah was identified as a religious social organization established within the framework of the state order, which it staunchly supported. Its birth signaled that even as Hinduism became deterritorialized from Bali, the religion's relationship with the state would be reinforced by the advent of a nationwide organization.

However, efforts to establish this new organization, which seemed to be progressing so smoothly, encountered a problem immediately after the general conference, one that culminated in the schism that would have such a serious impact in the future. It was common practice among Hindu organizations, including Parisada, for leading participants in the preparatory stages of a new organization to serve as its inaugural executives. However, Wayan Sudhirta, a Jakarta representative on the five-member Peradah Executive Organizing Committee, resigned from the committee over dissatisfaction with procedures undertaken after the general conference. Efforts to prevent a split in the committee failed, and the ensuing turmoil resulted in the selection of new members. Peradah's Dewan Pimpinan Pusat (Central Leadership Board) finally convened on April 15, 1985. The board attacked Sudhirta as the instigator of the turmoil—calling him an egotist who lacked consideration for the public and, particularly, for the Hindu religion—even as it appealed to him to rejoin Peradah at the next general conference in the name of maintaining organizational unity. However, Sudhirta cut his ties with Peradah and launched a different organization. Thus a disturbance over personnel led to an organizational split that destroyed the dream of a unified social organization immediately upon its inauguration. The new group founded by Sudhirta was, in fact, the aforementioned Pemuda Hindu.

Peradah sought to neutralize Pemuda Hindu by securing the support of the government. It persuaded the Religion Ministry and the Ministry of Home Affairs, which had jurisdiction over social organizations, to authorize Peradah as the sole Hindu social organization.[7] Parisada also actively cooperated with Peradah. At its fifth general conference, Parisada recognized Peradah as the only Hindu social organization, and newspapers and other media were advised that Pemuda Hindu was an 'unofficial' entity. Additionally, Parisada twice issued notices[8] to its regional branches requesting that they set up Peradah organizations in each locale. For its part, Peradah finalized its articles of association on March 27, 1987, and completed its registration with Ministry of Home Afairs bureaus in each regency as a Hindu social organization established in accordance with 1985 Law No. 8.

However, despite the organized efforts of Peradah and its allies to suppress Pemuda Hindu, it did not disappear. On occasion, the group changed its name and continued its activities as a foundation.[9] Peradah published a detailed report, dated March 11, 1989, on the circumstances of its founding; the reason it felt compelled to reassert its legitimacy at that juncture by affirming its origins was precisely because it could not ignore the existence of Pemuda Hindu (Dewan Pimpinan Pusat Peradah Indonesia 1989). Antagonisms engendered by the unfortunate circumstances of their founding led to ongoing harassment and sabotage between the two groups. Then, on November 12, 2000, after the collapse of the Suharto regime, Pemuda Hindu announced its reinauguration at a gathering of representatives from seven provinces and 500 participants at the Aditya Jaya Temple in Jakarta. Known by the name of its locale, Rawamangun, it is Jakarta's largest temple and the center of Hindu worship in the capital. Representatives of the Parisada national headquarters and the Religion Ministry attended the reinauguration ceremony and, for the first time, Pemuda Hindu received the approval of the state agencies that had kept it at arm's length for so long. In this way, Indonesian Hinduism came to possess two official social organizations. In a document, Pemuda Hindu expressed its determination to reorganize and described the 'long years and bitter experiences' to which Peradah had subjected Pemuda Hindu as the result of exclusionary practices by a small elite—further, it declared that these practices did not consist of direct, physical sabotage so much as political disempowerment via bureaucratic agencies, and that this was nothing less than clear evidence of the totalitarian tyranny of the Suharto regime (Dewan Pimpinan Pusat Pemuda Hindu 2000).

In the 1990s, the organizing of Hindus on a nationwide level further accelerated as it moved beyond the confines of the youth group framework. In 1991 Parisada held its sixth general conference at a Hindu temple at Taman Mini, Jakarta. Immediately thereafter, on September 29, people dissatisfied with the results of the conference (which, in their view, showed that Parisada was incapable of ridding itself of Bali-centrism) convened at Rawamangun temple to organize the Forum Cendekiawan Hindu

Indonesia (Indonesia Hindu Intellectuals' Forum). Ninety-one participants from Jakarta, Bali, Bandung, and elsewhere set up a steering committee to launch the forum. The leader of the forum was steering committee chair Putu Setia, a journalist with *Tempo* (the most influential magazine in Indonesia) and a prominent Hindu polemicist. That Pemuda Hindu was able to sustain its activities in the face of Peradah's ostracism was largely because of the political activities in Bali of Sudhirta, its founder, alongside active new efforts in Jakarta by Setia, including establishment of the forum, which solidified the group's presence in the capital. Setia's activities were permitted due to his association with the critique of endemic Bali-centrism that originated in Jakarta and spread from there.

Setia eloquently made the case for the forum, describing the sort of organization that it was and why it was necessary (Setia 1993: 129–74). The name 'forum' was meant to convey that it was an open organization—not a group with rules and a membership roster, but an arena for expression in which anyone could participate, the presence of a steering committee notwithstanding. Moreover, the term 'intellectuals' in the title did not refer to people associated with academic pursuits or religious authority; rather, it meant people capable of discussing issues related to religion and society from a broad perspective. Anyone with that capability and a desire to express their views was welcome to participate, regardless of educational background, institutional affiliation, profession, ethnicity, social status, or gender. The ultimate objective of the forum was to provide a place for communication, for dialogue among Hindu adherents at the national level. To ensure freedom of expression, the forum explicitly maintained an independent stance of paying respect to all Hindu organizations, including Parisada, but cultivating special relationships with none.

Why, then, was a forum for dialogue or communication necessary? Setia cited three reasons. First, Hinduism was viewed as a religion exclusively practiced by Balinese living in Bali, ignoring the reality that Hindus could be found throughout Indonesia. Second, because Hinduism was treated as a religion confined to a specific region, it was not afforded equal status with other religions, and was consequently denied the opportunity to participate in interfaith dialogue or contribute to nation-building efforts deriving from that dialogue. Finally, because of these circumstances, the voice of Hinduism remained indistinct on the national level and unheard in the decision-making processes of the state. These arguments demonstrate that Setia's position was an extension of the debate that led to the birth of a social organization in 1983.

Furthermore, there were strong indications that these three issues had become generalized as part of a pattern of discrimination against Hinduism, and this in itself provided a powerful incentive for Setia to set up the forum. In other words, he perceived a trend toward the normalization of such accusations as follows: Hinduism was limited to Bali, where religious practices involved devil worship and the wholesale slaughter of animals. It was an out-of-date religion that perpetuated a premodern caste system. The Hindus practiced an impure faith inconceivable to Muslims, even allowing Besakih, allegedly their main temple, to become a tourist spot. On top of these accusations, Hindu objects of worship and other religious elements were being indiscriminately incorporated into consumer culture: the famous Tanah Lot Temple was used in automobile advertisements, and the *griya* and *puri* residences of priests and nobles appeared in housing subdivision advertisements. The proliferation of mass media exacerbated this tendency, so that the improper use of Hindu elements for commercial purposes had become widespread. Problems of this sort occurred because Hindu adherents had no voice at the state level, Setia argued, and this was precisely why a place—in other words, a forum—was needed where Hindus could gather on a national scale to discuss these real-world issues. Setia went on to cite specific social issues faced by Hindus that merited discussion, among them the elimination of poverty, the improvement of education, and the problem of bank interest.

Along with launching the forum, Setia also set out to publish media for Hindus throughout the nation. Up to that point, there had been only one national Hindu magazine, *Warta Hindu Dharma* (Hindu Dharma News), with content limited mostly to speeches by government officials. By contrast, Setia envisioned a publication that would report on actual activities undertaken by Hindus nationwide. He launched his new magazine, titled *Raditya* (Sun), in 1995. Initially, he had been unable to secure permission to publish a magazine, so it took the form of a book, with one volume issued every two months. Once he obtained permission, he began issuing it as a semimonthly magazine publication in a larger, more readable format.[10]

The movement to organize Hindus on a national scale that began in the 1980s, as described above, was brought into the maneuvering between religious organizations and the state. The Hindus who initiated the formation of a nationwide organization within the Pancasila policy framework were obedient supporters of the status quo. Indeed, both Peradah and Pemuda Hindu were quick to assert their allegiance to the Pancasila and the 1945 Constitution, and to speak of contributing to the nation. In that sense, the co-optation of Hinduism into the state was clearly successful. Conversely, however, this co-optation resulted in the organization of the Hindu voice in the social sphere on a national level. What is more, such organizing yielded unanticipated results. A dispute over personnel ended up splitting the organization itself, with one side attempting to suppress the other through the use of government institutions. This, in turn, spurred the marginalized Pemuda Hindu to become more combative and intensify its criticism of the power structure. Thus co-optation into the state simultaneously produced critics of it.

Pemuda Hindu did not explicitly declare a political countermovement as its objective as a group. The goals articulated in the platform it had approved in 2000 were exceedingly moderate. Pemuda Hindu identified itself as a group based first and foremost on the Pancasila and the 1945 Constitution, as well as 1985 Law No. 8. Its activities would include research and education on Hindu doctrine and history, production and distribution of publications summarizing such studies, training of religious instructors, and construction of Hindu centers. Nonetheless, Pemuda Hindu's activities in Bali had a pronounced political flavor. One reason was that the group's policies regarding its activities accommodated the characteristics of communities in Bali, as I explain later. Another reason, however, was the political stance of Pemuda Hindu's founder, Sudhirta. When he shifted the base of his activities from Jakarta to Bali, he began issuing explicit political critiques of the tyrannical power structure in Bali.[11] No longer a youth himself, Sudhirta distanced himself from Pemuda Hindu, but one of his admirers became the group's director in Bali. In fact, Sudhirta's personal office served as the Bali office of Pemuda Hindu. As his attacks on the provincial government increased, the view spread that he was merely venting personal grudges, with suspicions growing in some quarters that his ostensible goal of a civil society was merely a tool for that purpose. Many others, however, admired Sudhirta's courage in pursuing his activities under the despotic Suharto regime and viewed him as a heroic figure. As opinions diverged on his behavior, Pemuda Hindu's avowed objective of achieving a civil society could not be taken as a neutral position, and support for Pemuda Hindu remained limited.

Communities and Hindu representative bodies

Amid these initial moves toward organizing Hindus on a national scale, plans were made for a Loka Sabha (regular meeting) of Bali Parisada after the conclusion of the Parisada general conference in 1986. This was when disunion between Bali Parisada and the group as a whole first became apparent. Subsequently, the status of Parisada at the national level became a primary issue at the group's sixth general conference in 1991. This conference marked the point at which the organization's basic provisions were rewritten, and the statement, 'The center of Parisada shall be in Denpasar,' was replaced with, 'Parisada shall be located in Denpasar, but administrators of day-to-day operations shall be located in the capital of the Republic of Indonesia.'[12] Although the priests' section of the organization would remain based in Bali, this change affirmed that Parisada's activities would now take place on a national scale. The establishment of Parisada headquarters in Jakarta and the institutionalization of its presence there generated unprecedented tension between headquarters and the Balinese-dominated Bali branch of Parisada. Parisada headquarters was constantly on guard against Bali-centrism tendencies; for example, when candidates for an executive position included both Balinese and non-Balinese, priority was given to the latter. Meanwhile, Peradah reiterated that Hinduism was not synonymous with Balinese ethnicity, thus conclusively discarding the notion that Bali occupied a central place in the Hindu framework. Underlying this growing tension between Jakarta and Bali was the special relationship between Parisada and Balinese communities, which dated back to the group's origins in Balinese society.

From individual rites of passage to community temples, ceremonies play a significant role in the daily life of Balinese society. The procedures for those ceremonies, the status of the priests conducting them, the offerings submitted and how they are made, the means by which the labor power and material resources for carrying out ceremonies are mobilized— all is determined by custom. The term *adat* is used to describe customs administered under a single body of law, including the rules for marriage. A distinctive feature of Balinese society is the continuing function of communities known as *desa* that are identified with *adat*. During the colonial era, the government set up an administrative structure with non-*adat* administrative units at the bottom of the bureaucratic hierarchy, but *adat* did not disappear. Instead, a situation emerged in which *desa adat* (customary villages) coexisted with *desa dinas* (administrative villages), the word *dinas* deriving from a Dutch term for public administration. Even amid changes in village administrative policy on the part of the Indonesian government, autonomous *adat* domains persist, and, as of 2001, there were still nearly 1400 *desa adat* in Bali.

The problem as it pertains to organizing Hindus on the national level is that the representative body institutionalized in Parisada is dependent on the *desa adat* and has deeply internalized the regional characteristics of Bali. As mentioned, the institutionalization of Hinduism that led to the establishment of Parisada began in the 1930s—the decade when the colonial ruling order achieved completion—and solidified during the process of negotiations between the Religion Ministry and the Bali Regional Assembly in the 1950s. Although that process included contacts with Hindu adherents outside Bali, little heed was paid to their presence. Born as it was from Balinese society, Parisada is an organization built on Balinese customs and predicated on the existence of the *desa adat*. The result was that only a religious authority with priests at its center was institutionalized, while activities in the social sphere were delegated to the *desa adat*; hence, Parisada failed to organize a presence in that domain. Parisada retained authority over such duties as promulgating *Bhisama* (religious decisions) by the priests, carrying out ceremonies at Besakih and other public temples, and approving qualifications for priests and Hindu converts. However, it recognized the autonomy of *adat* in matters of religious doctrine and maintained a policy of minimal involvement in *adat*.

In the 1990s, Parisada's reliance on the *desa adat* became a target of criticism from both inside and outside Balinese society. In Bali the problem was quite simply Parisada's powerlessness. Despite the group's status as the representative body for Hinduism and the fact that Hindus constituted a majority in Bali, Parisada enjoyed only a tenuous presence on the island. In practice, this meant Parisada participated in virtually no activities in the village communities where custom was predominant; in everyday life, the organization was essentially invisible. Outside Bali, the issue that came to the fore was Parisada's lack of an organizational presence in the social sphere. Hinduism's presence in Indonesia was by no means uniform. Hindus were scattered across the big cities like Jakarta, but there were also regions where Hindus—notably emigrants from Bali—gathered to form communities of notable size. In neither case was any set of customs in place to provide a foundation at the outset, and, in that sense, the Balinese community model could not be applied outside Bali. Hindus outside Bali had to construct their own versions of the domains conceptualized as *adat* in Bali. Hindus in Jakarta, for example, formed separate associations to oversee such tasks as burials, religious education, and temple construction. As the Hindu population grew, so did the size of these entities.[13] Thus Hindus outside Bali could hardly be satisfied with the stance of Parisada, which remained silent on and oblivious to such concerns in the social sphere.

Parisada's status as a representative body structurally lacking in a social-sphere presence because of its reliance on customary practice was reflected in the split between Peradah and Pemuda Hindu, and in the differences in their activities. Whereas Pemuda Hindu was particularly active in Bali, Peradah was virtually inactive, yet maintained a solid, active presence in other provinces. Peradah avoided the political sphere and focused on moderate social activities, while Pemuda Hindu's activities in Bali had a pronounced political tinge, as mentioned earlier.

Chapter 6

The existence of communities that retained their own autonomy was a motivating factor in Pemuda Hindu's overtly political stance in Bali. The *desa adat* basically had no opportunity to engage directly in politics on the national level, and Pemuda Hindu saw itself as providing these communities with a conduit, independent of political parties, for making their voices heard and energy felt in the political arena. Peradah, conversely, was an organization established for the purpose of conducting activities in the social sphere, which it pursued outside Bali in regions where community influence was negligible. Furthermore, Peradah consciously chose not to engage with the political sphere, identifying itself as a social organization strictly within a religious framework. These differences not only highlighted the gap between the two entities, but also inspired Pemuda Hindu's attacks on Peradah. That is to say, Pemuda Hindu impugned Peradah's stance of separating politics from religion as nothing less than a state of political impotence that was the fate of an organization that had accepted the backing of the Suharto regime's bureaucratic apparatus.

Peradah did, indeed, function as an organizing entity in the social sphere, as can be seen, for example, in its activities in Jakarta. It formed a mutual support society for families, Keluarga Pemuda Suka-Duka Hindu Dharma, which had as its most prominent undertaking an annual family excursion in the suburbs during school holidays to take courses on Hinduism. Sporting events and smaller lectures were also held on a monthly basis. For members scattered across a wide area who communicated primarily by telephone and email, such events were an opportunity—as important as those offered by temple ceremonies and school activities—to study religion while deepening their relations with one another. In Bali, where customs were firmly established, there was no need for such a group.

With the establishment of a nationwide Hindu organization came the opportunity to survey and compare Hindu activities in different parts of the country. This made it possible to view Peradah as an entity on par with *adat* in Bali. Indeed, Putu Setia, the editor of *Raditya*, argued that aside from the fact that one could not quit *adat* of one's own volition, an organization like Peradah served the same function as *adat* in the social sphere (Setia 1993: 72). In Setia's view, *adat* no longer possessed any special prerogatives. Framing *adat* and Peradah in the same context in this manner engendered a critical perspective of the *adat* in Bali from Peradah's side (i.e. among Hindus outside Bali), and this was one more factor in the heightening tensions between Bali and Jakarta.

Overt criticism of the *desa adat* was a new development. Until this point, these communities had been seen as an unequivocally positive element of Balinese society, and the prevailing view was that their potential should be used to the maximum extent possible. The idea was that *desa adat* provided a paradigm for autonomous social organizations, and their latent strengths could be applied to the creation of a stable society that would ensure the maintenance of social order. This position is still largely endorsed today by the Ministry of Home Affairs and other state agencies, as well as the provincial government of Bali, all of which promote expansion of the functions of the *desa adat*. The legislative trend toward decentralization since the fall of the Suharto regime has also reinforced the effective powers of the *desa adat*.[14] It is against this background that criticism of the *desa adat* has arisen within the Hindu community.

The criticism includes several arguments. First, there are challenges to the assumption that *adat* is characterized by mutual assistance and social awareness. Specifically, the criticism is that *adat* in Bali is rooted in the conduct of religious ceremonies, and any mutual support system is limited to these ceremonies. Hence Balinese society is fundamentally lacking in social assistance in the conventional sense, and its social awareness is inadequate at best. It has even been asserted that the Balinese fulfill ceremony-related labor duties because they are otherwise fined— not because they share a commitment to mutual social aid—and that they are in fact the most individualistic people in Indonesia. Doubts have also been cast upon the true nature of the social order ostensibly maintained by the *desa adat*, with critics citing the difficulties involved in resolving problems between communities. In the past, the kingdoms adjudicated disputes beyond the purview of *adat* law or those arising between *desa adat*, but today no entity is explicitly authorized to handle that role. As a consequence, such issues are left unresolved, and even if order is maintained within the *desa adat*, it cannot be said to constitute maintenance of the larger social order. Inserting itself into this situation, Pemuda Hindu argued that insofar as *adat* came under the purview of religion, Parisada should play a role in resolving problems of this sort, but because of its uncritical reliance on the *desa adat*, it had failed to serve any such function. Pemuda Hindu's intervention in these matters was a strategic means to expand its influence in the villages and attract supporters who shared the same demands.

Criticism targeting the state of public safety and the behavior of autonomous guards in the *desa adat* has also been heard from outside the Hindu community. The Indonesian National Police encouraged the activities of such security forces, which had the closest contact with the daily life of the community, and relied on them to supplement the power of the police. But although these security forces might play an important role in the larger objective of maintaining order, leaving them unchecked did not necessarily yield desirable results, as they did not always behave fairly or within the bounds of the law. In fact, newspapers carried reports of '*adat* incidents' in the villages, referring to punishments, lynchings, and other actions deviating from proper police conduct. Citing these reports, critics warned of 'executions' carried out by communities and of the ever-present danger that security forces operating outside the framework of the law could be exploited by private interests (Connor and Vickers 2003: 173–8). These critics saw a potential for *desa adat* to become an independent domain in which the legal apparatus of the state could not intervene, and viewed the expansion of the powers of the *desa adat* as evidence of declining faith in the state order.[15]

The viewpoint that juxtaposed Peradah with the *desa adat* engendered a critique of Balinese society that went beyond *adat* alone. This critique, moreover, had a strong moral component, with elements of Peradah in Jakarta embracing a utopian image of Balinese emigrant society and condemning the 'fall' of society in Bali. A former director of Peradah elaborated as follows. The tourism industry that had brought such wealth to Bali depended on the large disparity in currency value between Indonesia and the advanced industrial nations that sent tourists there, such as Japan. An industry such as tourism reinforced what was in essence a subordinate, slave-like order. Furthermore, tourism was an unstable industry vulnerable to rumors, as Bali had experienced with economic crises and bombing incidents. Despite these obvious shortcomings, Balinese society continued to deepen its dependence on tourism and neglect the development of other industries or investment in other districts, becoming ever more specialized in this one industry at the expense of all others. Before the advent of the tourism industry, Bali had been an agrarian society centered around rice cultivation. To restore Bali to a 'healthy' state required nothing less than reverting to agricultural production. However, having tasted the nectar of foreign currency, returning to the farming life of the past was no longer possible for the Balinese. The most feasible option was export crop production. If the same amount of money invested in Nusa Dua, a state-sponsored tourist enclave developed in Bali, had been used to develop farms to grow export crops, it would have been possible to restore the farming industry. By contrast, Balinese emigrating from the island had developed farmland using Bali's unique agricultural techniques and had built their own agrarian societies. A prime example could be seen in the large community of Balinese in Lampung, Sumatra, where they had been compelled to move after the 1963 eruption of Mount Agung. The essence of Balinese society was no longer to be found in Bali, but in these emigrant communities.

The Peradah members who disseminated this argument belonged to a generation of Jakarta born elite employees of large corporations. Working in the high-rise office buildings that lined Sudirman Road, the major north–south artery in downtown Jakarta, they certainly had no interest in returning to life on the farm themselves. Yet these urban elites did not hesitate to mouth idealistic platitudes and criticisms of Bali. Their view of Bali was clearly disdainful and their critique one-sided. While it would be easy to condemn this irresponsible stance, Balinese society for its part was almost entirely lacking in a broader perspective on Indonesia that would permit disdain in return. In reality, criticism of the tourism industry that had created such success for Bali was rarely heard in Bali itself. An environment conducive to criticism of their fellow Hindus in Bali by Hindus outside the island now pervaded Indonesian Hinduism. This criticism, moreover, extended to moral condemnation of the Balinese in Bali for having lost sight of their own Balinese nature.

A schism in religious authority

The tension between Hindus nationwide and Hindus in Bali revealed itself in Balinese society in an astonishing way: a schism in Parisada in Bali, the province that was the birthplace of the organization. Parisada convened its eighth general conference in Sanur from September 20 to 24, 2001. In keeping with a practice it had maintained since 1986, as mentioned earlier, the Bali branch of Parisada followed the conference with its fourth regular meeting on November 23 of the same year in Campuan. At this meeting, the decisions of the general conference—supposedly representing policy for all of Parisada—were rejected, with decisions made at the previous (seventh) general conference in Surakarta cited as grounds for the stance taken at the regular meeting. Parisada headquarters responded by denying the legitimacy of the Campuan meeting, and on March 29, 2002, held a new fourth regular meeting at Besakih Temple.

The events that transpired between the eighth general conference and the second of the two regular meetings can be described as a dispute between Hindus on the national level and a faction of Hindus in Bali. Though the eighth general conference was held in Bali, its decisions reflected the views of Hindus on the national level.

The conference was preceded by seminars in Denpasar, Palu, Medan, and Jakarta. These places were selected for their accessibility to large Hindu populations, the purpose being to hear the opinions of Hindus in each region and give them a voice at the general conference. The policy of listening to the views of Hindus nationwide was promoted by the Parisada headquarters director elected at the seventh general conference, as well as supporters of Pemuda Hindu, who also organized the seminars. In response to the seminars, participants in the eighth general conference debated—and ultimately incorporated into their decisions—two groundbreaking measures that represented a departure from previous conferences, including the seventh. The first was a decision to select the leader of Parisada from its secular membership, not from the priesthood as before. The second was a decision to recognize religious groups, notably the Sai Baba and Hare Krishna movement, as 'Hindu-type groups'[16] and grant them voting rights. These decisions were the trigger for the planning of the Campuan meeting by a number of participants from Bali who felt increasingly alienated from Parisada headquarters.

The Campuan meeting was essentially planned in secret, with no preparatory committee or meetings. When Parisada headquarters learned of the plan, it appointed a coordinating committee to serve as a conduit for dialogue. Parisada headquarters requested that the Campuan meeting organizers expand the preparatory process to include all of Bali Parisada, and that they modify the agenda to conform to the decisions made by the general conference. The coordination effort broke down, however, and Parisada headquarters ultimately left the outcome in the hands of the governor of Bali province, Dewa Beratha. It was customary for the provincial governor to deliver a speech at each regular meeting of the Bali branch of Parisada in his capacity as its patron. If the governor did not take part in this manner, the Campuan meeting would lose its legitimacy, and Parisada headquarters expected the governor to exercise his prerogative in this regard. Pemuda Hindu activists staged a sit-in at a provincial government building and awaited the governor's decision. The governor, while ultimately declining to play the role of patron, sent a representative to the Campuan meeting to deliver his speech in his stead, and this enabled the Campuan faction to assert that the meeting was in fact legitimate because the governor's speech had been delivered, albeit indirectly. The Campuan meeting observed the precedent of previous meetings—it summarized the activities of the past term of office, decided on a new operating framework and policies, and published a report—and, subsequently, the meeting organizers continued to refer to themselves as the Bali branch of Parisada and acquired a building to use as their own branch. Pemuda Hindu bitterly denounced the decision of the governor that led to this turn of events, and declared that Dewa Beratha was the first provincial governor to cause Parisada to split.

The Campuan meeting was unable to bring all factions together in Bali. From the outset, the Parisada offices in two regencies, Buleleng and Tabanan, sent no delegates to the meeting, and groups representing the three title groups of *Pasek*, *Pande*, and *Bhujangga* publicly rejected the decisions reached in the meeting. Meanwhile, organizers of the Campuan meeting sought to establish grounds for its legitimacy in the history of Parisada.

Indeed, this was why the meeting was held in a Campuan temple in the first place. Founded at the Udayana University Faculty of Letters in 1959, Parisada had issued a declaration at Campuan in 1961, as mentioned earlier. The Campuan Charter formally defined the character of the organization and initiated the compilation of the *Upadesa*, which would form the core of its religious teachings. The charter was adopted at the Gunung Lebah Temple in Campuan, and it was at this same temple, and on the same date, that the Campuan meeting convened forty years later in 2001. Ida Bagus Gde Doster, one of the very few surviving founders of Parisada, presented a detailed account of the history of Parisada since its beginnings to those present, followed by the provincial governor's speech (delivered by the proxy), which also reviewed Parisada's history. The chairman of the Campuan meeting was Cokorda Rai Sudharta, an editor of the *Upadesa* as a member of the India students group and right-hand man to Ida Bagus Mantra, the driving force behind the founding of Parisada. Finally, in addition to the usual subcommittees formed to discuss individual issues, a special subcommittee was established to affirm the Campuan Charter of 1961 as the basis for the present meeting and also to articulate a policy of 'returning to the origin' that applied to the subcommittees on religion, society, culture, and education.

This was not the first time that the Bali branch of Parisada had claimed a unique identity based on historical precedent at one of its regular meetings. The report of the second Bali Parisada regular meeting, held immediately after the 1991 Parisada general conference (at which the transfer of day-to-day operations to Jakarta had been decided), had declared that Bali was 'unique among regions' and therefore 'an exception,' and that it must be recognized as such by Parisada headquarters (Parisada Hindu Dharma Indonesia Propinsi Bali 1991: 59). This perception, which had percolated under the surface, now revealed itself in the split of Parisada.

After the Campuan meeting concluded, its organizers displayed an even more overtly confrontational stance. Ida Pedanda Gde Made Gunung, who had been the chief priest at the Campuan meeting, convened a conference in Denpasar on December 18, 2001, where he issued an official document rejecting the eighth general conference of Parisada.[17] Consisting of eight articles, the document began by reviewing the circumstances of

Parisada's founding. Then, in Article 6, it declared that the eighth general conference did not adhere to the decisions of the seventh conference, but instead betrayed the spirit and purpose of Parisada as articulated in the Campuan Charter of 1961; for this reason, Bali Parisada rejected the eighth conference. The Campuan faction then proceeded to engage in a propaganda campaign through handouts and emails, in which it claimed that the decisions of the eighth conference would destroy the traditions and customs of Bali, and that the decision to remove the priests as leaders of Parisada was harmful to priestly authority. Reaffirming that Bali was the source of Hinduism in Indonesia, the faction also declared its resolute rejection of voting rights for 'Hindu-type' groups. Furthermore, it appealed to Parisada branches outside Bali to hold a new general conference.

In the face of this unprecedented situation—an increasingly antagonistic attitude toward Parisada's top administrative ranks, including the rejection of their decisions, by a subordinate, provincial-level branch— Parisada headquarters was moved to act. On December 7, 2001, it reiterated its request for intervention by the governor of Bali, while coordinating committee members made the rounds of regency heads and police to explain that the Campuan meeting lacked legitimacy in its rejection of the Parisada general conference. Then, on February 20, 2002, the committee decided to hold a new regular meeting at Besakih Temple to bring the chaotic situation under control. A preparatory committee was formed on March 2 to plan the meeting, and on March 9 invitations were sent to all Parisada organizations in Bali province. The preparation process was intentionally open to everyone in Bali, including participants in the Campuan meeting.

The Campuan faction responded by planning a new action, a large-scale sacrificial ceremony, Wana Kretih, for the purpose of protecting the forests and other natural areas. The plan combined the calculated choice of an indigenous Balinese expression of concern for the environment with an opportunity to demonstrate the faction's legitimacy by displaying its capacity to perform religious ceremonies. Such a ceremony had never before been performed in Bali. The location chosen was Pura Luhur Batukaru, a temple on the slopes of Mount Batukaru that was in the most thickly forested environment of any temple in Bali, and the ceremony was announced on February 19 in the name of Bali Parisada, with Made Gunung as representative.

The coordination committee of Parisada headquarters took this decision as the final straw and, the next day, February 20, announced the convening of a new regular meeting at Besakih. The preparatory committee for the regular meeting fully understood the hidden agenda of the Campuan faction in organizing the ceremony: by getting the regency heads and *desa adat* leaders to attend, the faction could thwart the success of the regular meeting. The preparatory committee made continual appeals to the provincial governor, the regency heads, and the Parisada branches in each regency to secure their support. In response, the Campuan faction convened a meeting to plan the ceremony, demonstrating its determination to go through with it. Amid these maneuvers on both sides, a neutral position was no longer viable, and the Parisada branches in each regency were compelled to choose between the two. The preparatory committee for the Besakih meeting requested that invitees confirm by March 16 whether they would attend the meeting. The Parisada branches in Gianyar, Klungkung, Badung, and Denpasar did not respond, indicating their rejection of the meeting. Thus it became apparent that the schism in Bali Parisada extended to the regency level, the lowest organizational tier in Parisada.

Whatever their personal political views, the provincial governor and regency heads had no choice but to deny the legitimacy of the Campuan meeting because of its rejection of the decisions of the general conference. The villages in charge of the management of Besakih approved the holding of the new regular meeting there, and plans for the meeting moved forward (Parisada Hindu Dharma Indonesia Propinsi Bali 2002: 41–4).[18] In the end, the provincial governor delivered a speech, and all the regencies, except for Badung, sent representatives. Meanwhile, preparations for the Campuan faction's ceremony at Luhur Temple began on March 1, climaxed with the sacrificial rite held on March 29, and concluded on April 2. The climax of the ceremony coincided precisely with the day of the meeting at Besakih; thus, on March 29, 2002, Bali Parisada split completely in two, with one side at Besakih Temple on Mount Agung to the east and the other at Luhur Temple on Mount Batukaru to the west (Figure 6.1). The

Figure 6.1
A cartoon published in the magazine
Raditya satirizing the split in Bali Parisada,
showing the Besakih faction on the left
and the Campuan faction on the right.
The man at the bottom is saying,
'Make up your mind by yourself...'
(*Raditya* 2002, no. 58, p. 3)

consternation of the *desa adat* leaders who received invitations to both the ceremony and the meeting was incalculable, but the entities most torn by the schism were the Bali provincial government and the various regencies. The governor, who had approved the Besakih meeting, also appointed the members of the executive committee who carried out the ceremony at Luhur Temple, and the province and regencies all donated funds to both the ceremony and the Besakih meeting.[19]

If we compare the actual size of the two competing events, we find that registered participants at the Besakih meeting numbered 106 with voting rights and 118 without. Only 125 *desa adat* out of an official count of 1398 responded to the invitation to participate, and Besakih organizers acknowledged that not all respondents had actually sent representatives. In comparison, seventy priests and 400 *desa adat* representatives participated in the Campuan meeting. Thus the Campuan faction's plan to set up a ceremony in opposition to the Besakih meeting could be viewed as successful. However, the executive committee of the Besakih meeting reported that between 5000 and 10,000 people came to Besakih on the day of the meeting to offer prayers for its success, and asserted that the Besakih meeting clearly drew more participants and enjoyed greater public support (Dwikora 2002). By 2003 the split in Parisada was common knowledge in Bali. It became normal to refer to Parisada Campuan and Parisada Besakih, and the representative body of Indonesia Hinduism became known as the Parisada Kembar (Twin Parisadas) in its own birthplace.

The process that culminated in the schism should be clear from the description above. Bali Parisada ultimately split into a Besakih faction and a Campuan faction, with the Besakih faction consisting of people who supported the decisions of the Parisada general conference. In this sense, it was not so much a division into two factions but a secession from Parisada's national presence by Parisada organizations in Badung, Gianyar, Klungkung, and Denpasar, with Ubud at the center. Throughout this process, Sudhirta and Pemuda Hindu played important roles. It was Sudhirta's office that handled preparations for the Besakih meeting, and the chairman of the meeting's executive committee was a leading member of Pemuda Hindu. Thus the process of organizing Hindus nationwide that began in 1983 set the stage for revolutionary changes in Parisada, the Hindu community's representative body and religious authority. In response, one might say, a faction of Balinese unwilling to tolerate Parisada's deterritorialization from Bali resisted this trend by retreating back into what they claimed to be Parisada's 'traditions.'

The positions of the two camps were clearly defined. Members of the Campuan faction saw themselves as guardians of Balinese tradition and defenders of the status of the priesthood and *adat*, and castigated the Besakih faction as the violator of tradition, custom, and authority. For their part, members of the Besakih faction identified themselves as reformers. The eighth general conference of Parisada, which they claimed as precedent, had approved an eight-item list of demands addressed to the government. The list began with an affirmation of the unstable conditions prevailing in Indonesia amid rapid changes in the world at large, changes that had been brought about by economic globalization and scientific and technological advances. The Besakih faction then went on to assert the necessity of building a good government based on fairness and the rule of law, renouncing the practice of resolving issues through physical violence exercised by the police and military, pursuing regional decentralization, recognizing diversity of thought in society, and raising tolerance and social awareness among Hindu adherents.[20] A declaration of this nature was unprecedented in the annals of Parisada, and its content was nothing short of revolutionary.

The eighth general conference was, indeed, emblematic of a period of reform in Indonesian Hinduism. I Gusti Agung Mayun Eman, chair of the executive committee, declared that the conference's resolutions were the outcome of the fierce debate that accompanied the advent of an era of genuine reform triggered by the fall of the Suharto regime, and that Parisada must become a representative body independent of 'a single political force'—in other words, the Suharto order (Parisada Hindu Dharma Indonesia Pusat 2001: 12). There was, in fact, a strong perception within the Besakih faction post-schism that remnants of that order had created the Campuan faction. The people who had monopolized the administration of Parisada up to this point had connections to the Suharto order, and the epithet the Besakih faction used to describe the Campuan faction was 'feudalistic conservatives'; they accused a small number of individuals centered around the royal family in Ubud, which had profited from its associations with the Suharto regime, of rejecting the general conference to protect their own interests (Parisada Hindu Dharma Indonesia Propinsi Bali 2002: 2).

However, it cannot really be said that the Campuan faction was universally conservative. Made Gunung, the chief priest, was an activist who took to heart criticisms that Parisada should address the everyday problems people faced, and tirelessly worked for reform. After the sacrificial ceremony, he took the initiative to make time for speeches about the meaning of the ceremony and its significance to people's lives. Above all, his use of television in these activities made him a household name throughout Bali. In 2002 the Bali Post company launched its own television station, Bali TV. The station devoted considerable hours to religion in its programming, inviting prominent priests to speak about ceremonies, lifestyles, and other topics. Made Gunung made frequent appearances on these programs and drew a sizable audience with his easily comprehended and never-boring chats. Moreover, both the television station and the Bali Post company sold recordings of programs on which he appeared. In his utilization of the media, Made Gunung was an entirely new type of priest.

Be that as it may, many supporters of the Campuan faction were, in fact, economic beneficiaries of the Suharto regime. The salient example was the town of Ubud, which had grown as a tourist destination. What made Ubud different from other districts of Bali was the close connection between the economic benefits accruing from tourism and a social hierarchy dominated by the royal family at the top. Ever since Cokorda Gede Raka Sukawati rose to the pinnacle of the colonial elite, and in spite of ongoing internecine strife, the Ubud royal family profited from the tourism industry by exploiting Ubud's reputation as an 'art village.' As a result, Ubud is one of the most intensely hierarchy-conscious places in Bali. Furthermore, Campuan belongs to the Ubud royal family, and participants from Ubud were accorded special deference at the Campuan meeting. The 'tradition' espoused by the Campuan faction may be viewed as a crucial component of the symbolic capital that yields profits from the tourist industry, and, in point of fact, the Parisada branches that supported the Campuan meeting all belonged to districts with a high concentration of income from tourism.

Democratic Hinduism (1): Hindu-type groups

The Besakih meeting organizers, with Pemuda Hindu members at their core, were unable to prevent the Campuan meeting, but they did succeed in holding a new regular meeting. Two major factors contributed to this accomplishment: the legitimacy conferred by adherence to the decisions of the general conference, and the ability to mobilize Hindu-type and title groups in the name of democratic Hinduism. The democratic Hindu stance of denouncing, and calling for correction of, the inequities permitted by Hindu organizations had tremendous appeal for people who had historically been denied legitimacy by Parisada. These included members of religious organizations that belonged to international networks on the one hand and, on the other, local title groups whose status was of no significance outside Bali. Democratic Hinduism promised a voice for both of these utterly disparate groups.

At Parisada's general conferences and regional regular meetings, those in attendance were classified as either peserta (participants) or peninjau (observers), with only participants allowed to vote. The eighth general conference of Parisada granted participant status to groups recognized as belonging to a newly defined framework of 'Hindu-type' (yang bernafaskan Hindu, which can be translated as 'Hindu in essence') groups.[21] Representatives of Hindu-type groups had participated in the seventh general conference, but Bali Parisada, in particular, tended to treat them as Hindu Kelas Dua (second-class Hindus). The question of whether to legitimize their status and grant them voting rights was an issue debated among Hindus nationwide during the 1990s.

The two most visibly active Hindu-type groups were the Sai Baba and Hare Krishna organizations. A famous Hare Krishna guru visited Jakarta in 1973, and the group began engaging in organized activities around 1979. Its primary activities consisted of holding study meetings every Sunday to read the Hindu scriptures known as *weda*. Although the group's activities were banned for a time, it regained permission to function as a group after the collapse of the Suharto regime.[22] The heart of the Hare Krishna *weda* is the Bhagavad Gita, the official Indonesian translation of which was published in 1985 with an initial print run of 1000 copies. This grew steadily to a print run of 1500 copies in 1989, 2000 in 1995, 3000 in 1999, and 10,000 in 2000. The group is notable for stressing its compatibility with science, explaining that spiritual exploration is a natural aspect of the scientific age and that such exploration itself is a scientific undertaking. With a global presence, the Hare Krishna movement has a head office designated for each region. Indonesia is under the jurisdiction of the Tokyo office, so the materials it uses in its activities are sent from Tokyo.

The Sai Baba movement prioritizes not only scriptures, but also social activities. When a branch appeared in Jakarta in 1981, the Religion Ministry conducted an inspection (which the group protested) that ultimately led to its recognition as a religion. Acceptance of the group was facilitated when a senior member of Parisada became an adherent.[23] The group was first introduced into Bali around 1983; by 2003 it had 10,000 members and had built centers in thirty-three locations across the island. Placing emphasis on both social and spiritual activities, it promoted education and regularly organized meetings and discussion groups.

The Sai Baba centers did not look at all like Balinese temples. Upon entering one such building in Denpasar, for example, one was greeted at the entrance by a statue of Ganesh, and a portrait of Sai Baba hung on the facing wall. A Balinese temple sat next door, but this too contained a portrait of Sai Baba. Meetings began with a simple prayer, followed by a discussion on a predetermined theme. The leading members sat in the center facing the officiant, with rank-and-file devotees on the periphery. Referring to distributed materials, an officiant explained the reason for the choice of the meeting's theme and introduced the content of the discussion. Passing a microphone around, devotees—both men and women—were encouraged to talk about their personal experiences and share their own views about the theme, to which the officiant or one of the leading members would respond. The discussion would proceed in this format, ending with a prayer, some yoga, and a closing ceremony using fire. Whereas the Hare Krishna movement emphasized scriptural study, the Sai Baba movement focused on the sharing of individual experiences among participants. Opportunities to converse about one's personal experiences in this manner were a rarity in the public sphere in Bali.

As both the Sai Baba and Hare Krishna groups expanded during the 1980s, they shared obvious points in common in relation to Balinese society. Both were entirely new presences in the Balinese religious sphere, with its strong emphasis on texts, the priesthood, and ceremonies. In contrast with the custom-based communities of Bali, they displayed a pronounced individualist bent, stressing equality and rejecting hierarchy among their members. Participants in both groups joined of their own accord, as opposed to finding themselves in a pre-existing community owing to the circumstances of their birth. Though members of the two groups shared a sense of distance from their communities engendered by their religious consciousness, the degree of distance differed. Whereas the Hare Krishna adherents generally severed their ties with traditional customs, the Sai Baba adherents did not go so far. This difference was a function of relative degrees of emphasis on 'returning to the scriptures.' Hare Krishna devotees, who called for a return to the Bhagavad Gita, rarely participated in ceremonies in their home villages. Sai Baba devotees, however, continued to participate in village ceremonies.

This distinction was actually a source of criticism harbored against the Sai Baba group by the Hare Krishna group, although it was not made public. From the Hare Krishna viewpoint, the Sai Baba movement was nothing more than a personality cult that allowed for compromise with the communities and lacked a commitment to return to the scriptures—for one thing, the name Sai Baba did not appear anywhere in the Bhagavad Gita. Yet, even as they kept their distance from the communities, Hare Krishna adherents did not dismiss the significance of Bali itself as an environment. In the early 2000s, a director of Hare Krishna, who teaches at a university in Bali, stated that while studying at university in Surabaya, he decided to join the Hare Krishna movement because, whereas Islam encouraged earnest debate about personal spirituality, no such opportunity existed in Bali. Nonetheless, he became a teacher in Bali in order to live there, not because there happened to be a job available. For a Hindu, the environment of Bali is something impossible to duplicate elsewhere in Indonesia, and he chose to live in Bali even if it meant severing his ties with his home village.

Past research on Hinduism focusing on Bali has ignored the existence of these Hindu-type groups. An exception is Howe's (2001: 138–98) study, which devotes separate chapters to discussions of Sai Baba and Hare Krishna. Until the eighth general conference, Parisada, if anything, suppressed these Hindu-type groups. Howe's research, conducted during this period, makes clear the antipathy between the two entities. For Parisada, one negative aspect of the Hindu-type groups was participants' self-distancing from Balinese customs. Additionally, recognizing these influential groups that claimed to be Hindu would mean permitting the existence of organizations that might well emerge as rivals of Parisada in the Hindu sphere. However, the Hindu-type groups, which sought government approval, acknowledged the authority of Parisada. They accepted the tenets of Parisada and the Pancasila, and stressed their adherence to Hindu teachings and the preeminence of the *weda*. Yet, at the same time, there was unquestionable frustration with Parisada on the Sai Baba and Hare Krishna sides. According to Howe, this dissatisfaction centered around differing views on the inner life of the individual. Whereas both the Hindu-type groups attached great importance to the inner life, Parisada teachings substituted for this the abstract concept of kerohanian (spirituality), which group adherents found utterly inadequate. Where the Hindu-type groups were concerned, Parisada was an entity that not only suppressed them as groups, but also forced them to acquiesce to unsatisfactory teachings.

Howe (2001) goes on to say that both the Sai Baba and Hare Krishna groups held critical views of the communitarianism at the foundation of Balinese customs; an interview with a member makes it clear that severe criticism could be found even within the Sai Baba group, which tolerated customary ceremonies. It was characteristic of the group to urge the reform of customs rather than to reject them outright; in this sense, it did not refuse to participate in ceremonies. Conversely, the Sai Baba group aspired to put its critique against communitarianism into practice onsite at community ceremonies. The group's Bali critique, as described by Howe, was wide-ranging in content, extending from the status of the priesthood prioritized by Parisada to religious education and the significance of customs. The priests, it argued, cared only about carrying out ceremonies correctly, and never actually addressed real religious issues. Meanwhile, people felt compelled to request ceremonies at the priests' asking price to avoid harming their relations with the priests; in this sense, the priests were simply in the business of selling ceremonies. As for religious education, the group claimed that instructors would teach doctrine in the classroom, then leave school and go out gambling. In other words, religious education was just a job for them, and their instruction was fraught with hypocrisy and deceit. Finally, Balinese customs ultimately did nothing more than shackle people with the chains of caste, authority, offerings, and male chauvinism. Howe adds that these critiques were not in themselves motives for religious conversion, but rather part of an awareness that deepened after conversion. The reasons that people joined Sai Baba were diverse, ranging from persuasion by an acquaintance to a desire to heal an illness or an attempt to exorcize demons. In any event, there is no question that Sai Baba members viewed Parisada critically for its reliance on the communities.[24]

The fact that a number of prolific writers on religious issues were Sai Baba adherents may be viewed as a direct consequence of their desire for reform. It is also an indication that Sai Baba was already a presence that could not be ignored. Ketut Wiana, a regular columnist for the *Bali*

Post, and Wayan Jendra, a published author who lectured at Udayana University, are notable examples of polemicists who were publicly recognized as Sai Baba members. Both writers faithfully attended Sai Baba meetings and regularly engaged in dialogue with other participants. They also actively proselytized for Sai Baba. A portrait of Sai Baba adorned the door of Wiana's residence, while Jendra owned a small bookshop where he sold not only his own works, but also pictures of Sai Baba, cassette tapes featuring the guru's voice, and related books. Wiana was active in Parisada headquarters and worked closely with Pemuda Hindu to organize seminars at four locations prior to the eighth general conference. Thus the democratic Hindu movement played a significant role in obtaining official recognition of voting rights in Parisada for Hindu-type groups that had a history of being suppressed.

Democratic Hinduism (2): title groups

The mobilization of the *Pasek*, the largest of the title groups that supported calls for democratic Hinduism, was a major factor in the success of the Desakih meeting. I Made Artha, who was elected to head Bali Parisada at the meeting, was the leader of an all-Bali group representing the *Pasek*, which is discussed later. To understand why the title groups expanded and grew more active requires an understanding of the cultural factors associated with titles, and the historical perceptions that gave rise to the political sensibilities of these groups.

Titles in Bali are many. Priests and members of royal and other families associated with the former kingdoms employed titles to display their status, while titles were also used to indicate roles in village society. The *Pasek* were one of the latter village titles. Specific 'functional groups' also had their own titles, a prominent example being the title *Pande*, given to members of a group employed as blacksmiths. In the now-classic kinship study by Hildred and Clifford Geertz, titles are treated as an important object of analysis; the authors focus primarily on the relation to social status and conclude that possession or lack of a title, as well as the type of title, indicates one's place in the social hierarchy, and that social status correlates to the scale of the ceremonies conducted by a title group (Geertz and Geertz 1975). In Balinese society today, the notion that people bearing high-status titles automatically deserve respect is already on the wane. In contemporary workplaces, where people with high-status titles and those without titles work side by side, any emphasis on titles or status would only seem anachronistic. Despite this, titles remain meaningful in Balinese society and title groups continue to grow because of the association of titles with cultural factors other than status.

The concept of origin indicated by the word *kawitan* is described by Geertz and Geertz (1975: 64) as an 'ideology' shared among the Balinese. *Kawitan* means both 'origin-point' and 'origin-group.' The former refers to both a historical point of origin (one's ancestral progenitor), as well as a geographic point (the temple where one worships one's ancestors). The lineage so defined is basically patrilineal. Kinship is based on this concept, as are titles and their inheritance; indeed, title groups may be regarded as an extension of kinship groups. Further, behind the growth of title groups is the culturally accepted notion that the recognition of *kawitan* is subject to error or forgetting. In other words, 'no need is felt for the specification of a genealogical line of men linking the present members to the founding ancestors, as a charter for their legitimate membership in the origin-group' (Geertz and Geertz 1975: 64). This is because it is commonly accepted that such connections may be forgotten with the passage of generations, so that the lack of an ancestral deity or the worship of the wrong deity on the part of the current generation is the result of such forgetting. Since no concrete genealogy is required, it is possible to 'regain' a lost title, and this is what enables title groups to grow.

The actual process of regaining a title is carried out through ceremonies. In the example cited by Geertz and Geertz (1975: 77–82), the head of a family consults with a medium to ascertain the cause of a series of misfortunes befalling his family or kinship group, and is told that it is due to an erroneous origin, whereupon the entire kinship group changes its affiliation to what is indicated as its true origin. Similar cases continue to occur today, as I witnessed firsthand. After a series of misfortunes, members of a kinship group lacking a designated origin would begin to discuss the possibility that the group had neglected its origin-deity. Whereas the misfortunes in the example described by Geertz and Geertz are illness and 'ineradicable poverty,' those in the cases I witnessed involved not only illness, but also such problems as refusal by a middle-school-aged child to attend school. Discussion was accompanied by the search for a remedy; leaders of the kinship group would visit mediums in various locales, describe their recollections of family ancestors, and inquire who their true ancestors might be. The voices of the mediums were recorded whenever possible and played back at a meeting of the kinship group amid debate over the validity or legitimacy of their pronouncements. If consensus was reached, kinship group members would visit the title group in charge of the origin-temple of the indicated ancestral deity, describe the process that had transpired, and express their desire to join the title group. The title group would employ its own methods to evaluate the request; if approved, the kinship group would be allowed to adopt that title. This also meant that members of the kinship group would be obligated to participate in ceremonies dedicated to the ancestral deity.

All these cases are characterized by a process in which an illness or some other form of personal suffering comes to be perceived as a problem for an entire title group. The primary factor in this process is the perceived link between the physical body and ancestors via the *kawitan*. A human being consists of both body and soul, and the soul returns from one's ancestors. Any abnormal condition of the body is caused by the separation of the soul from the body and requires, first and foremost, that the soul be restored to it. When troubles befall an individual, they are believed to be caused by neglect of the ancestral deities and the appropriate rituals. Individuals and ancestors are connected through the relationship between body and soul; thus the suffering of the individual is treated not as a problem confined to the personal sphere, but as belonging to the much broader social sphere. Geertz and Geertz (1975: 78) view this linking of ancestors, soul, and body as a process that solves problems of both a psychological and sociological nature, and present it as evidence of the 'flexibility' of cultural conceptions in Bali.

The title groups that Geertz and Geertz discussed in general terms of psychology, sociology, and culture (based on their research in the 1950s) subsequently grew into an actual movement as they extended beyond village society, but the groups did not all expand under the same conditions. For example, the title *Pande* (associated with the occupation of blacksmithing) was an unusual case in that members had to use special altars at kinship-group temples and observe restrictions on which priests they could use for ceremonies. A title group of this sort had relatively little potential for expansion. The *Pasek*, by contrast, had few restrictions, and expanded throughout Bali. I Made Artha, who was elected head of Bali Parisada at the Besakih meeting, was leader of the *Pasek* title group Maha Gotra Pasek Sanak Sapta Rsi. The *Pande*, too, formed a group, Maha Semaya Warga Pande, that unified its local groups.

The primary reason that the *Pasek*, *Pande*, and *Bhujangga* title groups participated in Parisada Besakih was their shared desire for decolonization. During the colonial era, as described in Chapter 1, the government used titles for political purposes to establish a ruling order. The government determined that because Bali was a Hindu society, its ruling order must be built upon the caste system, which was an essential part of Hinduism, and it viewed titles as indicative of status in this hierarchy. The colonial government relied on titles to identify members of the *triwangsa* (three groups)—which consisted of the three classes of *brahmana*, *satria*, and *wesia* that had underpinned the monarchic order—and defined people without titles appended to their names as *sudra*, or commoners (*jaba* in Balinese). Classification by title did not merely indicate class differences but sustained a substantively discriminatory social structure. Titles recognized as belonging to the *triwangsa* enjoyed special protections, including the right to exemption from forced labor, while the *jaba* were subject to restrictions even in the sphere of religious custom—the number of tiers permitted in a cremation tower, for example. When the caste system grew more fluid with the collapse of the colonial order, title groups of people who had been classified as *jaba* began to grow. The title groups that came together at the Besakih meeting had all begun organizing in the 1950s after Bali joined the Republic of Indonesia. The initial motivation for people organizing these groups was to regain their honor by eradicating the low status imposed upon them. Underlying this desire to restore honor was intense criticism aimed at the *triwangsa*, who had been granted special privileges during the colonial era.

This criticism was brought into sharp relief through activities centering around Made Kembar Kerepun, adviser to the *Pande* title group, prior to the Campuan meeting.[25] On November 21, 2001, just before the meeting, Kerepun published a document, titled 'Is the Parisada regular meeting a meeting of certain kinship groups?' In it, he fiercely denounced the Campuan gathering, declaring that it not only ignored the decisions of the Parisada general conference, but was also undemocratic and entirely closed to the Hindus of Bali. He went on to analyze the roster of patrons and executive committee members listed as organizers of the meeting, and revealed that the list was dominated by people with *triwangsa* titles. Finally, Kerepun asserted that the conflicts between nobility and commoners fomented by the colonial era caste system had been 'revived on a larger scale and in a more dangerous form.' This document was sent to the provincial government and religious leaders and distributed to Pemuda Hindu members who were staging a sit-in at the governor's residence to call for a halt to the Campuan meeting. In addition to this written attack, Kerepun met directly with the governor and urged him to forgo attending, let alone speaking at, the Campuan meeting.[26]

For Kerepun, decolonialization meant the defeat of the *triwangsa*. The class was unequivocally a minority, comprising less than one-tenth of the population. It had been able to exercise its authority during the colonial era only because the *jaba* had remained divided and disorganized. If individual *jaba* title groups organized and allied with one another, he believed, the minority *triwangsa* had no chance of winning. That process was already taking place in the villages, where the *triwangsa* were rapidly losing their authority, and the gathering of the title groups at the Besakih meeting was clear proof that this was occurring throughout Bali. Kerepun saw the Campuan meeting as the last gasp of the minority *triwangsa*, the final stage of the decolonialization process.

Another reason for the emergence of this decolonizing impulse was the problem of implementation rights for Besakih Temple ceremonies. As mentioned in Chapter 5, after a major ceremony at Besakih in 1979 was judged to be insufficient, it was followed by even larger ceremonies in 1993 and 1996. Meanwhile, another major ceremony regularly held every ten years took place in 1989 and 1999. The result was that ceremonies at Besakih were held more frequently, and on a larger scale, in the 1990s than in any other decade of the twentieth century. The problem of implementation rights refers to the question of which priests carry out the sacrificial rites that are the climax of these ceremonies. Until this point, priests of the *Pasek*, *Pande*, and *Bhujangga* title groups were not permitted to participate in such rituals.[27] These three groups, in particular, asserted that the monopolization of implementation rights by a few priests was undemocratic, and that such rights should be extended to all priests on an equal basis. This demand, known as *Sarwa Sadaka* (all the priests), was first raised at the time of the 1989 ceremony, but the 1999 Panca Walikrama, held after the fall of the Suharto regime, was the first ceremony where it was adopted. As the *Pande* representative, Kerepun was a pivotal figure in this movement.

The provincial government controlled the finances for the major ceremonies at Besakih, so ultimate authority was in the hands of the governor. In 1989 the government acknowledged the demands of the *Sarwa Sadaka* movement, but did not take concrete steps to adopt them on the grounds that there was too little time before the actual ceremony. Kerepun saw this as a devious strategy by the governor to preserve the status quo, and in February 1999 he displayed an unyielding stance. On February 16, he met with Dewa Beratha, the first provincial governor of the post-Suharto era, and told him that whether he accepted the long-unresolved *Sarwa Sadaka* demands would be a 'major test' for him as the first governor in the new era. He then urged him to convene a meeting at Besakih to discuss the issue. As a champion of democratic Hinduism, Pemuda Hindu immediately announced its support, signaling the start of a joint struggle by Kerepun and Pemuda Hindu against the governor. The religious group Forum Penyadaran Dharma, led by I Gusti Ngurah Bagus, professor emeritus of anthropology at Udayana University, also declared its support for Kerepun, and a meeting was convened on March 4. In attendance were representatives of the *Pasek* and *Pande* title groups, leaders of the villages in charge of administering Besakih, members of the ceremony executive committee, and the provincial governor. The upshot of the meeting was that *Pasek* and *Pande* priests were granted the right to conduct ceremonies in 1999.

Enforcement of this decision, however, did not proceed smoothly. A regular ceremony, the Bhatara Turun Kabeh, was also held annually at Besakih. It was an important event that gathered together the deities of public temples belonging to Besakih. The Bhatara Turun Kabeh held after the 1999 Panca Walikrama followed traditional procedures, with *Pande* priests not allowed to participate. Prior to the Bhatara Turun Kabeh of 2001, Kerepun took action once again, with the provincial governor as his target, and demanded that the governor abide by his own previous pronouncements and reaffirm the principle of *Sarwa Sadaka*. On March 21, the governor publicly announced the use of all priests, cementing a policy under which *Pande* priests would participate in that year's Bhatara Turun Kabeh, and all priests would participate from the preparatory stages of ceremonies beginning in 2002.

In practice, it was no simple task to alter the procedures for carrying out these ceremonies. The power to create holy water, the most important element of the ceremonies, lay with the priests, and there was intense resistance to the adoption of *Sarwa Sadaka*, which would alter this arrangement. Certain priests overtly expressed their opposition to *Sarwa Sadaka*. However, opposition was not confined to the priests; there was a general belief that ceremony procedures were based on the traditional customs of Besakih Temple, as well as apprehension that altering customary practices would deprive them of their potency and cause unforeseen calamity. Believing that opponents of *Sarwa Sadaka* were exploiting this apprehension, Kerepun rejected the fear of altering customs by once again citing historical precedent. The priests who had conducted Besakih ceremonies to date had been appointed after the introduction of Hindu ceremonial practices in Bali; according to Kerepun's understanding of history, ceremonies had been held at Besakih since before the arrival of Hindu practices, and the practitioners of those ceremonies were none other than priests of such lineages as the *Pasek*, *Pande*, and *Bhujangga*. This could be argued precisely because those groups consisted of indigenous Balinese whose ancestors had lived on Bali from the outset. In that sense, *Sarwa Sadaka* could be said to conform to the oldest Balinese customs. Hinduization was a discourse central to the construction of the Balinese view of history under the colonial order, and Kerepun's interpretation of history was an attempt to relativize that view. Furthermore, his interpretation generated another discourse, that of indigenous Balinese.

Hinduism and pluralizing values

Hinduism in Indonesia since the 1980s has been marked by discontinuity; for example, 1985 Law No. 8 was a manifestation of the state's desire to reinforce the stability of its order through the penetration of the Pancasila into the nation. With their lack of a nationwide social organization, Hindus were sensitive to this development from the outset of debate on the law in the MPR (People's Consultative Assembly), and initiated efforts to organize on a national level. Parisada formally adopted the Pancasila, demonstrating the extent of obedience by Hindus to the Suharto regime. However, the organizing of Hindus yielded a number of consequences, not all of them consistent with the intentions of the state. For example, while the penetration of the Pancasila represented aggressive intervention by the state in the domain of morality, it did not mean the government favored the organizing of Hindus at the national level. Though the impetus was the debate over Law No. 8, the Hindus launched their effort to form a nationwide organization on their own initiative.

The discontinuity between the intentions of the state and the organization of Hindu adherents on a national scale was made conspicuous with the secession of Pemuda Hindu from Peradah. When the split first occurred over personnel issues, Pemuda Hindu did not display an antagonistic stance toward the state. It was the organized effort to ostracize Pemuda Hindu using the bureaucratic apparatus that resulted in the divide between the respective characters of Peradah and Pemuda Hindu. Peradah was permitted to expand nationwide, but restricted its activities to the social sphere, while Pemuda Hindu, having survived efforts to suppress it, became an oppositional force that increasingly confronted the established order. After announcing its reorganization in 2000, Pemuda Hindu rapidly augmented its political activities in Bali and, by attacking Peradah's apolitical stance, highlighted the reality of depoliticization under the Suharto regime.

The nationwide organizing of Hindus also brought to the fore the discontinuity that led to the schism in Bali Parisada. Behind the expansion of networks connecting Hindus in different locales lay a growing interest in the religion's activities in the social sphere. The desire to learn about one another's efforts and thereby develop possibilities for new undertakings grew in parallel with the organizing process. The formation of Peradah and Pemuda Hindu, followed by the launch of the Indonesia Hindu Intellectuals' Forum and the *Raditya* journal, signified the growing desire for a network not just among students, but among Hindus in general. Meanwhile, Parisada had decided in 1991 to move its administrative headquarters from Bali to Jakarta, a development that served to expose both the systemic shortcomings of Bali-based Hinduism, with its lack of an organizational structure in the social sphere, and the discontinuous nature of the relationship between Hinduism on a national scale and Hinduism in Bali.

It was Pemuda Hindu that introduced into Bali the aspirations of the national-level contingent of Hindu adherents. Supporters of Pemuda Hindu's avowed objective of democratic Hinduism envisioned a new Hindu order. The most concrete manifestations of this desire were the decisions of Parisada's eighth general conference held in Bali in 2001, which brought about momentous changes in the fundamental organizational principles of leadership status and voting rights eligibility. Pemuda Hindu not only provided a forum for Hindu voices nationwide by convening seminars in four locations around Indonesia, but also succeeded in mobilizing Hindu-type and title groups in Bali itself. This should have eased tensions, to some degree, between Balinese Hindus and those outside Bali that had been festering for more than a decade. However, support for Pemuda Hindu was tenuous, efforts to placate opponents of the general conference decisions failed, and the end result was the splitting of Bali Parisada. Pemuda Hindu denounced opponents as remnants of the Suharto order, while the opponents attacked Pemuda Hindu as destroyers of Hindu tradition. As of the early 2000s, the discontinuity between Hindus in Bali and those at the national level remained unresolved.

The Besakih meeting took place despite the weakness of Pemuda Hindu thanks to support by the Hindu-type and title groups for the

241

democratic Hindu movement. However, the presence of these two types of groups further highlighted a discontinuity in expectations regarding the individual and the community in Balinese society. First, the Hindu-type and title groups did not voice support for Pemuda Hindu because they agreed with its ultimate political goal of achieving a civil society; rather, each side harbored its own particular discontent with the status it had been accorded, and supported democratic Hinduism as a possible solution to their problems. Moreover, despite allying with each other in an effort to hold the Besakih meeting, the Hindu-type and title groups were mutually incompatible. Granted, members shared common motives in the personal realm—spiritual solace, illness, and so forth—for joining these groups, which existed in a domain where the individual and society intermingled (in the sense that solutions to personal issues of the body and spirit were sought in the social dimension). However, the Hindu-type groups, which distanced themselves from customary practices as part of their emphasis on returning to the *weda*, were utterly unlike the title groups, which were rooted in custom.

Being deeply rooted in Balinese society also meant that the title groups lacked a common cause with the social demands of Hindus nationwide. At the beginning of the 2000s, a university professor and former head of the Bali branch of Peradah expressed strong misgivings about the intensity of the Balinese interest in titles, citing two dangers: the fomenting of societal divisions and the obstruction of more open attitudes toward the future. In principle, all Balinese are eligible to acquire titles. If the title groups continue to expand, every Balinese living in Bali will eventually belong to one group or another. If these title groups should then enter into antagonistic relations with one another over issues of legitimacy, Balinese society will suffer irreparable divisions. Additionally, the obsession with titles is based on ancestor worship and is therefore always associated with inclinations to return to the past. The expansion of the title groups is internally grounded in ancestral genealogies—a foundation which, the professor warns, robs people of hope for the future and causes them to neglect possibilities for development and growth. He calls the fixation with titles a 'sickness of the heart' among the Balinese, and fears that it has spread even among his fellow teachers, despite their ostensible training in rational thought.

The reality behind calls for democratic Hinduism at the Besakih meeting was extremely discontinuous, and it was recognized that the demands of the Hindu-type and title groups could not be co-opted into a political ideology. At the meeting, separate pledges were therefore requested of the Hindu-type and title groups. The Hindu-type groups, which distanced themselves from custom, were required to promise not to introduce their own distinctive ceremonies at temples in Bali. Parisada headquarters conveyed this pledge to the Religion Ministry, and it was under these terms that the Hindu-type groups were granted voting rights. Regarding the title groups, a statement was added to the meeting minutes that *Sarwa Sadaka* was not an issue related to the legitimacy per se of title group lineages. The intention was to restrict discussion of *Sarwa Sadaka* to the question of ceremony implementation rights and thereby prevent the issue from expanding into areas affecting relations among the title groups over questions of legitimacy.

Such discontinuities could be viewed as symptoms of a struggle about aspirations regarding human life and the social order embraced by the streams of religious thought circulating globally via individuals, communities, nations, and bodies of scripture. Indonesian Hinduism today is an arena of contention among disparate demands by multiple agencies: the Suharto regime, which intervened in the moral sphere in the course of shoring up the legal system with the aim of reinforcing state order; Hindus who pursued organization on the national level so as to strengthen their participation in state governance, as well as their activities in the social sphere; Balinese Hindus who relied on community customs to maintain order; Hindu-type groups that looked to scriptures as the source of personal spirituality; and title groups that exhibited desires for decolonization. Insofar as there is no readily discernible shared value system among these agencies, Hinduism in Indonesia cannot be thought of as a closed, autonomous domain. Hinduism is a place to which these actors belong because they cannot abandon it, even as they recognize the profound divisions among themselves. This means that values are in the process of pluralizing within the framework called Hinduism, with a concomitant invigoration of public consciousness among Hindus. The new nationwide magazines provide a forum to discuss these diverse experiences of Hindus in Indonesia.

The pluralization of values in Hinduism presents an ambiguous situation with two aspects: relations between religion and the state mediated by the latter's religious policy, and the link between religious activities and concerns exemplified by the movement to achieve a civil society. Although one result was the birth of a persistent oppositional camp, Hindu organizations consistently acquiesced to the religious policies of the state. Behind this obeisance was the incontrovertible fact of Hinduism's minority status in Indonesia, and the reality that Hinduism could find a place for itself in the nation at large only by obtaining recognition on the terms of state religious policy. The policy of conferring membership in the nation through religious recognition can be said to have succeeded in co-opting Hindu adherents into the state. Ironically, however, this co-optation by the state effectively destroyed the relationship between Hinduism and Bali that had been the cornerstone of Hinduism's institutionalization under state religious policy.

Through its religious policy, the Indonesian government exercised powerful pressure to achieve the integration of religion, law, morality, and order, as can be seen in the state's intervention in the moral sphere through the first principle of the Pancasila, the system of official recognition of religions by the Religion Ministry, and the use of religion as a force for national order in the wake of the upheavals of 1965. When Hinduism was incorporated into this religious policy, a unique system emerged in which Balinese ethnicity, the political agency represented by the provincial government, and the island of Bali itself were all superimposed on the concept of Hindu religiosity. Thus the provincial government assumed a unique status in the religious domain, as exemplified by the jurisdictional powers pertaining to Besakih Temple. A type of religious community was formed in which religion and government partially coincided, and ethnic homogeneity and religious uniformity reinforced one another. However, the organizing of Hindus on the national level extended the awareness of Hindu adherents beyond Bali, and the previously self-evident identification of Hinduism with Bali became a thing of the past.

With the transfer of Parisada headquarters from Denpasar to Jakarta, the mindset of Balinese in Bali ceased to coincide with that of Hindu adherents nationwide. Hinduism was no longer a guarantor of religious community, an indicator of Balinese ethnicity, or representative of the interests of the Balinese. If that was not enough, now the Balinese—at least those who were Hindus—could no longer avoid acknowledging the voices of Hindus outside Bali or of Hindu-type groups that operated outside the parameters of Balinese custom. In Bali this reality gave birth to an impulse to return to the previous world in which historical legitimacy provided a form of self-protection. When forces sharing this inclination gathered at Campuan, the result was the schism of Bali Parisada. Yet, even as Parisada was splitting into two in the very place of its birth, nothing had changed in the arena of religious identity politics on the state level. Balinese who remained faithful to Balinese customs could not be denied their identity as Hindus, but neither could other Hindus be excluded.

It is a fact that an awakening of interest in civil society and democracy has been part of the narrative around Indonesian Hinduism since the 1980s. At present, however, it is difficult to argue that these goals are widely shared. First, the process of deterritorializing Hinduism from Bali began with the aim of improving the religion's presence in the social sphere and its status in the nation. As such, it does not directly correlate with the reform movement that arose alongside the collapse of the Suharto regime. Also, it is true that Pemuda Hindu has claimed that the success of the Besakih meeting demonstrated its mobilizing power and derived from spontaneous participation by individuals sharing the same political goals. Yet, as we have seen, the Hindu-type and title groups supported the democratic Hinduism espoused by Pemuda Hindu for different reasons. In particular, it is difficult to find a shared interest in political goals among the title groups, whose origins are found in cultural factors. In that regard, a democratic Hindu platform supported by such mutually incompatible groups appears cobbled together, fragile, and unstable. Hence, the success of the Besakih meeting could be viewed as nothing more than a chance product of historical circumstance.

The inherent weaknesses in Pemuda Hindu also threaten its avowed agenda of achieving a civil society. The notion of 'the channel of religion' adopted by Pemuda Hindu is actually a product of the Suharto regime. The government sought in religion a channel through which to insert itself into the moral and social order of the nation, a strategy made clear in the item devoted to religion in its five-year plan. The use of this same strategy by Pemuda Hindu meant that a force opposing government policy used that same policy, a practice that would rebound on Pemuda Hindu as a constraint on its activities. The treatment of religion as a channel signified that Pemuda Hindu, rather than earnestly contemplating the possibilities for religion in the social sphere, viewed religion as a means to inculcate political consciousness, just as the government did. However it might assert its identity as an opposition force, Pemuda Hindu anticipated the same role for religion as did the state, thus blurring the distinction between the two sides. As long as Pemuda Hindu clung to this notion of religion as a channel, it was difficult for the group to relativize the forces pressing for the integration of religion, law, morality, and order. This meant that the civil society it called for remained undifferentiated from the political world or the state and, indeed, that Pemuda Hindu itself was hindering the attainment of an autonomous civil society.

The situation surrounding Indonesian Hinduism was, in fact, extremely fluid. In 2003 Parisada headquarters publicly denied any schism in Bali Parisada, in effect adopting a wait-and-see attitude. Parisada headquarters has not acknowledged the existence of the Campuan meeting that rejected the decisions of the eighth general conference, and has taken the position that there is only one Parisada in Bali. In the *Raditya* journal, Putu Setia took pains to avoid using terms like 'split,' instead referring to the 'duality' of Bali Parisada. In reality, however, two Parisadas have continued to exist in the administrative units of Gianyar, Badung, Klungkung, and Denpasar, leaving the Balinese at a loss. In practice, this duality has caused serious confusion, such as the question of which Parisada to apply to for approval of priests' qualifications. It even affected the response to an incident of international significance—the Kuta bombings of 2002. About one month after the bombings, a large-scale ceremony was held to symbolically assuage the fears engendered by the destruction and the many lives lost. As no religious writings specifically addressed bombing incidents, the bombings were interpreted as a type of warfare and a ceremony for purifying the battleground was conducted. In the past, it had been customary for Parisada to conduct such ceremonies, and this was the wish of the provincial governor. However, Kuta belonged to Badung regency, so Parisada did not take part. Thus Parisada was kept distant from an activity—carrying out a ceremony—that was central to its role as a representative body.

Relations between Besakih Temple and the Bali provincial government are also undergoing profound changes—in short, the reorganization of a relationship between the island's political and religious centers that had been in place since the colonial era. After the adoption of the *Sarwa Sadaka* policy for the 1999 ceremony, the provincial government returned surpluses of funds for Besakih, which the government had been retaining since 1979, to the administering villages. This change loosened the ties between the provincial government and Besakih. On March 10, 2003, Parisada headquarters announced its intention to launch a group for the purpose of managing Besakih Temple and protecting its sacred status, and organized a preparatory committee to set up this group.[28] The committee was granted full decision-making power concerning Besakih, and the former leader of the *Pasek* title group was appointed as chairman. Then, on October 28 of the same year, Parisada headquarters issued a religious decision recognizing in principle the right of all priests who had received Parisada certification via initiation rites to conduct ceremonies.[29] Thus Parisada formally approved the application of *Sarwa Sadaka* to all temples.

EPILOGUE

After receiving official recognition, Hinduism expanded throughout Indonesia. People who had relocated to Lampung in southern Sumatra after the 1963 eruption of Mount Agung established themselves in the agricultural and transport industries, and formed influential Balinese Hindu communities outside Bali. Hinduism also proliferated among non-Balinese. In non-Islamic areas such as the Dayak regions of Kalimantan, South Sulawesi, and Sumatra's Karo highlands, Hinduism became the preferred official religion in lieu of non-recognized beliefs. Even in Islamic areas, there were converts to Hinduism, such as those among the practitioners of syncretistic religions in Java. This was a consequence of the intense pressure to belong to one of the official religions in the aftermath of the massacres of 1965 and 1966. The Sai Baba movement also expanded its network, primarily in the cities, regardless of region or ethnicity.[1]

However, the situation changed dramatically in the mid-1980s when the Suharto regime shifted its policy toward Islam 'from one of hostile confinement to strategic co-operation' (Hefner 2004: 94). For official religions other than Islam, this resulted in the end to funding for education and new religious facilities, as well as in more aggressive proselytization by Islamic groups to gain more converts. For the first time under the Suharto regime, non-Islamic religions were forced to come to terms with their status as minority religions.[2] The growth of the Hindu reformist movement described in Chapter 6 may be said to reflect a sense of crisis in the face of these circumstances.

The development of this reformist movement resulted in the schism in Parisada between Parisada Besakih and Parisada Campuan.[3] As reported by Picard (2011a), Parisada Campuan failed to hold a leading position in the ninth national congress in Jakarta in October 2006. Consequently, in January 2007, it convened its fifth congress at the Samuan Tiga Temple in Bali. On this occasion, it changed its name to Parisada Dharma Hindu Bali and announced its independence from Parisada Hindu Dharma Indonesia on the grounds of returning 'to the "true self" (jati diri) of the Balinese religion' (Picard 2011a: 134).[4]

The most remarkable characteristic of Hinduism in Indonesia has been its expansion throughout the country since receiving official recognition at the same time as the expansion of rituals in Bali. Instead of a spiritual individualism taking the place of a communal ritualism in decline, both forms of religious practice expanded concurrently. As Pitana (1999) pointed out, with the establishment of modern educational and medical institutions, more and more people began living and working in the urbanized capital of Denpasar in hotels and other businesses. In addition, as Bali became an international tourist destination with large numbers of foreign visitors, more Balinese began associating frequently with non-Balinese. Thus Bali was arguably the place in Indonesia most susceptible to 'homogenizing global forces' (Pitana 1999: 197). Despite this, far from declining, religious ceremonies in Bali continued to expand, as we saw in Chapter 5. In light of this phenomenon, I would like to reconsider the split of the Campuan faction from Parisada.

As mentioned in Chapters 3 and 4, Parisada was formed as a result of the Hindu religious recognition movement after Bali became an autonomous province in the late 1950s. Also, as Schulte Nordholt (2007: 21) has reminded us, the establishment of Bali as a province came at the insistence of the Islamic Masyumi Party, and had nothing to do with either the national government's initial plans or the religious recognition movement. However, the loose correspondence that existed between the provincial government, the Hindu religion, the territory of Bali island, and the ethnicity of the Balinese provided the foundation for the construction of a new ritual environment that brought administrative and religious functions together.

As mentioned in Chapter 5, in 1968 the provincial governor declared that Besakih Temple was 'the center of worship for the adherents of Hinduism' (Stuart-Fox 2002: 316), and formally assigned responsibility for administration of the temple and its ceremonies to Parisada, as the representative Hindu organization. At the same time, the governor stated that the *guru wisesa* (holder of power), who had the authority to enact rituals, had to be the governor himself.[5] This arrangement redefined the relationship between Besakih, the provincial government, and Parisada; for the first time in Bali's history, ceremonies were to be conducted by priests approved by Parisada, together with a governor playing the same role as the kings once had. It seemed entirely natural to reimagine, in this manner, the kingship concept of having religious ceremonies carried out by those in power.

This structure—which, however traditional it may appear, is actually very contemporary—embodied the state ideology of the Suharto regime. Suharto himself visited Besakih after becoming president. The spread of both tourism and grand religious ceremonies on Bali was emblematic of the Suharto regime, which had eradicated the Communist Party (by claiming its members were blaspheming atheists), emphasized the belief in the 'one and only God' clause of the Pancasila, and promoted development as fundamental to Bali's existence. Furthermore, income from the tourism industry helped sustain the large-scale rituals of the 1990s, through which the priests of Parisada established a cosmology with Bali as its symbolic space.

While the provincial government and Parisada collaborated in establishing a system under which ceremonies were implemented from the top down by authorities who provided both the organization and the funding, there were also forces from below supporting ceremonies with the proliferation of *kawitan* (ancestral origin) searches and the *Sarwa Sadaka* movement they engendered, as described in Chapter 6. As mentioned earlier, the search for *kawitan* grew into what might be termed the largest grassroots social movement in Bali, addressing the problems and afflictions of people in day-to-day life amid rapid social change. The *kawitan* searches gave birth to groups known as *warga,* of which three title groups, in particular, enjoyed substantial growth. Each title group had its own *kawitan* origin-temple, where priests belonging to the temple prepared holy water. *Sarwa Sadaka* was a movement through which these title groups sought the participation of their own priests, who had been excluded up to that point, alongside priests from the *brahmana* class (who were authorized by Parisada in ceremonies held at public temples such as Besakih), so that the holy water they prepared would be treated in the same manner as that prepared by Parisada priests.

I Gde Pitana, who has studied the growth of the *warga* and the *Sarwa Sadaka* movement, identifies this movement as a 'potent indicator' of changes in Balinese society. In seeking approval of *jaba* (commoner) priests and asserting the equal status of the holy water they prepared, the movement cited contemporary values such as social justice and human rights. In this respect, Pitana (1999: 198) argues, the movement was not merely a quest for participation in an existing tradition of religious ceremonies, but an indicator of new changes in society and culture based on contemporary values.

As described in detail in Chapter 6, the participation of the *Sarwa Sadaka* movement in Parisada Besakih and its support for the principle of decolonialization helped bring about the schism in Parisada.[6] However, it is important to note that both Parisada and *Sarwa Sadaka* agreed in principle on the validity of the rituals. The movement had already grown conspicuous by 1989 and, in a case study, Pitana (1999: 185–7) analyzes its development in the context of the ritual of the Tri Bhuwana of 1993. In short, this movement was in complete agreement with the implementation of these rituals and the objective of the Parisada priests to consolidate the Hindu cosmology. It was precisely because *Sarwa Sadaka* shared this view of the rituals that it sought the participation of its own priests. Though they appeared to be in conflict, both sides were of the same mind regarding the role of temples and rituals in Balinese society.

As mentioned in Chapter 6, I Gusti Ngurah Bagus, a former professor of anthropology at Udayana University and a leading intellectual commentator on Balinese society, supported *Sarwa Sadaka*. He made an urgent plea for the rapid reform of Parisada, which still retained the old pro-Golkar establishment of the Suharto era and, he argued, had utterly failed to respond to the social changes occurring not only in Bali, but also in Indonesia at large. He also viewed the provincial government's involvement in religious rituals as problematic, and further stressed the necessity of integrating rituals with the spiritual life of the individual, citing the importance of 'simplifying the rituals and improving the quality of moral education' (Bagus 2004: 87). However, it must also be noted that Besakih had been redefined as the central temple not only for Balinese, but also for Hindus throughout Indonesia, and that the rituals performed there were strongly supported by ordinary Balinese, particularly in these times of rapid social change, as evidenced by the stance of *Sarwa Sadaka*.

Even after the collapse of the Suharto regime, the provincial governor of Bali continued to play the role of king in these ceremonies. Hauser-Schäublin (2011) has reported on the role of the governor in a ritual that he witnessed from 2007 to 2008 at Batur Temple, on the shore of Lake Batur. The ritual, the supreme ceremony for good harvests, concluded with the destruction of the main offering, which was stabbed with a dagger known as a *kris* and buried beneath the altar for the god of the lake. In the past, only a king was believed to possess the spiritual power necessary to wield the *kris*, which contained the spiritual power known as *sakti*. In the ritual, the priest handed the *kris* to the governor, who 'raised the *kris* first to his forehead and meditated for a moment. Then, with a jerk, he stabbed one of the huge offerings' (Hauser-Schäublin 2011: 208). According to Wiener (1995: 68), the forehead is the invisible 'third eye,' through which the king 'sees what is the invisible world (*niskala*).' By connecting this link to the invisible world, the governor represented the action of the former kings, which strengthens the efficacy of *sakti*.

The historical process by which Hinduism became institutionalized as it spread from Bali to the rest of Indonesia resulted in the separation of Bali Parisada from the nationwide Parisada. This could also be viewed as a withdrawal of the priests from Parisada—which had functioned as both the representative organization of Hindus and the representative agency of the religious authority embodied in the priesthood—to concentrate exclusively on carrying out ceremonies. Alternatively, it could be viewed as a split between two tendencies: one toward a ritualism based on Balinese culture, and the other toward Hinduism as a global religion. Nonetheless, the ceremonies at Besakih were carried out in the name of Hinduism, not Balinese culture, and were supported by contemporary Balinese experiencing massive social change. The 'true self of Balinese religion' espoused by Bali Parisada is a newly reimagined contemporary 'self.'

NOTES

Introduction

1. The Constitution of the Republic of Indonesia guarantees freedom of religion. However, the Pancasila (or Five Principles) that serves as the national policy of the republic stresses the importance of belief in God, referring to the 'Tuhan yang Maha Esa' (one and only God). For its part, the Religion Ministry distinguishes between agama (religions) and mere kepercayaan (beliefs), as determined by the presence or absence of holy prophets and holy scriptures. To religions, it accords mutually equal status and recognizes their participation in education and other aspects of public policy. Official recognition of a religion in this sense is the purview of the Religion Ministry. After the fall of the Suharto regime, Confucianism was added to the list of ministry-recognized religions, for a present total of six (Islam, Protestan, Katolik, Hindu, Buddha, and Kong Hu Cu). According to 2010 statistics, 87.18% of the Indonesian population adheres to Islam, and only 1.69% to Hinduism (Statistics Indonesia (Badan Pusat Statistik)).

Chapter 1

1. The expansion of Ubud's power occurred against the backdrop of the decline of the royal court of Gianyar from the 1880s to the 1890s. By accepting the protection of the Dutch, Sukawati hoped to preserve the gains he had recently achieved.
2. Stbl. 1882 No. 124, 143 (cf. Vickers 1987)
3. For the term translated here as 'native' for indigenous people, the Dutch had traditionally used the term inlander. According to Sears (1996: 146), however, with the advent of the 'ethical policy' period, this was replaced by the more neutral, less derogatory term inheemsche (indigenous).
4. Stbl. 1882 No. 143 art. 12.
5. Volkstelling 1922 Deel II, p. 265. According to the 1920 survey, there were 464,364 Hindu Balinese males and 477,691 females; 6460 Muslim Balinese males and 6870 females; 1607 Buddhist Balinese males and 1523 females; and 509 Bali Aga males and 566 females. Hence, it was evident to the government that the vast majority of Balinese were Hindu.
6. Volkstelling 1936 Deel V, p. 14.
7. See the passage about Liefrinck and Schwartz in Lekkerkerker (1920).
8. Notulen van het verhandelde op de Bestuurconferentie (Col. Korn: 166).
9. The regional government compiled statistics on these castes. In Gianyar, for example, which had a relatively large titled nobility, 2.5% of Hindu Balinese were *brahmana*, 9.5% were *satria*, and 5.3% were *wesia*. Thus the total number of *triwangsa* came to 17.3%, with the rest of the population designated as *sudra* (Col. Korn: 211).

10. Penalties were determined by the degree of class disparity between the parties involved. For example, marriage between a *satria* woman and a *sudra* man was punished by a fine of up to 80 *peks* (one *pek* was the equivalent of 1000 of the Chinese coins used in trade) and ten years imprisonment, whereas marriage with a *wesia* man would result in a fine of up to 20 *peks* and five years imprisonment. Marriage between a *wesia* woman and a *sudra* man was punished by up to 40 *peks* and five years imprisonment. In any case, marriage to a *sudra* man was always subject to the severest penalties.

11. Korn (1932: 147) states that in Buleleng, sixteen out of twenty-six heads did not have noble rank.

12. Stbl. 1922 No. 168.

13. *Ayahan* is a standard term for labor obligations. *Kadaleman* is the nominal form of the word *dalem*, which generally means 'inside,' referring in the context of the social order to a person of high (close to holy) status, and more narrowly to the king himself.

14. Stbl. 1916 No. 162–4.

15. References on the 1917 earthquake: Anonymous 1917; Kemmerling 1918; Lekkerkerker 1920: 204–05; Marcel 1917; MvO 1919 van Stein; MvO 1923 Damsté; Nieuwenkamp 1922: 207; Col. Moojen: 10; Col. Korn: 265. A memorandum cited in Col. Korn: 265 clearly describes the actions and discussions on the part of the ruling government following the earthquake. Moreover, numerous letters, petitions, and reports were exchanged from immediately after the earthquake into 1921. The pertinent reports in the possession of the Algemeen Rijksarchief (Royal Library of the Netherlands) in The Hague are numbered as follows: V28-8-1917-62, V12-8-1918-68, V18-6-1918-39, V14-4-1919-77, V24-10-1919-52, V15-6-1920-38, and V16-7-1920-68. The description that follows is based on these documents (see Nagafuchi 1994).

16. The Balinese-language document, titled '*Bhuwana winasa*,' was written in 1918 by the Tabanan priest Ide Pedanda Ngurah. From the content of this text and the fact that it was written in 1918, Schulte Nordholt (1996: 259) concluded that the 1917 earthquake was perceived to be the deciding factor in the collapse of the southern Balinese kingdoms, and that this perception was widespread among the general Balinese populace. For interpretations and cosmological meanings of this document, see Wiener 1995: 275–313.

17. For more about Moojen, see Nagafuchi 1998.

18. Some colonial officials, like R. M. Statmo, who was sent to Bali as a monitor for the Public Works Department, took such an adamant stance in favor of abolishing royal privileges that they did not even accept the existence of the *puri*. Under Dutch rule, they asserted, there was fundamentally no justification for recognizing such structures as *puri* that depended on royal privileges for their maintenance. They argued that even if the prohibition of *ayahan kadaleman* made it problematic for the current Balinese officials to rebuild their

own residences (i.e. the former *puri*), that still did not necessitate government assistance in their reconstruction.

19. The actual claim of divine punishment did not originate with the regent of Karangasem. Rather, it was said, the father-in-law of a Besakih *perbekel* (village official) received a revelation that the earthquake was the wrath of the gods. The *perbekel* reported this to the *punggawa* of Rendang, who conveyed it to the regent of Karangasem (Stuart-Fox 2002: 300).

20. Letter dated June 6, 1917, V18-6-1918-39.

21. The episode concerns Besakih Temple and Rsi Markandeya, an ancient Indian sage with supernatural powers (Stuart-Fox 2002: 262).

22. This account states that Besakih Temple was built by the tenth-century king Sri Kesari Warmadewa. Stuart-Fox (2002: 263) suggests that it is highly likely that the Balinese text relating this legend was based on the discovered inscription.

23. Letter dated June 6, 1917, V18-6-1918-39, pp. 8–9.

24. Letter from the Resident to the Governor-General dated May 15, 1917, 3294/1, V18-6-1918-39, p. 5.

25. Schwartz filled this position from 1915 to 1918. For more about Schwartz, see Kats (1939).

26. The examples cited were the *puri* of Gianyar, which sustained damage in 1883, and Batur Temple, which was partially damaged in a volcanic eruption in 1905.

27. Report dated September 20, 1917, V18-6-1918-39, p. 19.

28. Stuart-Fox (2002) estimates that the funding provided by the Dutch toward restoration of Besakih Temple comprised 25,000 guilders from the government, 1000 guilders from the Queen, plus some contributions from private companies. However, by the end of the project an estimated 100,000 guilders had been spent; hence, Stuart-Fox (2002: 303) concludes, the Balinese paid close to 75% of the total expenditure.

29. After moving to his next place of employment, Damsté gave an interview to a newspaper (*Java Bode* 1923/03/21) to which Moojen responded with a bylined article (*Java Bode* 1923/04/02), an exchange that highlights the disparity between the two men's viewpoints. Damsté regarded Moojen with enmity for what he perceived to be Moojen's unilateral declaration that Besakih Temple would be rebuilt with government money.

30. Damsté commented that while they remained culturally authentic, handicrafts made in Bali for foreigners also included shoddy, inferior goods. To this Moojen retorted that Damsté was ignoring Moojen's own efforts since his posting to Bali to maintain the quality of handicrafts made for tourists. With government approval, Moojen had carried out a project based on a proposal he had drawn up with the former Resident and Assistant Resident to fund Balinese craft groups with the objective of preserving traditional cultural values. Moojen

claimed that when Damsté became Resident, he cut off funds for the project because he disparaged the funding of cultural value preservation efforts as an idealist's fantasy.

Chapter 2

1. Stbl. 1928 No. 337 art 1.

2. Ektos, Pengharapan, *Bhawanagara* 3/2–3 1933/07–08, pp. 20–3. (Quotations from periodicals are generally cited in the sequence volume/issue publication year/month/day, page numbers; citations reflect as much of this information as the author could access.) This article says that there were many instances in which ceremonies were cancelled due to an inability to pay the slaughter tax.

3. *Bhawanagara* pre-inaugural issue, pp. 20–4.

4. In the document this is spelled *mantjabalikrama*, which became *panca wali krama* in 1960. In 1999 *wali* was changed to *bali*; the difference between *w* and *b* is not semantically significant, but the change to *bali* invited controversy over whether this was a sign of ethnocentrism. In this regard, it is worth noting that the first ceremony in the twentieth century used the word *bali*.

5. For an account of how tourism in Bali began under the guidance of the colonial government, see Nagafuchi (1998). In the 1930s there was still only one hotel on the island, the Bali Hotel in Denpasar, and the number of people involved in tourism was limited to taxi drivers and the proprietors of souvenir stands along the roads used by tourists.

6. The Public Works Department was in charge of irrigation system maintenance and the Land Rent Bureau was in charge of tax collection, thus actual implementation of the land tax system was handled by agencies independent of the regional government. This meant that the system of land development and tax collection now in place had the sole purpose of maximizing productivity without any regard for the local culture and technology that had evolved through maintenance of the traditional productivity system represented by irrigation system management. This caused a fundamental change from the era of the kingdoms in how obligatory labor and taxation were viewed.

7. As of 1927, about two-thirds of the land tax collected from regions east of Java came from Bali. The tax per hectare of paddy was markedly higher in Bali, averaging 10.87 guilders compared to 4.20 guilders in Madiun and 4.42 guilders in Semarang on Java (Robinson 1995: 56; Schulte Nordholt 1996: 286).

8. Government Decisions No. 26 1911/11/27 and No. 38 1913/10/09.

9. After the collapse of the kings' monopoly on trade, women took the lead in initiating commercial activities. For an account of the rapid increase in women engaged in business, see Schulte Nordholt (1996: 282).

10. The currencies used in Balinese society were the Chinese-derived *pis bolong* and *kepeng* which, combined with the currency of the colonial government, meant that Bali had a dual-currency system.

11. Notulen openbare vergadering Karangasemraad pada hari Kemis tanggal 24 September 1931 (MvO Beeuwkes 1932: 89–108). Some districts reported that the percentage of people who could not afford to pay taxes jumped from 10% in 1930 to 50% in 1931. Conference participants cited declining prices as the cause of the crisis and recognized that farmers' livelihoods were directly affected by exports and imports (MvO Beeuwkes 1932: 29). The most directly impacted commodity was coffee; assigning a value of 100 to export prices in 1930, the prices for three varieties of coffee in 1931 had fallen to 53, 39, and 65 respectively (MvO Beeuwkes 1932: 182). At the conference, it was decided to reduce the amount of the payment in place of obligatory labor from five to three guilders.

12. The *pipil* were administered by the heads of the *subak* irrigation groups, which were subordinate to the *sedahan* (Schulte Nordholt 1996: 252).

13. For a discussion of the weak oversight of the *sedahan* by the colonial government, see Schulte Nordholt (1996: 253). The following is a specific example cited of the abuse of their position. In certain districts, the government implemented a system of enforced taxation with the objective of 'educating' people about their tax obligations. If tax went unpaid, a mortgage was placed on the land; if payment was forthcoming by a certain deadline, the delinquency was forgiven on payment of a fine, but if payment was not made, the mortgage was auctioned off. Since this system was ostensibly for purposes of education, the question of whether to implement such measures was often left to the discretion of the tax collectors, which also gave them the opportunity to pocket the fines they collected for their personal use. Moreover, the auctioned land was sold at a bargain price, often to the tax collectors themselves. Initially with native Balinese as its target, this system was implemented in districts like Kintamani, which had suffered the direct impact of falling coffee prices; later, however, only Chinese owners of coffee plantations were singled out for such treatment. I. W. Goebah, Keadaan masjarakat kita di Bali. *Djatajoe* 4/2 1939/09/25, pp. 55–63.

14. Since these developments were occurring in an economic domain invisible to the government, no statistical data are available, but scholars are uniformly dire in their assessments of the extent of the farmers' distress. Robinson (1995: 59), who sees their poverty as having triggered profound changes in Balinese society (with a visible class rift growing between those who owned land and those who did not), notes that there are few recorded instances of farmer protests in the 1930s; he suggests that the tax system, 'both in the absolute burden it placed on the rural sector and in the way that burden was distributed, placed Bali's peasants in a peculiarly powerless position, making open rebellion less likely.' Thus the farmers' position was so precarious as to preclude even protest.

15. Stbl. 1929 No. 226. The establishment of the Negarabestuur occurred during the same period as the abolition of the slaughter tax on animal sacrifices.

16. From the standpoint of the Dutch, 'good rulers' (who understood the indigenous culture while pretending to leave untouched the unique customs of the Balinese) occupied a position from which they could look down from above upon a domesticated Balinese populace. For the link between this attitude and the process leading to establishment of the autonomous regions, see van der Kaaden (1938).

17. Damsté argued for the reconstruction of the kingdoms, citing the royal family of Karangasem as an example to follow (MvO Damsté 1923: 81–99).

18. N, Karja ring Poera Besakih, *Bhawanagara* 3/7 1933/12, pp. 108–10.

19. While recognizing the royal courts as the center of Balinese culture, Resident Beeuwkes viewed village society as a separate domain independent of the courts and called for a restoration of religiosity. This viewpoint was one inherited from Liefrinck, and it was accepted by Beeuwkes through the time of establishment of the autonomous regions (MvO Beeuwkes 1932: 76). For a discussion of the building-construction metaphor and the evaluation of Karangasem as a model, see MvO Beeuwkes (1932: 60–88).

20. Nota van Toelichtingen betreffende het in te stellen Zelfbesturend Landschap (Notes on the Territories Designated as Autonomous Regions) ends with a list of the names of eight territories.

21. The first such group, Stiti Bali, is known to have formed in Karangasem in 1917, the year of the earthquake (Vickers 2000: 91).

22. Several writers have discussed this dispute (Atmadja 1987; Putra Agung 1974; Robinson 1995: 59–67; Schulte Nordholt 2000; Vickers 2000). The specific cause of the dispute was an incident in which I Nengah Metra, a leader of Surya Kanta, married a woman of the *brahmana* caste with the title of Ida Ayu in 1926 and was consequently banished to Lombok by the colonial government (Vickers 2000: 92).

23. Statuten Soerya Kanta, *Surya Kanta* 1925 No. 2. Hidoeplah perkoempoelan Surya Kanta, setialah sekalian lid-lidnja !!! *Surya Kanta* 1926 No. 2.

24. Kaoem Djabakah jang mereboet haknja Triwangsa ? *Surya Kanta* 1926 No. 4.

25. Schulte Nordholt (2000: 79) makes the same point.

26. Openbare oprichtingsvergadering Surya Kanta Singaradja, *Surya Kanta* 1926 No. 1. Kaoem Djabakah jang tiada tahoe membalas goena? *Surya Kanta* 1926 No. 8. Madjoelah, hati bangsakoe Bali, *Surya Kanta* 1926 No. 9/10.

27. Statuten Perhimpoenan Tjatoer Wangsa Derja Gama Hindoe Bali, *Surya Kanta* 1926 No. 5.

28. Pemandangan, *Surya Kanta* 1925 No. 1. Sikap Kita, *Surya Kanta* 1926 No. 3.

29. Akan meradja lelakah bahaja merah di poelau Bali dan Lombok? *Bali Adnyana* 1926 No. 16. Pemandangan, *Bali Adnyana* 1926 No. 19.

30. The government relaxed rules concerning the banishment of lower-caste men who married women of the priest class (Schulte Nordholt 2000: 75).

31. Groups known to be active in the 1920s include Tjwadega Hindu Bali (Catur Wangsa Derja Gama Hindu Bali) and Stiti Gama Siwa Buda; the latter was formed under the leadership of the royal family of Karangasem. These groups shared common goals of studying and disseminating religious knowledge, but also included among their objectives the promotion of ethical policies improving the welfare of the indigenous population (Vickers 2000: 94–5).

32. Ni K. Setiari dan Ni G. Ajoe Rai, 'Poeteri Bali Sadar,' *Djatajoe* 1/9 1936/04/25, pp. 263–5. I Gst. P. Merta, 'Poetri Bali Sadar.' (P. B. S.) *Djatajoe* 2/3 1937/10/25, pp. 69–71.

33. Meisjes Vervolgschool, meaning a school for continuing education at a higher level after the completion of basic education. The Indonesian translation of Vervolgschool was Sekolah lanjutan, a term also used by Taman Siswa.

34. I. G. G. Raka, Orang Bali dengan perkoempoelannja, *Djatajoe* 3/10 1939/05/25, pp. 297–312. Raka was from Mengwi and worked in a tax office; while appreciating nationalism, he also petitioned the government for restoration of the Mengwi kingdom in anticipation of the establishment of the autonomous regions. Thus, even as he criticized the autonomous region system, he sought recognition of his own home kingdom as an autonomous region. Raka's dual stance was emblematic of the position in which lower-level civil servants found themselves (Schulte Nordholt 2000: 82).

35. According to the recollections of A. A. M. Jelantik from the royal family of Karangasem, around twenty Balinese students were enrolled in the two middle schools, and a group formed spontaneously among them for purposes of socializing and conducting religious ceremonies. If we take these recollections at face value, a group by the name of BDL already existed in the early 1930s. Ngurah Rai, who led the independence movement in Bali for the republican government but died in battle early on, was also a member of the Java BDL (Jelantik 1997: 69–70).

36. BDL was founded on July 26, 1936.

37. G. P. M. Menoedjoe Masjarakat Baroe, *Djatajoe* 3/12 1939/07/25, pp. 387–91.

38. While regular members paid 0.1 guilder per month, contributors paid 25 guilders per year or 2.5 guilders per month.

39. Kehadapan Madjelis Paroeman Agoeng di Denpasar, *Djatajoe* 4/7 1940/02/25, pp. 217–22.

40. Congres 'BDL.' Jang pertama pada boelan Juli 1937 di Singaradja, *Djatajoe* 1/7 1937/02/25, pp. 192–3. Congres 'BDL.' Jang Ke II, *Djatajoe* 2/9 1938/04/25, pp. 257–8. Congres BDL. Jang Ke III, *Djatajoe* 4/1 1939/08/25, pp. 27–30. Congres 'BDL.' Jang Ke IV Pada Boelan Juli 1940 di Tabanan, *Djatajoe* 4/9–10 1940/04–05/25, pp. 259–61.

41. Gst. Pt. Merta, Menoedjoe kerapatan besar BDL. *Djatajoe* 2/10 1938/05/25, pp. 312–14. Merta concluded by declaring that the second general meeting would be critical in determining the future course of the organization, and that self-awareness on the part of each and every member was imperative.

42. Openbare Vergadering Comite Badan-Boenda, *Djatajoe* 4/9–10 1940/04–05/25, pp. 295–8.

43. Kirtya was determined to be a Balinese word derived from a Sanskrit stem, kirti, that had the same meaning as the Dutch word for foundation, stichting. However, Jelantik, the Buleleng ruler who proposed the use of the word, acknowledged that this Sanskrit stem was not used in Balinese. C.C. Berg en R. Goris, De Lontar-Stichting genaamd Kirtya Liefrinck-van der Tuuk, Rapport van 10 November 1928, *Mededeelingen* 1 1929/10/01, p. 2.

44. Verslag van het Congres van het Java-Instituut, gehouden op Bali 18–23 October 1937, *Djawa* 18/1–2 1938, pp. 1–96.

45. Pemboeka Kata Redaksi, *Bhawanagara* pre-inaugural issue, pp. 4–7. The extent to which these conditions for publication were met is unclear.

46. H. Beeuwkes, Soerat ideran 1930/04/29, *Bhawanagara* pre-inaugural issue, pp. 7–8.

47. Kabar Redactie, *Bhawanagara* 1/7 1931/12/01, p. 97.

48. In an explanation of the meaning of the title *Djatajoe*, emphasis was placed on the spirit of korban (self-sacrifice or devotion) to a mission. Sampai Dimana 'Madjoe dan Modern,' *Djatajoe* 3/11 1939/07/25, pp. 345–8.

49. The title of the novel is *Melantjaran ka Sasak* (Traveling to Lombok). Many relatives of Bhadra and others from the same district were activists and narrators active in the 1950s (Putra 2000: 137–8).

50. I. G. N. Sideman was a contributor to *Bhawanagara* but worked as a secretary for the Klungkung chapter of BDL and also published poems in *Djatajoe*. Pers Meninggikan Deradjat Bangsa, *Bhawanagara* 3/1 1933. Sja'ir Seroean 'Djatajoe,' *Djatajoe* 1/7 1937/02/25, p. 185. He later became known by the name Anandakusuma when he began actively writing about religious matters during the 1950s.

51. See, for example, K. M. Cultuur Kita, *Djatajoe* 3/7 1939/02/25, pp. 200–04.

52. Goebah, Kebingoengan kita tentang agama, *Djatajoe* 2/4 1937/11/25, pp. 97–100, 2/5 1937/12/25, pp. 131–2.

53. I. B. Manoeaba, Pertimbangan oentoek Kitab Soetji, *Djatajoe* 2/4 1937/11/25, pp. 112–13.

54. W, Manak Salah dengan metoenjang, *Bhawanagara* 3/7 1933/12, pp. 106–08.

55. MvO Winkelman 1937, Bijlage 2 Tijgrekening en Feestkalender.

56. Stbl. 1925 No. 20.

57. Balinization was promoted under the leadership of H. Te Flierhaar; for details on Balinization, see Flierhaar (1941), Nakamura (1990), and Parker (2000: 57–9).

58. G. P. M. Disekitar 'Baliseering,' *Djatajoe* 4/5 1939/12/25, pp. 145–9, 4/7 1940/02/25, pp. 214–17.

59. The author's criticism was directed at teachers who were actually engaged in Balinization practices. He mentions by name individuals who were surveying and teaching music in Denpasar and Klungkung; while recognizing the significance of their efforts, which extended to the study of musical notation, he critiques them for indulging their own personal interests and failing to talk about the overall historical background of the songs they introduced. Moreover, he claims, these practitioners of Balinization arbitrarily assumed that the majority of indigenous songs were love songs, ignoring what the author believes are the many songs about the beauty of nature or other themes. This assumption on the part of the practitioners is, to him, a flagrant example of the diminution of Balinese culture. In response, the practitioners named in the article published a short rebuttal in *Djatajoe*, emphatically declaring that it was a misunderstanding to think that they were only interested in love songs. Wajan Djirne, Sekali lagi: Disekitar Baliseering Salah Faham, *Djatajoe* 4/9–10 1940/04–05/25, pp. 283–4.

Chapter 3

1. A deep rift existed between the Japanese army and navy, but in Bali there was some intermingling between the two branches, and this tendency grew as the end of the war approached. Studies of Japanese military administration in Asia suggest that, if anything, Bali (where the army–navy rift was relatively mild) was an exception.

2. The formation of the Federated States of Indonesia was part of the diplomatic policy of the Netherlands in the period immediately after the war. The policy called for the establishment of a federation that included the Netherlands, the Federated States of Indonesia, and Suriname and Curaçao, which had been Dutch colonies in South America and the Caribbean, so that these territories could jointly deal with common diplomatic, defense, and economic issues (cf. Cheong 1982; Djajadiningrat 1958).

3. Lombok, which had been continually subjected to direct rule, lacked a body of indigenous representatives such as that established in Bali during the colonial period. A council, Dewan Lombok, was first established when Lombok became part of East Indonesia, and an executive organ for carrying out administrative tasks, Badan Pemerintah Harian, was organized at the same time, consisting of members of a committee elected by the council. The representatives who participated in the Denpasar Conference took on the responsibilities of both the council and the executive organ (Schiller 1955: 106–07). With the formation of this administrative apparatus, Lombok achieved some parity with indirectly ruled territories that already had a representative system in place. However, the

administrative structure thus established was at most a theoretical framework devised by the government of East Indonesia; the degree to which it actually functioned in practice is unclear. Even in the analysis by Magenda (1989: 347), who provides one of the few perspectives on political conditions in Lombok during this period, details are lacking about the political basis upon which Lombok's Denpasar Conference representatives were selected. Although the representatives belonged to the nobility, they were unable to cultivate political connections beyond the island, a failing that contributed to their precarious position after the establishment of a unitary Indonesia.

4. Undang–Undang Negara Indonesia Timur No. 44 1950.

5. Undang–Undang No. 22 1948.

6. Undang–Undang No. 1 1957.

7. Undang–Undang No. 9 1954.

8. Realisasi Swatantra Tingkat I Bali, SI581110. Setelah petugas2 ditundjuk menjusul pembubaran2 DPD/DPRD, SI581111. Daerah Bali beserta pemerintahan bubar, SI581202. Hut Propinsi Daerah Tingkat I Bali ke-30 Tgl. 14 Agustus 1988.

9. *Nusa Tenggara* (Djawatan Penerangan R. I. Propinsi Nusa Tenggara) 2/7 1955/02, pp. 5–6, 9–10. Pendjelasan Pembagian Nusa Tenggara, SI571021. Pembagian Nusa Tenggara setjepatnja dilaksanakan, SI580227.

10. During the Japanese military occupation, Bali had been divided into three military districts, and it was tentatively proposed that this division be applied.

11. Tadjuk Rentjana: Meringankan atau beratkan beban rakjat? SI581127. Realisasi Swatantra Tingkat I Bali (II), SI581022. *Nusa Tenggara* 2/8 1955/03, pp. 4–6. Pembagian Nuteng Juli selesai di DPR, SI580619.

12. For the merchants and landowners who supported Masyumi, the fact that Singaraja was the seat of government for Nusa Tenggara presented a major problem. During the East Indonesia era, the flow of budgetary funds, as well as personnel in both the administrative and educational spheres, took place between Makassar and the various districts. But this flow was altered when Singaraja became the capital of the Lesser Sunda province under a unitary Indonesia. In education there was an increase in direct interaction with Java, but in budgetary and administrative matters Singaraja became the intermediary with Jakarta for the first time in the history of the region. For the Balinese, this represented a new form of privilege; consequently, the representatives from Bali reacted nervously to proposals to move the capital as part of the division plan. For their part, representatives from regions east of Lombok felt their regions had been placed in a dependent and therefore unequal relationship with Bali. This was particularly the case where the government's licensing system was concerned, as the system dispensed specific advantages and disadvantages. Twice-yearly inspections of those engaged in trade, along with the issuing and renewal of permits, continued until 1961.

These procedures became linked to political party membership, so that party politics emerged as a significant factor in the economic sphere. Because the capital, Singaraja, was located on Bali, most of the government workers there were Balinese. This put Masyumi supporters at a disadvantage, one that could most effectively be eliminated by achieving autonomy as a new regional administrative district, through which they could manipulate the system to their own advantage (Robinson 1995: 248–9). In fact, says Magenda (1989: 360), from the 1950s onward, trade between Bali and Lombok was increasingly monopolized by Balinese and Chinese merchants. The preeminent Balinese-run trading company was P. T. Nusatenggara, one of whose employees was Sugriwa, a leader of the religious recognition movement to be discussed later.

13. Puja was an important presence in Jakarta, both for the Hindu religious recognition movement and for the regional administrative reform process. Mr. I Gst. Kt. Pudja: Kehendak Rakjat jang Menentukan–Kesatuan Bali Tetap Ideeel, SI580527. Meski Berat Sw.I Bali dapat berdjalan, SI580711.

14. In his analysis of the regional administrative reform, Legge (1961: 82) remarks that the government ultimately recognized the disparity between neighboring islands and the essential, pervasive unity of Bali. This explanation certainly dovetails with the views of the Balinese representatives, but in fact adopts the viewpoint of Magenda (1989), who treats Bali's cultural identity as indisputable and assigns priority to the political situation. Magenda (1989: 392) asserts that the province of Bali is a historical product of political circumstances, and that the three-way division of Nusa Tenggara was born less from administrative than political needs. According to Magenda, the fact that a three-way split was adopted after the proposition of a two-way split with clearly valid grounds can only be attributed to bargaining in parliament and the political agendas that propelled it.

15. Pendit (1979a: 305) provides a vivid description of the extent of the shock felt by the Bali independence movement when the Republic of Indonesia recognized the Federated States of Indonesia, even quoting a poem on the subject. One verse is as follows:

> Our struggle is for independence
> Even if they say we are already independent
> Our struggle is for a unified nation
> Even if the republic calls for a federation
> Bali hopes to become one with Java
> Even if the republic recognizes East Indonesia
> Even if the republic places Bali in East Indonesia.

16. Robinson notes that even the Dutch administrators assigned to Bali at the time expressed misgivings about the Gianyar royal family amassing power and its draconian measures against the republicans; the Dutch viewed the royals as having an irredeemably feudalistic point of view (Robinson 1995: 169–78).

17. Robinson (1995: 183) attributes this situation to the fact that 'Bali was suddenly left without a strong local state apparatus.'

18. See the table below.

    Table: Incidence of crime in the 1950s

	1951	1952	1953	1954	1955 (Oct.)	Total
Murder	207	47	66	97	106	523
Arson	193	80	60	49	39	421
Looting	317	179	209	198	101	1004
Robbery	118	66	65	80	73	402
Theft	1521	1792	1417	1235	1061	7026

    Source: Sekitar Keamanan di Bali, *Dhamai* 3/14 1955, p. 6; *Nusa Tenggara* 3/1 1956/01, pp. 3–4

19. The situation regarding intimidation and fraud in the villages is mentioned by readers who contributed to the 'Question corner'; 'Djawaban Redaksi!' *Dhamai* 2/24 1955, p. 2; 3/1 1955, p. 2; 3/2 1955, p. 2; 3/13 1955 p. 2; 3/14 1955 p. 2.

20. Pertahanan Rakjat di Bail, *Dhamai* 1/6 1953, pp. 19–2l; l/7 1953, pp. l7–20. Robinson (1995) analyzes the vigilante groups formed during this period as having set a precedent for the tactical forces involved in the massacres of 1965.

21. These groups called themselves Lanjutan Organisasi Gerila Indonesia Seluruhnya (LOGIS, Continuation of the All-Indonesia Guerrilla Organization).

22. The objective of JKP was to protect veterans, but the veterans themselves did not become members and look after their own interests. Rather, it was an auxiliary organization of the Bali Regional Assembly in terms of both funding and operations, with assets to revert to the assembly in the event of its dissolution.

23. The official name of the monument is Candi Pahlawan Margarana (Margarana Memorial Park). The structure itself is an aggregation of symbols of independence. Its pentagonal shape represents the Pancasila; its eight tiers and 17-meter height stand for Independence Day, August 17, and a four-step staircase and five pillars indicate the year, 1945. The statue at the top symbolizes the revival of the spirit of the Proclamation of Independence and the unity of movement participants and, by extension, of the entire Indonesian people.

24. J. K. P. Daerah Bali – B. R. N.Sunda Ketjil, *Dhamai* 1/3 1953, pp. 43–5. Tjilik: Jajasan Kebaktian Pedjuang (J. K. P.), *Dhamai* 1/4 1953, pp. 7–14. Usaha dan Perkembangan Jajasan Kebaktian Pedjuang Daerah Bail, *Dhamai* 1/18 1954, pp. 8–9; l/19 1954, p. l2; 1/20 1954, pp. l3–l4. I Gst. Bgs. Sugriwa: J. K. P. Tjukup Terkenal, *Dhamai* 3/11 1955, pp. 7–9, 18.

25. *Dhamai* began publication as a monthly on March 17, 1953, then became a semi-monthly that August (cf. Putra 2000: 139–41).

26. The student support organization, Kantor Urusan Demobilisan Pelajar, began its activities in 1950, but was abolished on October 1, 1953, after which no support for student veterans was forthcoming until a new organization, Gerakan Pelajar Pejuang, was formed. On December 5 that same year, this organization announced that it would work with JKP to remedy the current neglect of youthful talent. Pengumuman Bersama, *Dhamai* 1/15 1954. Masalah Hasrat & Usaha Pemuda Pelajar, *Dhamai* 1/16 1954, pp. 9–10.

27. Cilik was an alias for Nengah Tamu.

28. I Gst. Bgs. Sugriwa, Tjeramah Bathin (Rochani) kepada Warga J. K. P. di Denpasar, pada Tgl. 9 November '53, *Dhamai* 1/14 1953, pp. 27–8; 1/15 1953, pp. 28–30, 32.

29. The bemo terminal was built in the 1960s.

30. No. J 18/1/61 1950.

31. Based on the following report on the establishment of the Bali Regional Assembly: Peringatan 1 Tahun Dewan Perwakilan Rakjat Daerah Bail, Denpasar, 25 Sep. 1951.

32. As will be discussed in Chapter 4, an East Indonesia regional administrative law was also cited as legal grounds for the Bali Regional Assembly's creation of the Autonomous Religion Bureau.

33. Panitia Penjelenggaraan Pembentukan D. P. R. Daerah Bahagian/Swapradja. Even with the establishment of assemblies, the authority of the royal families was not subjected to legal restrictions, as mentioned earlier.

34. Pedoman untuk Dewan Perwakilan Rakyat Bail, Pasal 1(2).

35. See 50 Tahun RRI.

36. The actual provider of funding was I Gusti Ngurah Pemecutan of the Puri Pemecutan clan (Vickers 2000: 96).

37. No. 17678/Kab.No.K/1/9180, 1951/07/16.

38. No. P/21/DPRD/1953, 1953/05/19.

39. It changed its name to *Suara Indonesia,* then *Suluh Marhaen.* This newspaper was the forerunner of what would later become Bali's leading newspaper, the *Bali Post.*

40. The official view, according to the print shop, is that printing in Bali began with the *Bali Shimbun.* Equipment from the time of the first printing operations still exists, though it cannot be ascertained whether this was shipped from Java or was already present in Singaraja.

41. In tracing the activities of I Nengah Metra, whose marriage to a woman of the *brahmana* caste triggered a dispute between Surya Kanta and Bali Adnyana, Vickers (2000: 96) suggests that support for Metra was backed in large part by the solidarity of Balinese who had studied in Java, particularly Malang, and that the philosophical bond they shared was based on theosophy.

42. According to research by Subagiasta (1999: 109–10), he collected 567 titles on Hinduism and Indian philosophy, primarily in English, and translated 116 of these into Indonesian, several of which were published by the Saraswati Foundation's publishing house, Bhuvana Saraswati Publications.

43. Cokorda Rai Sudharta gave the author information on the situation in Sanglah during this period.

44. Nyoman Pendit is the source of the information that Sukawati was the person who provided Mantra with the opportunity to study in India. The same opportunity subsequently given to Oka and Sudharta was circumstantial, and it is unclear whether their political position was their own choice or not. Both had attended high school in Singaraja in the early 1950s, and one of their teachers was Ibu Gedong, who taught English and was also the wife of the governor of the province. Dr. Idora Raguvira, director of the International Academy of Indian Culture, saw Sanskrit as having had a profound impact on Indonesia and particularly Bali. On a visit to Bali, he had met the governor and his wife, and proposed to them that high school graduates be sent to India to study. Sudharta had been interested in the classical Balinese language from his high school days, and while in school had studied Sanskrit with Goris. He maintained that Goris's knowledge of Sanskrit was extremely poor and that he had not found his studies satisfactory.

45. An exemplar of this viewpoint is Oka, who, after studying in India, became a priest in his birthplace, Kediri.

46. For interpretations of Sang Hyang Widi in the 1950s, see Swellengrebel (1984: 52–3).

47. Shastri's interpretation of the negotiation process for religious recognition was simple: he viewed recognition as a product of Sukarno's judgment.

48. As mentioned earlier, this name also appeared in *Djatajoe*. Furthermore, as we will see in Chapter 4, it was used by Ida Pedanda Made Kemenuh, who played a central part in organizing the priests, and was employed by the eminent philologist Hooykaas in one of his titles.

49. Shastri's portrait adorns the first page of his book *Intisari Hindu Dharma* (Essence of Hindu Dharma), which takes the form of a volume of scripture, with no year or place of publication indicated.

50. When interviewed by the author (August 18, 1999), Shastri initially behaved as if he was an old man who was hard of hearing and on the verge of dementia. But upon learning that the author was not Balinese but Japanese, he suddenly began speaking clearly and described the events of the 1950s in considerable detail. At the end, he declared that he had talked because the author was a foreigner, and that he would not have spoken to a Balinese.

Chapter 4

1. The Pancasila (Five Principles) are as follows: (1) belief in the one and only God, (2) just and civilized humanity, (3) the unity of Indonesia, (4) democracy guided by the inner wisdom in the unanimity arising out of deliberations among representatives, and (5) social justice for all people of Indonesia.

2. Several analyses and descriptions of the religious recognition movement have been published (Bakker 1993; Diantari 1990; Fukushima 1991; Kagami 2000; Mulder 1978; Subagiasta 1999; cf. Atkinson 1987; Kipp 1996; Kipp and Rodgers 1987; Schiller 1997; Schrauwers 2000; Tsing 1987, 1993).

3. The general conference was held at irregular intervals, and conference reports articulate the policies of the Religion Ministry at the time. The reports are titled *Komperensi Kementerian, Departemen, Djawatan Agama Seluruh Indonesia,* or *Komperensi Dinas Kementerian Agama,* hereafter cited as *Komperensi*. These reports sometimes refer to Christianity by the general term Masehi, with Protestantism and Catholicism treated as subdivisions thereof, and sometimes to Protestantism and Catholicism as separate entities from the outset.

4. However, Bali alone was assigned four part-time employees; also, after a Religious Education Office was opened in Bali on October 1, 1953, instructors in Balinese Hindu religious education were authorized, albeit few in number (*Komperensi* 1954, pp. 148, 151–2).

5. No. 31 1952.

6. *Komperensi* 1954, pp. 189–97.

7. *Komperensi* 1954, pp. 37–8.

8. The document consisted of nine statements. (1) The Religion Ministry was founded to implement the revolutionary spirit in fulfillment of the first of the Five Principles. (2) The ministry is not a Kementerian Islam (Ministry of Islam), but serves all religions and beliefs in conformity with the law. (3) The ministry does not distinguish between 'nobles' and 'commoners' according to religion. (4) The ministry is not an agency for intervention in particular religions or beliefs, but rather one that observes the constitutional guarantee of religious freedom. (5) The ministry is not an agency for imposing restrictions on religious organizations, but rather one that supports them within the limits of the law. (6) The ministry is an agency for resolving problems associated with religion in concert with the citizenry. (7) The ministry serves as an intermediary among different religions so as to foster the unity of the Indonesian nation. (8) The ministry fully recognizes that, as a new government agency, problems have arisen in the implementation of its policies. (9) The ministry will continue to make efforts to resolve those problems. Kementerian Agama Melajani Segara Aliran Aliran Agama, Pengumuman Kementerian Agama, *Warta* 3/8 1954/04/17, pp. 4–6. Surat Kagri No. A/VII/4940 1954/04/14 (Pedoman tentang Tugas Mendjaga Kemerdekaan Agama).

9. Bagaimana dengan Kantor Agama? *Bhakti* 1/12 1952/12/01, p. 19.

10. Religion Minister Decision No. 2447/A-7/53 1953/09/30. *Komperensi* 1954, p. 160.

11. Kebebasan Beragama, *Mimbar Agama* 1953 No. 3, pp. 14–16. Katholik di Bali Selajang Pandang, *Mimbar Agama* 1953 No. 10–11, pp. 40–2. The problems occurring at this time were in the villages of Badung and Gianyar.

12. The Religion Ministry made a point of declaring that it made the shift to a more detached policy stance in deference to the views of Anak Agung Gede Agung, who had been in Bali at that time and said that a wait-and-see attitude was preferable to a positive one that produced mistakes (*Komperensi* 1954, p. 104). A central figure in the federation-era State of East Indonesia, Anak Agung was known to be an old adversary of the republican faction that dominated the Bali Regional Assembly.

13. For example, in regard to the *nabi* (holy figures) viewed as important by Islam, one document hints at the existence of Hindu holy figures, mentioning the name Bhagawan Wyasa, albeit with a footnote stating that this was not a formal determination. However, this name was not generally used in Bali.

14. *Komperensi* 1954, pp. 156–60; 1955, pp. 513–14.

15. The name of the column was 'Ruangan Mimbar Agama Hindu Bali.' Dasar2 Agama Hindu Bali, *Mimbar Agama* 1953 No. 7, pp. 22–3. 'The voice of Hindu-Bali religion' appeared in Suara Agama Hindu-Bali, *Mimbar Agama* 1953 No. 9, pp. 14–17.

16. The change of the election day is described in *Nusa Tenggara* 2/15 1955, pp. 16–18. It was stipulated that holidays should be separately determined for Bali (and Lombok). Religion Minister Decision No. 12 1955 Pasal 3.

17. For more on the background of Ida Pedanda Gede Nganjung, see Subagiasta (1999: 121–3).

18. See footnote 50 in Chapter 2.

19. Regarding the name of the religion, Paruman Para Pandita rejected the name 'Hindu-Bali' advocated by Sugriwa and others, instead promoting the name 'Religion of Holy Water' and declaring that its patron saint was Siwa-Buddha.

20. The Religion Ministry's questions were as follows: (1) the name of the religion, (2) the content of its teachings and its philosophical background, (3) the meaning of its various ceremonies, (4) its most important temples, (5) whether there were religious schools, and (6) what the holy scriptures were.

21. Bali Regional Assembly Decision No. 2/S. K/DPRD 1953/03/24. *Komperensi* 1955, pp. 512–13. Djawaban Pemerintah (i.e. Kementerian Agama), SI580721. The Religion Ministry did not use the name Dinas Agama Otonom Daerah Bali, choosing the term Djawatan Agama Daerah Bali instead.

22. The main topics of discussion at the general conference were standardization of the day of Nyepi in order to make it a national holiday, and establishment of a system for marriages. Menjosong Hari Raya Njepi, *Warta* 314 1954/02/14, p. 8; 3/8 1954/04/ 17, p. 15; 3/9 1954/05/03, p. 11.

23. 1954/01/09 No. A/VII/394.
24. The Autonomous Religion Bureau was referred to as a sect using the words perkumpulan/persekutan.
25. *Komperensi* 1954, p. 103. Djaja-Negara, *Dhamai* 2/13 1954, pp. 2–4.
26. No. A/VII/269/R 1953/06/09.
27. Bali Regional Assembly Decision P/21/D. P. R. D./1953/06/25.
28. *Komperensi* 1955, pp. 512–13.
29. The eight religious groups were as follows: (1) Satya Hindu Darma Denpasar, (2) Jajasan Dwidjendra Denpasar, (3) Partai Nasional Hindu Bali Klungkung, (4) Madjelis Hinduisme Klungkung, (5) Paruman Para Pandita Singaradja, (6) Panti Agama Hindu Bali Singaradja, (7) Angkatan Pemuda Hindu Bali Denpasar, (8) Eka Adnjana Sempidi Badung.
30. Djawaban Pemerintah: Sedia Adakan Bagian Agama Hindu Bali, SI571220,21. Kerdjasama Organisasi2 Agama Hindu Bali Tuntut Kedudukan Agama Hindu Bali sedjadjar dlm Kem. Agama, SI580628. Pres. Sukarno Setudju Tuntutan Bagian Agama Hindu Bali, SI580701. Delegasi Umat Hindu Bali berangkat, SI580714. Umat Hindu Bali Mendjawab Tantangan, SI580715. Delegasi Umat Hindu Bali Kembali dgn Hasil Gemilang, SI580728. 'Umat Hindu-Bali' Menjambut Kedatangan Menteri Agama, SI580729. Dinas Agama Otonom Daerah Bali akan masuk Lingkungan Kem. Agama, SI580802,04.
31. Departments in the Religion Ministry at this time were as follows: (1) Biro Menteri, (2) Bagian Umum, (3) Bagian Kepegawaian, (4) Bagian Keuangan, (5) Bagian Pengawasan Keuangan, (6) Bagian Urusan Hukum, (7) Bagian Urusan Perguruan Tinggi Agama, (8) Bagian Urusan Hadji, (9) Bagian Urusan Kristen, (10) Bagian Urusan Katolik, (11) Bagian Urusan Hindu Bali, (12) Bagian Urusan Agama-Agama Lain dan Gerakan/Aliran Kerohanian. *Komperensi* 1961, pp. 49, 53.
32. Rapat Pamongpradja/Para Pendeta Bali Rentjana Membentuk Suatu Dewan A. H. B. SI581009. Panitia Perantjang 'Hindu-Bali Shaba' (Dewan Agama Hindu Bali) Bersidang, SI581014. Participating religious groups were Paruman Pandita, Panti Agama Hindu-Bali, and Angkatan Muda Hindu Bali. Kemenuh participated as a representative of Paruman Pandita, and Kandia as a representative of Panti Agama Hindu-Bali.
33. Umar Hindu-Bali di Lombok Menjokong Idée Hindu-Bali Sabha, SI581027.
34. As noted in Chapter 3, the India students group actively involved itself in the editing of the *Upadesa*, representing the voice of truth from a holy prophet. However, Sudharta, one of the editors, adopted an extremely cautious stance in responding to perceptions that this holy text was a product of the group. Even if the group had handled the compilation, he argued, ultimately it was published with the blessing of the priests of Parisada and, in that sense, the *Upadesa* was the result of a collective consensus by Parisada.
35. *Komperensi* 1961, pp. 219–21.

36. No. 100 1962.

37. The Religion Ministry approved the following document as reflecting its official views regarding the creation of the Hindu-Bali department and subsequent developments: Sejarah Berdirinya Kanwil Departemen Agama Propinsi Bali, *Dharma Bhakti*, XVI 1993, pp. 8–11.

38. In addition to the three leaders discussed in this chapter, petitioning delegation members and their affiliations were as follows: I Md Pugeg Tantrawan (Nationalist Party), Sdr Sudjono (Communist Party), I Md Narsin (Biro Pantja Sila), I Gede Puger (Pengusaha Nasional), and I Gusti Anandakusuma (Satya Hindu Dharma).

39. The new name was Gerakan Kumara Bhuvana.

40. In fact, a political party espousing the Hindu cause was formed during the 1955 election, but failed to attract supporters.

41. The Jakarta Hindu Bali Association called for both the creation of a Hindu-Bali department at the Religion Ministry and the preservation of the Bali regional government's Autonomous Religion Bureau. It argued for a distinction between Hindus throughout Indonesia and Hindus in Bali, asserting that while the Hindu-Bali department served the nationwide Hindu population, it was not unlawful to maintain a separate Autonomous Religion Bureau in Bali to serve Hindus there.

42. The association invited religious leaders and priests from Bali to celebrate Galungan in Java; Sugriwa and the priest Ida Pedanda Oka Telaga responded. Departing from Bali on February 28, 1955, they performed ceremonies and Sugriwa gave a speech on March 2, the day of Galungan. They then proceeded to Bandung and Yogyakarta, where they participated in the Kuningan ceremonies following Galungan. One question addressed to Sugriwa prior to the ceremony was whether it was acceptable for people who had never touched holy water before to receive holy water directly from a high priest. Sugriwa replied that all people were equal before the holy water and there was no need to separate them into classes. I Gst. Bgs. Sugriwa: Galungan dan Kuningan dirayakan di Djawa, *Dhamai* 3/2 1955, pp. 5–6, 12.

43. The contents of this seminar are described in a report: Kementerian Pendidikan, Pengadjaran dan Kebudajaan, Seminar Sedjarah: Laporan Lengkap Atjara I dan II tentang Konsepsi Filsafat Sedjarah National dan Periodisasi Sedjarah Indonesia, Jogjakarta, 14 dan 15 Desember 1957.

44. The other four members were Gusti Putu Merta (head of the political section), Gusti Gde Subamia (head of the social section), Wajan Dangin (head of the economic section), and Wajan Bhadra (head of the general section) (Pendit 1979a: 353–4).

45. No. 11/D. P. R. D. 1951.

46. I Gst. Bgs. Sugriwa: Apakah Hari Raja Njepi Itu? *Dhamai* 3/2 1955, p. 10.

47. Resolutions were passed in Bangli on November 7, Gianyar on November 11, Jembrana on November 28, and Badung on December 14.

48. Bagaimana dengan Otonomi Propinsi Sunda Ketjil? *Bhakti* 2/1 1953/01/01, pp. 3–4. Nusa Tenggara 2 Propinsi, *Bhakti* 3/14 1954/07/01, p. 8. Daerah Istimewa atau Daerah Swatantra Biasa? SI571130. Pernjataan DPRDP Daerah Bahagian Buleleng, SI571230.

49. In the 1955 election, the Socialist Party gained far more support in Bali than in other regions. The success of the party in that election enabled it to form a coalition of support from diverse political bodies, ranging from the republicans to their greatest adversaries, the Gianyar royal family. However, the issue of the status of the districts highlighted the rifts among these support bases, plunging the Socialist Party into crisis. Meanwhile, on the national level, the government banned activities by the Socialist Party in 1960 (cf. Robinson 1995: 200–5).

50. Resolusi Tuntut Djadi Daerah Swatantra, Sidang Luar Biasa DPRD Swap. Gianjar, SI571112,13. Suara Pembatja: Kembalilah Kedjalan jang Benar, SI571114. Anak Agung Gde Oka Takut Kehilangan Pengaruh, SI571121. Hukum Rimba di Gianjar? SI571130. Suara Pembatja: Ada apa di Abian Seka? SI571130. Surat Kiriman, Surat Pembaca, SI571205.

51. The problem lay with the system of land use known as *pecatu*, described in Chapter 1. Under this system, those who tilled rice fields owned by the royal family could keep the entire harvest; the term *pecatu* refers to such fields. Originally, the right to use *pecatu* was granted in exchange for labor and fealty to the royal family; for the royals, the system provided a large source of manpower. According to Schulte Nordholt (1996: 129–30, 252–3), at its greatest extent during the colonial era, an estimated 50% of all land in southern Bali was *pecatu*; however, with the introduction of land taxes in the 1920s, the colonial government established individual ownership of land, leading to a reduction in the area of *pecatu*. These dramatic reforms notwithstanding, some royal families (notably that of Gianyar) still retained vast land holdings into the 1950s.

52. The regional administrators known as *perbekel* were to receive a minimum monthly stipend of 125 rupiah for up to 500 people under their jurisdiction, with the amount increasing at a rate of 25 rupiah per 500 people over that number. The village heads known as *kelihan desa* were to receive a minimum monthly stipend of 50 rupiah for up to 400 people under their jurisdiction, increasing by 10 rupiah for each additional 400, up to a maximum of 70 rupiah. The assembly determined that there was a total of 572 *perbekel* and 3000 *kelihan desa* in Bali, calculating that 161,075 rupiah per month would be required for the *perbekel* and 172,000 rupiah for the *kelihan desa*. Based on these estimates, the annual expenses for these officials came to 3,996,900 rupiah; thus the government would have to cover disbursements of four million rupiah per year. Soal Nafkah Perbekel (Pamong Desa), *Dhamai* 1/13 1953, pp. 22–3. Bagaimana Nasib Perbekel dan Kelihan sekarang? *Dhamai* 1/15 1953, pp. 12–15.

53. PKI Djembrana Pertahankan Stelsel 'Radja'? SI571119. There were many republicans among members of the nobility under the royal family, and they, too, supported the Nationalist Party (Robinson 1995: 207). However, concerns were also raised that support for the royals was perpetuated by a deep-rooted class consciousness, exemplified by a 1952 call by the governor of Lesser Sunda province for the abolition of titles. Masjarakat Bali Sesudah Repolusi, *Bhakti* 1/11 1952/11/20, pp. 1–2.

54. Negara Indonesia musti berdasarkan National, *Bhakti* 2/7 1953/03/01, pp. 2–4.

55. For Sugriwa's statements, see Negara Indonesia Mendjadi Islam? (1)(2) *Bhakti* 2/5 1953/02/10, pp. 5–6; 2/6 1953/02/20, p. 4. Kegelisahan Dewan Pemerintah Daerah Bali di Sekitar Kantor Urusan Agama Daerah, *Bhakti* 2/7 1953/03/01, pp. 4–5. Guna Kementerian Agama, *Bhakti* 2/15–16 1953/06/01, pp. 8–9.

56. For Suyasa's statements, see Agama Hindu Bali Terantjam, *Bhakti* 2/19 1953/07/10, pp. 10–11, 19. Ummar Hindu-Bali Membangun, SI570926. Hapuskan Kementerian Agama (Islam), SI571224.

57. I Gst. Bgs. Sugriwa: Pantja Sila dan Negara Islam, *Dhamai* 1/2 1953, pp. 1–7. I Gst. Bgs. Sugriwa: Rasa-tjinta terhadap kesatuan-bangsa, *Dhamai* 1/3 1953, pp. 3–6.

58. In the early 1950s, in its internal communications, the Religion Ministry used both Tuhan and Allah for the word 'God' in the phrase 'one and only God' of the First Principle of the Pancasila.

59. R. I. Berdasarkan Islam Mendjamin Kemerdekaan Agama dan Kebudajaan Lainnja? *Bhakti* 3/3 1954/02/01, pp. 5–8. This article was published under the title 'Reaction from Jakarta' as a rebuttal to the following: Nasional dan Agama tidak dapat dipisahkan? *Bhakti* 2/27 1953/10/17.

Chapter 5

1. Bupati Wajan Dhana Adakan Kesatuan Tingdakan Dalam Menghadapi Situasi Dewasa Ini, SI651015. Keputusan Gub. Kepala Daerah Bali Tentang Idjin Menjimpan Beras/Gabah/Padi, SI651019. Djangan Ada Aksi Tjorat-tjoret Tingkatkan Kewaspadaan thd. Anasir2 Subversif, SI651020.

2. Pangdam XVI/Udayana G-30-S di Bali Digagalkan ABRI, SI651105.

3. Brigdjen Sjafiudin Rakjat bersemangat tinggi tumpas habis G-30-S, SI651111. Pernjataan 5 Parpol di Bali Bubarkan PKI dan Ormas2nja, SI651121. 19 Tahun Puputan Margarana Gestapu Pendurhakaan Revolusi Didalangi PKI, SI651122.

4. After this, the fate of Suteja is unknown.

5. Djenderal2 ke Bali Masalah Bali Dapat Perhatian Penuh, SI651210.

6. Brigdjen Sjafiudin Kewadjiban kita mepulihkan keadaan Bali jang tjukup parah, SI660103. Kolonel Sarwo Eddy Sepeninggal RPKAD, SI660104. HIDUP PRAKAD Penumpasan G-30-S Berdjalan Lantjar, SI660104. Pangdam XVI/

Udayana Kontrev G-30-S di Bali, SI660104. Brigdjen Sjafiudin Tidak Ada Alasan Untuk tidak Gotong Rojong setelah Tertumpasnja Gestapu/P. K. I. SI660107.

7.   Djam Malam Seluruh Bali Dihapuskan, SI660120. Madjen. R.Askari Keamanan di Bali Pulih Kembali, SI660126.

8.   In terms of the ratio of deaths to population, the Bali massacre ranks with what occurred under the Pol Pot regime in Cambodia; however, it remains largely ignored in academia and other arenas. Robinson suggests that this is due to the prevailing cultural explanation for the massacre, which argues that a ruthless response to perceived violators of the harmonious social order is a fundamental aspect of Balinese culture, and that the PKI was viewed as such a violator (cf. Robinson 1995: 129–46, Ch. 6 'The ideology of tradition'). The cultural explanation has clear political ramifications, and to avoid being seduced by such an explanation requires a careful examination of the process by which events unfolded. Robinson himself has made a detailed study of the course of events following the September 30 Incident, which the author has confirmed through examinations of newspaper articles from the period. For a broader overview of the circumstances surrounding the September 30 Incident, see Cribb (1990).

9.   While the general discourse related to religion has been discussed here, Robinson (1995: 301) cites *nyupat* as an example of the use of religious terminology to justify the massacre: *nyupat* is a Balinese word meaning 'the shortening of someone's life in order to free them from their suffering and give them a chance to be reincarnated as a better person.' The Nationalist Party spread the story that Suteja himself wanted to be killed in this manner. By framing murder as a moral act for the purpose of ritual purification, forces within the Nationalist Party and army who sought the destruction of the PKI skillfully and deliberately redefined the massacre as a religious duty, thereby mobilizing people to kill as if it were their natural obligation.

10. Madjen Suharto G-30-S Bertudjuan Hapuskan Pantjasila, SI651225.

11. Shortly before the September 30 Incident, on June 19, 1965, a Hindu social organization, Prajaniti Hindu Indonesia, was formed in Bali. The aim of the group was to extend the presumed religious authority of Parisada to the social and political spheres. The organization explicitly acknowledges its role in the destruction of the PKI.

12. Confucianism is referred to in the law as 'KhongFuTju (Confucius).'

13. Presidential Decision No. 1, 1965 (Pentjegahan Penjalah Gunaan dan/atau Penodaan Agama).

14. Kolonel Sukarmen: Dengan Agamalah Kita Membikin Diri Kita Kebal Thd. Pengaruh Komunisme, SM670610. Berapa Djumlah Korban Akibat G30S di Bali? SM670920. Pd.Gubernur Merta Djangan Ada Usaha2 Tidak Akui Agama dan Tuhan, SM671016. Setiap Agama Diturunkan Tuhan untuk Peranan Perbaikan, SM671202.

15. Parisada Hindu-Dharma Pusat dengan persetudjuan Pds. Gubernur Kepala Daerah Bali, SI660117.

16. Seruan Kepada Umat Hindu Bali di Kab. Djembrana, SM670325. Menjongsong Hari Raya Galungan & Kuningan Mari Pandjatkan Rasa Pengaju-Bagia Sebesar-besarnja, SM670326. Perajaan Galungan & Kuningan Serti Dengan Penerangan Agama (Upanisa), SM670326. Hari2 Sutji Ke-Agama-an Djangan Biarkan Lewat Begitu Sadja Sikap Bathin jg. Sehat Manifestasi dp. Adjaran Agama, SM670327. H.B.B.Kebandjiran Galungan Dirajakan Setjara Khusus, SM670327.

17. I have translated this as 'support,' but in the original document it is called *memperbaiki mental* (mental improvement), which has a more education-oriented nuance.

18. It was reported that as of September 1967, the course had been taught in Karangasem sixty-four times, with another four courses still in progress, while in Gianyar, fifteen of fifty-one villages had held the course by the end of 1967, and 1277 people (1234 men, 43 women) had participated.

19. Pidada Adnjana: Agama Membentuk Masjarakat Susila dan Tertib, SM670919. Gianyar: Desa Keliki Tamatkan 72 Kader Hindu Dharma, SM670925. 15 Desa Dapat Penjuluhan Agama Hindu, SM680227.

20. Agama Unsur Mutlak dlm Pembinaan Moral dan Mental Orba, SM671202.

21. Three Hindu groups, the third being Prajaniti Hindu Indonesia, joined Golkar at this time. Each group came under the jurisdiction of a different division of Golkar as follows: Parisada joined Unsur Alim Ulama Hindu; the Indonesia Hindu Youth Alliance joined Unsur Pemuda/Paradjar/Mahasiswa; and Prajaniti Hindu Indonesia joined Unsur Sosial Politik.

22. Panitia 'Seminar Tampaksiring' SM680613. Panitia Seminar, SM680627. LK. 10 Djuta Hindu di Indonesia, SM680704. Seminar Pembangunan AMHI Dibuka, SM680704. Seminar A.M.H.I. Berachir, SM680709.

23. Menjambut: Sabha ke-II 'Parisada Hindu Dharma' SM681129. Sebuah tjatatan buat: 'SABA (Musjawarah Sutji) Parisadha Hindu Dharma di Denpasar, SM681201, 03. Presiden Soeharto Kehidupan Keagamaan Salah Satu Prinsip jang harus diwudjudkan, Sabha Parisadha Hindu Dharma ke II Dibuka Resmi, SM681203. Gubernur Prop. Bali Kol Soekarmen: Parisada agar tetap pertahankan kemurniannja, SM681204. Hindu Indonesia Djiwa Murni Pantja Sila, Galungan di Ibukota Dirajakan Ditingkat Nasional, SM681208. Ketua Umum Sekber Golkar tentang Hasil Parisada Hindu Dharma ke-II di Denpasar, SM681213.

24. In 1968 Mantra was selected for the national Dewan Perwakilan Rakyat Gotong Royong (People's Representative Council), along with Ibu Gedong (introduced in Chapter 3 as the wife of the governor of Lesser Sunda province) and Ida Bagus Oka Punyatmaja, a member of the India students group. Their qualifications as representatives were certified by Sekber Golkar. Representatives were selected

in February 1968, before the Parisada conference, so it appears that Mantra and others may have decided to join Golkar early on (Tim Peneliti Jurusan Sejarah Fakultas Sastra 1998: 103).

25. One staunch opponent of membership in Golkar was Cokorda Bagus Sayoga. Born at Puri Satria, where the palace was newly built when he became autonomous region head in 1938, he participated in the war for independence, then became a member of the Nationalist Party and served as head of the party in Bali. From the outset, he distanced himself from Golkar, eventually coming to support the Democratic Party. When the Suharto regime collapsed, he became a leading ally of Megawati Sukarnoputri (Tim Peneliti Jurusan Sejarah Fakultas Sastra 1998: 104–05; Izarman 1999: 58–61).

26. Parisada concluded that its organizational membership in Golkar and the political activities of its members were two separate issues.

27. Construction of temples required the acquisition of a written permit to function as a 'religious venue.'

28. No. B6/5/14, 1951/08/31.

29. As Stuart-Fox (2002: 311–13) acknowledges, the stance of the republic's central government toward Besakih Temple was, like that of the Bali Regional Assembly, extremely ambivalent, but despite its apparent rejection of the requests submitted by Sugriwa, it did in fact provide funding for the temple.

30. With the 1960 ceremony, the central government began to view the rituals at Besakih Temple as having a positive significance in terms of cultural publicity directed abroad. The Department of Information published an English-language pamphlet about the ceremony with numerous photographs (Department of Information 1960).

31. Nyoman Wijaya, Organisai Spiritual di Bawah Bayang-Bayang Kepentingan Politik. Manuscript of a report given at a seminar, entitled 'The role of organizations in maintaining security in Bali,' held in Denpasar on March 26, 2003.

32. The Nationalist Party supported the Sabda Palon movement. Because of this, a number of individuals in government positions were involved in the movement, making the incident a political issue.

33. Although the provincial government had jurisdiction over the funding, Stuart-Fox (2002: 330) suggests that the money came from the military.

34. At the Parisada meeting held in 1961 at Campuan, which was the most important gathering convened since the founding of the organization, it is said that the Dewa Agung left after attending only the opening session.

35. Vickers (2000) analyzes the activities of the Dewa Agung in the 1950s as having both elitist and democratic aspects. In terms of the former, the Dewa Agung consolidated his ties with the local priesthood and, being extremely well versed in religious texts, was in an optimal position to provide counsel to the priests. From a democratic standpoint, he was also involved in the descent

movement that had spread throughout Bali in the 1950s. This movement was concerned with the search for *kawitan* (family origins)—in other words, one's ancestral deities—who were closely associated with personal hardships. Most of Bali's ancestral deities were connected to the Klungkung area, particularly to Gelgel, located just south of the town of Klungkung, hence the involvement of the Dewa Agung with this movement. He devoted himself to the restoration of local temples and, conflicts with certain groups notwithstanding, was fundamentally a patron of the descent movement's search for ancestral deities (Vickers 2000: 265–6).

36. From testimony by I Gusti Agung Gede Putra, who would become head of the administrative agency for Besakih Temple. Putra participated in the 1963 ceremony as a private individual, and states that the chaotic conditions he witnessed at the time served as the impetus for establishing an administrative framework later on.

37. No. 526/B6/5/113.

38. Buleleng was reportedly the regency most resistant to carrying out the cremation directive due to the particularly strong bias there in favor of large-scale ceremonies. Although the government circulated the directive there, it is claimed that the Dewa Agung had to personally persuade the local priests to accept it. Moreover, the Dewa Agung was said to have discovered the document outlining the non-calendar justifications for holding the Ekadasa Rudra, and to have worked with the priests to devise procedures for carrying out the ceremony. However, this last assertion appears only in the Dewa Agung side's own account and has not been verified from other sources.

39. Linda Connor (1996: 193) suggests that the declaration that it was acceptable to economize on the ceremonies was based on a document titled *Yama Purwana Tattwa*.

40. Ida Bagus Gede, who served as director of publicity for the Ekadasa Rudra, wrote a detailed account of the cremation directive (Dinas Agama Daerah Bali 1962; cf. Stuart-Fox 2002: 316–17). One stipulation was that appropriate rites must be held for each non-Hindu religion. There was also a list of categories of the dead: those who had simply been buried, those who had died very recently, infants who had died just after birth, suicides and *salah pati* ('abnormal' cases), and those without heirs. For the last category (i.e. those with no one to carry out the cremation), the directive made clear that the government would conduct the rite. It also stipulated the use of simplified rites for those who died just before or during the designated period of the ceremony. Regarding the designated day, it stressed that it was unnecessary to consider the month in the case of those dying just before the ceremony, nor even to consider the day in the case of those dying during the designated period. In all cases, it asked that the rites take place immediately after death.

41. Tawur Agung di Pura Besakih, SI660415.

42. Pengumuman No. 25/Peng./1966, 1966/09/16. SM660919.

43. Pengumuman No. 5/Peng./1967, 1967/06/28. SM670724.

44. Bulan Djuni Pem. Dan Masjarakat Tabanan Menjelenggarakan Karja Agung 'Panca Wali Krama,' SI660313.

45. Bali Provincial Governor's Decision No. 50/Pemb. 206/I/c/1968, Denpasar, 1968/08/10.

46. 'Pura Besakih' Mulai Diperbaiki, SI650914.

47. Beryadnjalah utk Keluhuran Pura Besakih, SM660801.

48. Pura Besakih Mulai Diperbaiki, SM670302.

49. Atjara 'Atji Bhatara Turun Kabeh' di Pura Besakih, SM670423.

50. Submissions of donations were defined for (1) civil servants, (2) government-related businesses, (3) private businesses, (4) students, (5) hotels and other tourism-related businesses, and (6) *subak* (irrigation groups). The designation of the last category indicates that farmers were also fundraising targets. Pengumuman No2/Peng. Pen/1968, SM680325.

51. Umat Hindu Bersiap-siap Menjongsong Upatjara 'Betra Turun Kabeh' di Pura Besakih, SM680318. Gubernur Kol. Soekarmen Hindu Dharma Berkembang Diseluruh Pelosok Nusantara, SM680402. Upatjara Turun Kabeh di Pura Besakih Ribuan Umat Hindu dari Seluruh Pelosok Bersembahjang, SM680415. Pangdam XVI/Ud. Brigdjen Sukertijo Kita harus patuh dan tunduk atas perintah2 Tuhan, SM680415. Pura BESAKIH Tempat utk memohonkan kekuatan untuk menegakkan Dharma, SM680416.

52. Program Kundjungan Bapak Pd. Presiden R.I. ke Bali, SM671122. Pd. Presiden Djenderal Soeharto ditunggu hari ini, SM671123. Kembalilah kpd. Landasan Perdjoeangan Jang Sebenarnja, SM671124. Pd. Presiden Soeharto datang untuk saksikan partisipasi rakjat Bali dlm sukseskan program Kabinet Ampera, SM671124. Gubernur Kdh. Bali Kol. Soekarmen Rakjat Bali Bertekad Tegakkan Pantjasila dan UUD 45 setjara murni & konsekwen, SM671124. Pd. Presiden Djenderal Soeharto di Desa Pandak Gde Tuntutan ORBA adalah perbaiki kehidupan rakjat, SM671125. Saksikan Tekad Umat Hindu Bali, SM671128. Pak Harto sembahjang Bersama Umat Hindu Bali di Besakih, SM671129.

53. The colonial government reorganized the villages that had traditionally existed under customary law and established a new configuration of villages as administrative units, which the republican government preserved after independence. However, due to the continued maintenance of customs even after the formation of these administrative units, the traditional villages retained a parallel existence. To distinguish between the two types of villages, they are commonly referred to as *desa adat* (customary villages) and *desa dinas* (administrative villages) (cf. Warren 1993). On the recent discussions about *desa adat*, see 'Communities and Hindu representative bodies' in Chapter 6.

54. The classification of temples described here reflects the situation from the 1970s to the early 1980s, when Stuart-Fox conducted his survey; the actual temples at Besakih have continued to develop since then.

55. Bali Provincial Governor's Decision No. 26/Kesra. II/c/339/74, Denpasar, 1974/11/15.

56. Bali Provincial Governor's Decision No. Bappeda III/c. 4/3/1977, Denpasar, 1977/05/24.

57. A detailed description of policies by the Bali provincial government in relation to Besakih Temple is provided in a report titled Rencana Induk Pembinaan dan Pemgembangan Pura Besakih.

58. From 1979 on, the Panca Walikrama was held every ten years (Parisada Hindu Dharma Pusat 1981: 4).

59. Bali Provincial Governor's Decision No. 716, Denpasar, 1992/12/07. The 1996 ceremony was initially scheduled for 1994 but was postponed to 1996 because repairs to one of the altars at Besakih Temple could not be completed in time and because of renewed uncertainty about the details of the ritual.

60. The provincial government provided 50 million rupiah in reserve funding. As of June 1993, when the ceremonies were completed, a total of 994,076,927 rupiah had been collected, whereas total expenditures for the ceremonies came to 893,801,120 rupiah. Out of this balance the reserve funds were returned to the government, leaving an outstanding surplus of 50,275,807 rupiah. In the 1960s, it was impossible to carry out ceremonies without using reserve funds from the government. For the 1960 Panca Walikrama, the local governments covered 13 million rupiah of the total cost of 24.7 million. For the 1963 Ekadasa Rudra, government funding came to 50 million rupiah (consisting of 15 million rupiah as a gift from the president, 25 million from the provincial government, and 10 million from the regencies), out of the total cost of 88.9 million (Stuart-Fox 2002: 318–19). The surplus from funds for the 1993 ceremonies was spent on the construction and repair of Hindu temples both inside and outside Bali. One example of this was support for the Mandara Giri Temple in Java, pilgrimages to which were once popular with the Balinese, particularly civil servants.

61. Although a façade of cooperation was presented by these four entities—local government, Parisada, the Religion Ministry, and the Customary Entities Development Committee—their autonomy vanished after the formation of the Central Committee, under whose name all work on the ceremonies was undertaken. Leading the committee was the provincial government, with the governor at the helm.

62. Under the administrative framework of the Bali provincial government in 1993, this post occupied a position under the governor and vice-governor, and had below it four administrative departments. Thus the heads of these departments received their instructions directly from the bureaucrat in this post, not the governor. The Religion Section belonged to the Third Department, which handled social welfare. This department was divided into a Social Bureau and Environmental Bureau, with the Social Bureau (Biro Binsos) made up of four sections respectively in charge of religion; education

and culture; health; and youth, athletics, and women. The Religion Section handled not just Hinduism but all religions. Meetings about Besakih were organized by this section, which also provided funding and assistance for Parisada's meetings and publishing activities.

63. Born in Peliatan in 1946, Cokorda Raka Krishna had been involved in the operation of Besakih Temple since 1967. As his title indicates, he was born into the nobility, but it is impossible to identify a connection between this background and his role in the ceremonies at Besakih Temple. His assumption of the role of de facto administrator of the ceremonies can be attributed, first, to his individual ability (his willingness to handle any task, however trivial, and execute it effectively, coupled with his religious knowledge and his years of experience at Besakih Temple) and, second, to his resume (his educational background as a graduate of the Hindu Dharma University, his experience working in the Religion Ministry, and his active membership in Parisada).

64. For details on Hindu Dharma University, see Tim Peneliti Jurusan Sejarah Fakultas Sastra (1998: 176–80).

65. Several conditions were taken into account in the allocation of tasks. First, work on each ceremony was allotted to regencies close to the location of the ceremony. Next, regency populations were considered, with the larger regencies assigned more work. Finally, the availability of priests and people skilled in the preparation of offerings was a concern; regencies with few such human resources were viewed as problematic for carrying out the necessary tasks, which were allocated or not allocated accordingly. For example, work on the central altar for the Tri Bhuwana, which required the most offerings of all the ceremonies, was assigned to Klungkung, which had the largest number of offering preparation veterans.

66. The regencies were notified that, as with the ceremonial tasks, it was their responsibility to procure the materials for the offerings, as well as food for those working at the temples. The genres of performance associated with each ceremony were also assigned in regency units. In Bali the costumes, music, and choreography for a given genre of performance varied from locale to locale. The Central Committee, however, took the position that such differences notwithstanding, performances in the same genre served the same objective as far as the ceremonies were concerned. Even if the style of performance in a regency assigned by the committee to a given ceremony differed from that of performances traditionally held at the temple, they would be acceptable as long as they belonged to the same genre.

67. Work procedures at the regency level varied from regency to regency. The Central Committee included regency-level representatives from local governments, Parisada, the Customary Entities Development Committee, and the Religion Ministry, and these individuals formed committees within the regency administrations. Central Committee directives were passed on to these regency-level committees, which consulted with the leading priests of

their regency in deciding how to proceed with the tasks assigned to them. As a result, tasks were carried out in different ways based on the circumstances of each regency. In Gianyar, for example, the production of offerings was divided among all villages, whereas in Klungkung and Karangasem the work was concentrated in one particular village, to which workers from other villages were recruited to prepare the offerings. In Tabanan, meanwhile, tasks were allotted among several designated villages.

68. *Caru* offerings were made at nine locations for the Candi Narmada, five for the Panca Walikrama ring Danu, and three for the Tri Bhuwana, for a total of seventeen venues.

69. A manuscript (*Lontar indik Ekadasa Rudra*) about the Ekadasa Rudra (which was archived in the library established during the colonial era, as described in Chapter 2) was re-examined, while similar *lontar* (palm-leaf texts) were found in the possession of individual priests.

70. Panitia Plaksana Karya Agung Tri Bhuwana, Candi Narmada, Panca Walikrama ring Danu dan Bhatara Turun Kabeh Tahun 1993 di Pura Besakih, Palihan Upakara, Denpasar, 1992.

71. Parisada Hindu Dharma Indonesia Pusat, Yasa Kerti Umat Hindu dalam rangka menyongsong Karya Agung Tri Bhuwana, Candi Narmada, Panca Walikrama ring Danu dan Bhatara Turun Kabeh Tahun 1993, Denpasar, 1992.

72. Piagam Besakih III/TAP/M. Sabha/1996.

73. Widnyana Sudibya (1996) has written a highly detailed account of ceremonies at Besakih Temple from the 1989 Panca Walikrama onward. I have referred to this account for my descriptions of the ceremonies.

74. This refers to the *tirtha panglukatan* (holy water) produced in the Nuwasen ceremony. In the case of the Eka Bhuwana performed on March 20, 1996, this ritual was carried out on February 14 (Agastia 1996: 44–9).

75. The second largest malasti after the one conducted in 1966 was actually carried out in Tabanan.

76. Atjara 'Atji Bhatara Turun Kabeh' di Pura Besakih, SM670423.

77. Written texts are able to serve a dual function as sources for the reconstruction of ceremonies and also for ideological authority because they can be read in different ways depending on the objective. When the purpose is to enact ceremonies, the approach taken is that of an information search in which texts are actually scrutinized to elicit facts. In this case, only a very few texts are selected for perusal. In the case of religious instruction, or when there is a need to furnish support for an abstract concept such as the objective of a ceremony, pertinent passages will be selectively quoted from a much wider range of sources, including Indian scriptures, without the need to specify quotations.

78. The *Bali Post* published daily listings of donations submitted to the newspaper for ceremonies at Besakih Temple, along with the names of the donors. The newspaper passed the funds it collected on to the provincial government. Thus

donations submitted via the newspaper provided the donor with a means of self-promotion and public notice of one's participation in worthy causes. This donation route was used not only for the ceremonies at Besakih Temple, but also for those at other large temples, as well as aid for the sick.

Chapter 6

1. In Indonesian, the term used for 'civil society' is generally masyarakat madani, which has a strong Islamic association, or masyarakat sipil, a literal translation from the English. Hindus naturally preferred not to use the Islam-tinged term, and there was little resistance to English expressions in Bali.

2. Members of Pemuda Hindu did not necessarily accept this line of thought as self-evident. One former leader of the group admitted that it took him five years to accept the idea of conducting activities within the framework of Hinduism. Speaking from his present-day perspective, the former leader, who is university-educated, said that, initially, he could only view the use of a religious framework to engage in a social movement as extremely 'primitive' and behind the times, and it took a very long time for him to discover the meaning of religion.

3. No. II/MPR/1983.

4. For details on the founding of Peradah, see Dewan Pimpinan Pusat Peradah Indonesia (1989).

5. Parisada Priests' Conference Decision No. 016/Tap/IV/PA.PHDP/1984.

6. The guidelines mentioned here refer to the Pedoman Penghayatan dan Pengamalan Pancasila, commonly abbreviated as P4.

7. Religion Ministry Notice No. H/362/1985.

8. No. 851/Org/VII/PHDIP/1986, No. 1032/Org/VIII/PHDIP/1986, 08/26.

9. For example, it used the name Ikatan Pemuda Hindu Indonesia.

10. Putu Setia's house in Denpasar served as an office where staff members, including members of Setia's family, received edited manuscripts sent by post or email from Hindus in different locales. Setia himself read the final version of the manuscript and wrote an introduction. The magazine was printed in Bali. With Hindu subscribers throughout Indonesia, the magazine was published as a family operation.

11. Wayan Sudhirta moved from Jakarta to Bali to run as a candidate for the representative of a local constituency following the institutional reform of the Indonesian parliament.

12. Anggaran Dasar Parisada Hindu Dharma Indonesia Bab 1 Pasal 3 (Parisada Hindu Dharma Indonesia Pusat 1991: 36). At the fifth general conference in 1986, it had been stipulated that 'the center shall be in Denpasar' (Parisada Hindu Dharma se Indonesia 1986: 14).

13. Excluding temple-related associations, at present Jakarta has such associations as Yayasan Pitra Yadnya, which handles burials; Yayasan Mandira Widhyaka, which is concerned with Hindu education; Yayasan Dharma Nusantara, which is involved with book publication and school construction; and Yayasan Dharma Sarathi, which oversees temple construction. There is also Yayasan Manunggal Karsa Nusantara, an organization of Hindus of relatively high social status residing in Jakarta. This group plays an important role, providing funding for Hindu activities in Jakarta (including the construction of Parisada's headquarters building) and having a major voice in the selection of Parisada executives.

14. The term *desa adat* has been replaced by the Balinese-derived *desa pakraman*; by 2003 such importance was attributed to the existence of the customary villages that the *Bali Post* carried a debate over the pros and cons of abolishing the *desa dinas*.

15. This situation drew the attention of a human rights group. See the November 7, 2003, report by the International Crisis Group titled *The Perils of Private Security in Indonesia: Guards and Militias on Bali and Lombok*.

16. The actual text, which anticipates an exceedingly large number of groups and organizations, reads as follows: Utusan, Organisasi, Lcmbaga, Forum, Yayasan, Sampradaya dan Komunitas umat yang bernafaskan Hindu (Parisada Hindu Dharma Indonesia Pusat 2001: 20). A similar description had already appeared in 1996, but only applied to qualifications for observers at regular meetings of regional branches, not general conferences: Organisasi-organisasi Hindu/Forum/Lembaga/Yayasan yang bernafaskan Hindu yang ada di daerah (Parisada Hindu Dharma Indonesia Pusat 1996: 99).

17. 1/TAP/PHDI,B/XII/2001 01/12/18.

18. Parisada headquarters Decision SK-05/Parisada Pusat/XII/2001 01/12/07. 02/ST/Parisada Pusat/XII/2001 01/12/07. 02/REK/PHDI-P/B/2002 02/01/15. Parisada Bali Decision 05/SK/PLT PHDI BALI/III/2002 02/02/20. 06/SK/PLT PHDI BALI/III/2002 02/03/02. 07/SK/PLT PHDI BALI/III/2002 02/03/09.

19. Ceremony executive committee members were appointed in accordance with Bali Provincial Governor's Decision No. 454/1368/BKPP, dated March 7, 2002. Total expenses for the ceremony were 119,795,425 rupiah, of which the province and regencies donated 76,000,000 rupiah. See Dwikora (2002: 72) for details on the funding provided by the province and regencies for the Besakih meeting; the head of the village with jurisdiction over Luhur Temple remarks that he was utterly unaware of the schism in Parisada at the time and was surprised by the sudden notification that a ceremony would be held there, thinking it did not provide sufficient time for preparations, but abided by the governor's decision.

20. Eighth Parisada General Conference Decision No. III/TAP/Maha Sabha VIII/2001, titled 'Pedoman Pengamalan Dharma dalam Kehidupan Berbangsa dan Bernegara' (Parisada Hindu Dharma Indonesia Pusat 2001: 104–05).

21. The expression 'Hindu-type groups' was only used in written documents. Ordinarily these groups were referred to by the Hindu term 'Sampradaya.' However, associates of these various groups limited their use of the word to the activities of groups deemed 'suspicious' by the courts and the Ministry of Home Affairs. In this sense, the term 'Sampradaya' could be applied to Hare Krishna, but not to Sai Baba.

22. The Ministry of Home Affairs had jurisdiction over not only religious activities, but also group activities. The 'permission' mentioned here was granted to groups by the Ministry of Home Affairs. In the case of Hindus, agencies such as the Religion Ministry or Parisada did not undertake their own respective registrations of religious groups.

23. Gusti Agung Gede Putra, who had become a representative of Parisada in 1968 and head of the Hindu department at the Religion Ministry in 1985, became a Sai Baba convert when he heard Sai Baba's voice firsthand in Bangalore, India (Bakker 1993: 155–6).

24. After Parisada granted them recognition, members of Hare Krishna could be seen adopting the same strategy as Sai Baba. Having obtained the status of Parisada priests at the eighth general conference, Hare Krishna priests began applying the methodology of displaying new Hindu religious practices as part of community activities.

25. Kerepun summarized his views in two pamphlets titled as follows: Pande Menggugat: Telaah Singkat atas Dokumentasi Masalah Pande. Perjuangan Penggunaan Sarwa Sadaka di Pura Agung Besakih.

26. Kerepun had served as the governor of Gianyar regency, and the current provincial governor had worked under him. As his former superior in their previous workplace, Kerepun was therefore in a position to speak with the governor. Kerepun says that the governor's ultimate decision to allow his speech to be given at the Campuan meeting enraged him and led him to sever his ties with the governor.

27. In the case of the *Bhujangga*, the *Bhujangga* title was used to refer to a role of priests in the ceremonies, but priests of the *Bhujangga* title group were not employed to perform that role.

28. Parisada headquarters Decision No. 036/KEP/PARISADA PUSAT/III/2003. This decision reflected the results of the Parisada meetings of December 16, 2002, and March 7, 2003.

29. No. 02/Bhisama/Sabha Pandita Parisada Pusat/XI 2002.

Epilogue

1. See the articles in Ramstedt (ed.) (2004) for details about Hinduism in Indonesia outside Bali.

2. Hefner (2004), who surveyed Hindu converts around Yogyakarta, Java, introduces examples with implications for the future of Indonesian Hinduism. Terrible massacres occurred in 1965 and 1966 in this region, after which people who were pressured by the government to join one of the official religions converted to Hinduism. However, they were dismayed by the training provided by Parisada, which seemed intended to inculcate them with Balinese traditions more than Hinduism per se, extending to temple styles and modes of dress, as well as doctrine; at the same time, they found the content of religious education in the schools under the Suharto regime to be 'controlled and formalistic.' Then, in the 1980s, government support was withdrawn, and Hinduism seemed certain to decline. In this situation, well-educated Hindu youth and intellectuals independent of Parisada started a new Hindu movement. Hefner (2004: 106) writes that a 'feature of this new Hindu movement is its vigorous pluralism and concern for inter-religious dialogue.'

3. The bombings in Kuta in 2002 destroyed Bali's image as a peaceful tourist spot and imperiled the security of the Balinese themselves. This was a period during which reaction to the highly centralized Suharto regime prompted the promulgation of the decentralization laws (Nos. 22/1999 and 25/1999), which promised more regional autonomy. It was in this context that, in 2002, the Bali Post group launched a campaign to extend the discourse to emphasize *ajeg Bali* (the strength of Balinese culture) for the purpose of returning to its origins, recovering a pure, peaceful, and safe Bali, and putting up resistance to terrorism. Schulte Nordholt (2007: 57–8) describes how Pedanda Made Gunung, representative of the Campuan faction, made this discourse comprehensible to ordinary people.

4. In his examination of the Parisada schism, Picard (2004, 2011a, 2011b) traces it back to the origins of the Hindu recognition movement in Bali, enhancing our understanding of the perception of Hinduism in the colonial era and the recognition movement of the 1950s.

5. From a letter by Provincial Governor Sukarmen dated August 10, 1968. A thorough analysis of this letter can be found in Stuart-Fox (2002: 316–20). As mentioned in Chapter 5, the governor announced that he had already played the role of *guru wisesa* at the Bhatara Turun Kabeh ritual at Besakih Temple in 1967.

6. Pitana (1999) asserts that the confrontation between the priests of the commoner groups and Parisada, which supported the *brahmana* priests, represented a struggle over social status and signified the re-emergence of a caste conflict that had persisted since the colonial era. Picard (2011a: 134) and Schulte Nordholt (2007: 20–6) make the same argument. See Nala (2004) for a discussion of the selection and education of priests by Parisada.

BIBLIOGRAPHY

Archives

Algemeen Rijksarchief (ARA), DenHaag
    Memories van Overgave van het Bali en Lombok (MvO)
    Staatsblad van Nederlandsch-Indie (Stbl)

Koninklijk Instituut voor Taal-, Land- en Volkenkunde (KITLV), Leiden
    Collectie Korn, or.435 (Col. Korn)
    Collectie Moojen, H1169 (Col. Moojen)

Newspaper, Bali
    Bali Post (BP)
    Suara Indonesia (edisi Bali) (SI)
    Suluh Marhaen (SM)
    ex. SI591128: *Suara Indonesia* Nov. 28, 1959

Agastia, Ida Bagus Gede (1996), *Eka Dasa Rudra Eka Bhuwana*, Denpasar: Parisada Hindu Dharma Indonesia Pusat.

Agung, Ide Anak Agung Gde (1985), *Dari Negara Indonesia Timur ke Republik Indonesia Serikat*, Yogyakarta: Gadjah Mada University Press.

Agung, Ide Anak Agung Gde (1993), *Kenangan Masa Lampau: Zaman Kolonial Hindia Belanda dan Zaman Pendudukan Jepang di Bali*, Jakarta: Yayasan Obor Indonesia.

Anderson, Benedict (1991), *Imagined Communities: Reflections on the Origin and Spread of Nationalism* (revised edition), London, New York: Verso.

Anonymous (1916), Bali. Oudheidkundig Verslag 4, pp. 107–17.

Anonymous (1917), De Ramp op Bali, *Weekblad voor Indie*, 13 (43), pp. 990–3.

Atkinson, Jane Monning (1987), 'Religions in dialogue: the construction of an Indonesian minority religion,' in Rita Smith Kipp and Susan Rodgers (eds), *Indonesian Religions in Transition*, Tucson, AZ: University of Arizona Press, pp. 171–86.

Atmadja, Nengah Bawa (1987), Surya Kanta sebagai Perkumpulan Sempalan dan Gagasannya dalam Mewujudkan Kemahuan dan Kesumpurnaan Masyarakat Bali (1925–1927), Program Studi Sejarah, Universitas Udayana.

Bagus, I Gusti Ngurah (2004), 'The Parisada Hindu Dharma Indonesia in a society in transformation: the emergence of conflicts amidst differences and demands,' in Martin Ramstedt (ed.), *Hinduism in Modern Indonesia: A Minority Religion between Local, National, and Global Interests*, London and New York: Routledge Curzon, pp. 84–92.

Bakker, F. L. (1993), *The Struggle of the Hindu Balinese Intellectuals*, Amsterdam: VU University Press.

Benda, Harry J. (1983), *The Crescent and the Rising Sun: Indonesian Islam under the Japanese Occupation 1942–1945*, Holland: Foris Publication.

Boland, B. J. (1971), *The Struggle of Islam in Modern Indonesia*, The Hague: Martinus Nijhoff.

Boon, James A. (1977), *The Anthropological Romance of Bali 1597–1972: Dynamic Perspectives in Marriage and Caste, Politics and Religion*, Cambridge: Cambridge University Press.

Caldwell, Ian (1985), 'Anak Agung Panji Tisna: Balinese raja and Indonesian novelist, 1908–78,' *Indonesian Circle*, 36, pp. 55–79.

Cheong, Young Mun (1982), *H. J. van Mook and Indonesian Independence: A Study of His Role in Dutch-Indonesian Relation, 1945–1948*, The Hague: Martinus Hijhoff.

Connor, Linda H. (1996), 'Contesting and transforming the work for the dead in Bali: the case of Ngaben Ngirit,' in Adrian Vickers (ed.), *Being Modern in Bali: Image and Change*, New Haven: Yale Southeast Asia Studies, pp. 179–211.

Connor, Linda and Adrian Vickers (2003), 'Crisis, citizenship, and cosmopolitanism: living in a local and global risk society in Bali,' *Indonesia*, 75, pp. 153–80.

Cribb, Robert (ed.) (1990), *The Indonesian Killings of 1965–1966: Studies from Java and Bali*, Clayton, Vic.: Centre of Southeast Asian Studies, Monash University.

Department of Information (1960), *Karya Pudja Pantja Wali Krama*, Djakarta: Department of Information.

Dewan Pimpinan Pusat Pemuda Hindu (2000), *Buku Pedoman Pemuda Hindu*, Jakarta: Dewan Pimpinan Pusat Pemuda Hindu.

Dewan Pimpinan Pusat Peradah Indonesia (1989), *Mengungkap Kelahiran Ormas Peradah-Indonesia*, Jakarta: Dewan Pimpinan Pusat Peradah Indonesia.

Diantari, Ni Putu (1990), Gerakan Pembaruan Hindu: Studi tentang Perkembangan Pemikiran Intelektual Hindu di Bali Tahun 1925–1958, Skripsi Sarjana Dalam, Fakultas Sastra, Universitas Udayana.

Dinas Agama Daerah Bali (1962), *Almanak Hindu Bali*, Denpasar: Dinas Agama Daerah Bali.

Dirks, Nicholas B. (2001), *Casts of Mind: Colonialism and the Making of Modern India*, Princeton and Oxford: Princeton University Press.

Djajadiningrat, Idrus Nasir (1958), *The Beginnings of the Indonesian-Dutch Negotiations and the Hage Veluwe Talks*, Ithaca, NY: Cornell University, Monograph Series.

Djelantik, A. A. M. (1997), *Memoirs of a Balinese Prince*, Hong Kong: Periplus Edition.

Dwikora, Putu Wirata (2002), *Menjadi Pelayan Umat*, Denpasar: Parisada Hindu Dharma Indonesia Propinsi Bali.

Feith, Herbert and Lance Castles (eds) (1970), *Indonesia Political Thinking 1945–1965*, Ithaca, NY, and London: Cornell University Press.

Flierhaar, H. Te (1941), 'De Aanpassing van het Inlandsch Onderwijs op Bali aan de Eigen Sfeer', *Koloniale Studien jrg*, 25, pp. 135–59.

Fraser, J. J. (1910), 'De Inheemsche Rechtspraak op Bali', *De Indische Gids*, 32 (2), pp. 865–910.

Friederich, R. (1847), 'De Oesana Bali', *Tijdschrift voor Nederlandsch-Indie*, 9 (3), pp. 245–373.

Friederich, R. (1959), *The Civilization and Culture of Bali*, Calcutta: Susil Gupta.

Fukushima Mabito 福島真人 (1991), Shinkō no Tanjyō (The birth of 'belief'), Tōyōbunka, Kenkyūsho Kiyō 113, pp. 97–210.

Geertz, Clifford (1980), *Negara: The Theatre State in Nineteenth-Century Bali*, Princeton, NJ: Princeton University Press.

Geertz, Hildred and Clifford Geertz (1975), *Kinship in Bali*, Chicago and London: University of Chicago Press.

George, Kenneth M. (1996), *Showing Signs of Violence: The Cultural Politics of a Twentieth-Century Headhunting Ritual*, Berkeley, CA: University of California Press.

Harvey, Barbara S. (1985), 'South Sulawesi: puppets and patriots,' in Andrey R. Kahin (ed.), *Regional Dynamics of the Indonesian Revolution: Unity from Diversity*, Honolulu: University of Hawaii Press, pp. 207–35.

Hauser-Schäublin, B. (2011), 'Spiritualized politics and the trademark of culture: political actors and their use of *adat* and *agama* in post-Suharto Bali,' in Michel Picard and Remy Madinier (eds), *The Politics of Religion in Indonesia: Syncretism, Orthodoxy, and Religious Contention in Java and Bali*, London and New York: Routledge, pp. 192–213.

Hefner, Robert W. (2004), 'Hindu reform in an Islamizing Java: pluralism and peril,' in Martin Ramstedt (ed.), *Hinduism in Modern Indonesia: A Minority Religion between Local, National, and Global Interests*, London and New York: Routledge Curzon, pp. 93–108.

Hoadley, M. C. and M. B. Hooker (1981), *An Introduction to Javanese Law: A Translation and Commentary on the Agama*, Tucson, AZ: University of Arizona Press.

Howe, Leo (2001), *Hinduism and Hierarchy in Bali*, Oxford and Santa Fe, NM: James Currey, School of American Research Press.

Hurgronje, C. Snouck (1906), *The Achehnese*, Leyden: E. J. Brill.

Inden, Ronald (1990), *Imaging India*, Cambridge and Oxford: Blackwell.

International Crisis Group (2003), *The Perils of Private Security in Indonesia: Guards and Militias on Bali and Lombok*, ICG Asia Report no. 67, Jakarta and Brussels: ICG, www.crisisgroup.org/asia/south-east-asia/indonesia/perils-private-security-indonesia-guards-and-militias-bali-and-lombok

Izarman (1999), *Memoar Tjokorda Bagus Sayoga: Melangkah di Jalan Kebenaran*, Denpasar: Penerbitan Nusa Tenggara.

Kagami Haruya 鏡味治也 (2000), *Seisakubunka no Jinruigaku* (The Anthropology of The Culture of Policy Making), Kyōto: Sekaisisōsha.

Kahin, George, M. (1952), *Nationalism and Revolution in Indonesia*, Ithaca, NY: Cornell University Press.

Kats, J. (1939), 'In Memoriam H. J. E. F. Schwartz,' *Djawa*, 19, pp. 86–8.

Kemmerling, G. L. L. (1918), De Aardbeving van Bali op 21 Januari 1917, Jaarboek van het Mijnwezen in Nederlandsch Oost-Indie 1917, pp. 1–49.

Kempers, A. J. Bernet (1991), *Monumental Bali: Introduction to Balinese Archeology & Guide to the Monuments*, Berkeley, CA, and Singapore: Periplus Editions.

Kipp, Rita Smith (1996), *Dissociated Identities: Ethnicity, Religion, and Class in an Indonesian Society*, Ann Arbor, MI: University of Michigan Press.

Kipp, Rita Smith and Susan Rodgers (1987), 'Introduction: Indonesian religions in society,' in Rita Smith Kipp and Susan Rodgers (eds), *Indonesian Religions in Transition*, Tucson, AZ: University of Arizona Press, pp. 1–31.

Korn, V. E. (1932), *Het Adatrecht van Bali (Tweede Herziene Druk)*, 's-Gravenhage: G. Naeff.

Lane, Max (1972), Wedastera Suyasa in Balinese Politics, 1962–1972: From Charismatic Politics to Socio-Educational Activities, Bachelor of Arts thesis. Department of Indonesian and Malayan Studies, The University of Sydney.

Legge, John D. (1961), *Central Authority and Regional Autonomy in Indonesia: A Study in Local Administration 1950–1960*, Ithaca, NY: Cornell University Press.

Lekkerkerker, C. (1920), *Bali en Lombok: Overzicht der Litteratuur omtrent Deze Eilanden tot Einde 1919*, Rijswijk: Blankwaardt & Schoonhoven.

Lyon, Margaret, l. (1977), Politics and Religious Identity: Genesis of Javanese-Hindu Movement in Rural Central Java, doctoral thesis, University California, Berkeley, CA.

Magenda, B. D. (1989), The Surviving Aristocracy in Indonesia, doctoral thesis, Cornell University.

Marcel, Max (1917), Zuid-Bali. De Reflector, 2 (5) pp. 116–18, 2 (6) pp. 143–5.

Meidiary, F. D. A. (1999), Bibliografi I Gusti Bagus Sugriwa 1900–1977, Skripsi untuk Sarjana Dalam, Universitas Udayana.

Moojen, P. A. J. (1920), *Bali: Verslag en Voorstellen aan de Regeering van Nederlandsch-Indie*, Batavia: Bond van N.I. Kunstkringen en N. I. Heemschut.

Moojen, P. A. J. (1926), *Kunst op Bali: Inleidende Studie tot de Bouwkunst*, Den Haag: Adi Pustaka.

Mulder, Neils (1978), *Mysticism and Everyday Life in Contemporary Java*, Singapore: Singapore University Press.

Nagafuchi Yasuyuki 永渕康之 (1994), 1917 nen Bali Daijishin: Shokumintijyōkyō niokeru Bunkakeisei no Seijigaku (Colonial narratives on demolished culture: the Great Earthquake in Bali, 1917), Bulletin of the National Museum of Ethnology 19 (2), pp. 259–310.

Nagafuchi Yasuyuki 永渕康之 (1998), *Bali Tō* (The Island of Bali), Tōkyō: Kōdansha.

Nagafuchi Yasuyuki 永渕康之 (2005), Shūkyō to Tagenkasuru Kati: Indonesia niokeru Hindu o meguru Kyōkaisen o sadameru Tōsō (Religion and proliferating pluralism of values: negotiating the boundaries on Hinduism in Indonesia), Bulletin of the National Museum of Ethnology 29 (3), pp. 375–428.

Nagafuchi Yasuyuki 永渕康之 (2007), *Bali Shūkyō Kokka: Hindu no Seidoka o Tadoru* (Bali, Religion, States: The History of The Institutionalization of Hindu), Tōkyō: Seidosha.

Nagazumi Akira 永積昭 (1980), Indonesia Minzokuisiki no Kēsē, Tōkyō: Tōkyō Daigaku Shuppankai. (1972, The dawn of Indonesian nationalism: the early years of the Budi Utomo, 1908–1918, Institute of Developing Economies.)

Nakamura Kiyoshi 中村潔 (1990), 'Balika' nitsuite (On 'Balinization'), Shakaijinruigaku Nenpō 16, pp. 179–91.

Nala, Ngurah (2004), 'The development of Hindu education in Bali,' in Martin Ramstedt (ed.), *Hinduism in Modern Indonesia: A Minority Religion between Local, National, and Global Interests*, London and New York: Routledge Curzon, pp. 76–83.

Nieuwenkamp, W. O. J. (1922), *Zwerftochten op Bali*, Amsterdam: Elsevier.

Panitia Catur Windu Yayasan Dwijendra (1985), Catur Windu Yayasan Dwijendra, Denpasar: Panitia Catur Windu Yayasan Dwijendra.

Parisada Hindu Dharma (1970), *Piodalan Ekadasa Warsa Parisada Hindu Dharma 1959–1970*, Denpasar: Dharma Bhakti.

Parisada Hindu Dharma (1978 [1967]), Upadesa tentang Ajaran-Ajaran Agama Hindu, Denpasar: Parisada Hindu Dharma.

Parisada Hindu Dharma Indonesia Propinsi Bali (1991), *Lokasabha II*, Denpasar: Parisada Hindu Dharma Indonesia Propinsi Bali.

Parisada Hindu Dharma Indonesia Propinsi Bali (2001), *Sejarah Parisada dan Hasil Lokasabha IV*, Denpasar: Parisada Hindu Dharma Indonesia Propinsi Bali.

Parisada Hindu Dharma Indonesia Propinsi Bali (2002), *Hasil-Hasil Lokasabha IV*, Denpasar: Parisada Hindu Dharma Indonesia Propinsi Bali.

Parisada Hindu Dharma Indonesia Pusat (1991), *Keputusan dan Ketetapan Maha Sabha VI, Tanggal 9–14 September 1991 di Jakarta*, Jakarta: Parisada Hindu Dharma Indonesia Pusat.

Parisada Hindu Dharma Indonesia Pusat (1996), *Hasil-Hasil Maha Sabha VII Parisada Hindu Dharma Indonesia, Surakarta, 18–20 September 1996*, Jakarta: Parisada Hindu Dharma Indonesia Pusat.

Parisada Hindu Dharma Indonesia Pusat (2001), *Hasil-Hasil Maha Sabha VIII Parisada Hindu Dharma Indonesia, Denpasar, 20–24 September 2001*, Jakarta: Parisada Hindu Dharma Indonesia Pusat.

Parisada Hindu Dharma Pusat (1981), *Karya Agung Eka Dasa Rudra: Bali, Once in a Century Ceremony*, Denpasar: Parisada Hindu Dharma Pusat Bagian Penyalur dan Penerbitan.

Parisada Hindu Dharma se Indonesia (1986), *Keputusan/Ketetapan Maha Sabha V Parisada Hindu Dharma se Indonesia Tanggal 24 s/d 27 Peburuari 1986 di Denpasar*, Denpasar: Parisada Hindu Dharma se Indonesia.

Parker, Lynette (2000), 'The introduction of Western-style education to Bali: domination by consent,' in Adrian Vickers and I Nyoman Darma Putra with Michele Ford (eds), *To Change Bali: Essays in Honour of I Gusti Ngurah Bagus*, Denpasar: Bali Post, pp. 47–69.

Pendit, Nyoman S. (1979a [1954]), *Bali Berjuang*, Jakarta: PT Gunung Agung.

Pendit, Nyoman S. (1979b), *Mencari Inovasi*, Jakarta: PT Gunung Agung.

Picard, Michel (1999), 'The discourse of Kebalian: transcultural constructions of Balinese identity,' in Linda H. Connor and Raechelle Rubinstein (eds), *Staying Local in the Global Village: Bali in the Twentieth Century*, Honolulu: University of Hawai'i Press.

Picard, Michel (2004), 'What's in a name? Agama Hindu Bali in the making,' in Martin Ramstedt (ed.), *Hinduism in Modern Indonesia: A Minority Religion between Local, National, and Global Interests*, London and New York: Routledge Curzon, pp. 56–75.

Picard, Michel (2011a), 'From Agama Hindu Bali to Agama Hindu and back: toward a relocalization of the Balinese religion?' in Michel Picard and Remy Madinier (eds), *The Politics of Religion in Indonesia: Syncretism, Orthodoxy, and Religious Contention in Java and Bali*, London and New York: Routledge, pp. 117–41.

Picard, Michel (2011b), 'Balinese religion in search of recognition: from Agama Hindu Bali to Agama Hindu (1945–1965),' *Bijdragen tot de Taal-, Land- en Volkenkunde*, 167 (4), pp. 482–510.

Pitana, I Gde (1999), 'Status struggles and the priesthood in contemporary Bali,' in Raechelle Rubinstein and Linda H. Connor (eds), *Staying Local in the Global Village: Bali in the Twentieth Century*, Honolulu: University of Hawai'i Press, pp. 181–201.

Putra, Anak Agung Putu Oka (1989), Perkeumpulan Bali Darma Laksana: Sebuah Organisasi Sosial di Bali 1936–1942, Skripsi Sarjana Dalam, Fakultas Sastra, Universitas Udayana.

Putra, I Nyoman Darma (2000), 'Bali and modern Indonesian literature: the 1950s,' in Adrian Vickers and I Nyoman Darma Putra with Michele Ford (eds), *To Change Bali: Essays in Honour of I Gusti Ngurah Bagus*, Denpasar: Bali Post, pp. 135–53.

Putra Agung, Anak Agung Gde (1974), Perobahan Sosial dan Pertentangan Kasta di Bali Utara, 1924–1928, Universitas Gadjah Mada.

Ramstedt, Martin (ed.) (2004), *Hinduism in Modern Indonesia: A Minority Religion between Local, National, and Global Interests*, London and New York: Routledge Curzon.

Reid, Anthony (1979), 'The nationalist quest for an Indonesian past,' in Anthony Reid and David Marr (eds), *Perceptions of the Past in Southeast Asia*, Singapore: Heinemann Educational Books, pp. 281–98.

Robinson, Geoffrey, B. (1995), *The Dark Side of Paradise: Political Violence of Bali*, Ithaca, NY, and London: Cornell University Press.

Robson, Stuart (1995), *Desawarnana (Nagarakrtagama)*, Leiden: KITLV Press.

Schiller, Anne (1997), *Small Sacrifices: Religious Change and Cultural Identity among the Ngaju of Indonesia*, Oxford and New York: Oxford University Press.

Schiller, A. Arthur (1955), *The Formation of Federal Indonesia 1945–1949*, The Hague: W. van Hoeve.

Schrauwers, Albert (2000), *Colonial 'Reformation' in the Highlands of Central Sulawesi, Indonesia, 1892–1995*, Toronto, Buffalo, NY, and London: University of Toronto Press.

Schulte Nordholt, Henk (1981), 'Negara: a theatre state?', *Bijdragen tot de Taal-, Land- en Volenkunde* 137 (4), pp. 470–6.

Schulte Nordholt, Henk (1986), *Bali: Colonial Conceptions and Political Change 1700–1940: From Shifting Hierarchies to 'Fixed Order'*, Amsterdam: Erasmus University.

Schulte Nordholt, Henk (1991), *State, Village, and Ritual in Bali: A Historical Perspective*, Amsterdam: VU University Press.

Schulte Nordholt, Henk (1996), *The Spell of Power: A History of Balinese Politics 1650–1940*, Leiden: KITLV Press.

Schulte Nordholt, Henk (2000), 'From Wangsa to Bangsa: subaltern voices and personal ambivalences in 1930s colonial Bali,' in Adrian Vickers and I Nyoman Darma Putra with Michele Ford (eds), *To Change Bali: Essays in Honour of I Gusti Ngurah Bagus*, Denpasar: Bali Post, pp. 71–88.

Schulte Nordholt, Henk (2007), *Bali: An Open Fortress, 1995–2005: Regional Autonomy, Electoral Democracy and Entrenched Identities*, Leiden: KITLV Press.

Sears, Laurie J. (1996), *Shadows of Empire: Colonial Discourse and Javanese Tales*, Durham and London: Duke University Press.

Setia, Putu (1993), *Kebangkitan Hindu Menyongsong Abad Ke-21*, Jakarta: Pustaka Manikgeni.

Stuart-Fox, David J. (1992), *Bibliography of Bali: Publications from 1920 to 1990*, Leiden: KITLV Press.

Stuart-Fox, David J. (2002), *Pura Besakih: Temple, Religion and Society in Bali*, Leiden: KITLV Press.

Subagiasta, I Ketut (1999), Reformasi Agama Hindu dalam Perubahan Sosial di Bali, Tesis Derajat Magister, Program Pascasarjana, Universitas Udayana.

Sudibya, Made Widnyana (1996), *Kilas Balik Karya Agung Candi Narmada, Panca Walikrama ring Danu, Tri Bhuwana & Bhatara Turun Kabeh Pura Agung Besakih 1993*, Denpasar: Pelawa Sari Offset.

Supartha, Ngrah Oka (1993), *Karya Agung Candi Narmada, Panca Walikrama ring Sagra Danu, Tribhuwana dan Bhatara Turun Kabeh Pura Agung Besakih*, Denpasar.

Supartha, Wayan (ed.) (1995), *Dharma Agama dan Dharma Negara*, Denpasar: PT. BP.

Supomo, S. (1979), 'The image of Majapahit in later Javanese and Indonesian writing,' in Anthony Reid and David Marr (eds), *Perceptions of the Past in Southeast Asia*, Singapore: Heinemann Educational Books, pp. 171–85.

Suryadinata, Leo, Evi Nurvidya Arifin, and Aris Ananta (2003), *Indonesia's Population: Ethnicity and Religion in a Changing Political Landscape*, Singapore: Institute of Southeast Asian Studies.

Sutherland, H. A. (1979), *The Making of a Bureaucratic Elite: The Colonial Transformation of the Javanese Priyai*, Singapore: Heinemann.

Swellengrebel, J. L. (1984), 'Introduction,' in *Bali: Studies in Life, Thought, and Ritual*, Dordrecht: Foris Publications, pp. 1–76.

Tim Peneliti Jurusan Sejarah Fakultas Sastra (1998), *Prof. Dr. I. B. Mantra: Biografi Seorang Budayawan 1928–1995*, Denpasar: Upada Sastra.

Tsing, Anna Lowenhaupt (1987), 'A rhetoric of centers in a religion of the periphery,' in Rita Smith Kipp and Susan Rodgers (eds), *Indonesian Religions in Transition*, Tucson, AZ: University of Arizona Press, pp. 187–210.

Tsing, Anna Lowenhaupt (1993), *In the Realm of the Diamond Queen: Marginality in an Out-of-the-Way Place*, Princeton, NJ: Princeton University Press.

Tsuciya Kenji 土屋健治 (1982), *Indonesia Minzokushugi Kenkyū—Taman Sisawa no Seiritsu to Tenkai*, Tōkyō: Sōbunsha. (1987, Democracy and leadership: the rise of the Taman Siswa movement in Indonesia, trans. Peter Hawkes, University of Hawaii Press.)

van der Kaaden, W. F. (1938), Geschiedenis van de Bestuurvoering over Bali en Lombok van 1898–1938, *Tropisch Nederland*, 11, pp. 203–08, 219–24, 234–40, 253–6, 265–72.

van Goudoever, W. A. (1947), *Denpasar: Bouwt Een Huis*, Batavia: Regeerings Voorlichtings Dienst.

Vickers, Adrian (1987), 'Hinduism and Islam in Indonesia: Bali and the Pasisir world,' *Indonesia*, 44, pp. 31–58.

Vickers, Adrian (1996), 'Modernity and being "modern": an introduction,' in Adrian Vickers (ed.), *Being Modern in Bali: Image and Change*, New Haven, CT: Yale Southeast Asia Studies, pp. 1–36.

Vickers, Adrian (2000), 'I Nengah Metra, 1902–1946: thoughts on the biography of a modern Balinese,' in Adrian Vickers and I Nyoman Darma Putra with Michele Ford (eds), *To Change Bali: Essays in Honour of I Gusti Ngurah Bagus*, Denpasar: Bali Post, pp. 89–112.

Volkstelling (1922), *Uitkomsten der in de Maand November 1920 gehouden Volkstelling*, Batavia: Drukkerijen Ruygrok & Co.

Volkstelling (1936), *Volkstelling 1930*, Batavia: Landsdrukkerij.

Warren, Carol (1993), *Adat and Dinas: Balinese Communities in the Indonesian State*, Oxford and New York: Oxford University Press.

Wiener, Margaret J. (1995), *Visible and Invisible Realms: Power, Magic and Colonial Conquest in Bali*, Chicago and London: The University of Chicago Press.

Wijaya, Nyoman (2000), '1950s lifestyles in Denpasar through the eyes of short story writers,' in Adrian Vickers and I Nyoman Darma Putra with Michele Ford (eds), *To Change Bali: Essays in Honour of I Gusti Ngurah Bagus*, Denpasar: Bali Post, pp. 113–34.

INDEX

Subject ——————————————

Personal name

Organization

www.ingramcontent.com/pod-product-compliance
Lightning Source LLC
Chambersburg PA
CBHW060149280326
41932CB00012B/1689